BONNIE PRINCE CHARLIE

BONNIE
PRINCE
CHARLIE

A Biography
CAROLLY ERICKSON

Quill
William Morrow
New York

Library of Congress Cataloging-in-Publication Data

Erickson, Carolly, 1943–
    Bonnie Prince Charlie / Carolly Erickson.
    p.   cm.
    Bibliography: p.
    Includes index.
    ISBN 0-688-10006-6 (Pbk)
    1. Charles Edward, Prince, grandson of James II, King of England,
1720–1788. 2. Jacobite Rebellion, 1745–1746. 3. Great Britain—
Princes and princesses—Biography. 4. Scotland—History—18th
century. I. Title.
DA814.A5E7 1989
941.07′2′0924—dc19
[B]   88-13438
                                                              CIP

Printed in the United States of America

2   3   4   5   6   7   8   9   10

BOOK DESIGN BY RICHARD ORIOLO

CONTENTS

BONNIE PRINCE CHARLIE

The small boat that approached Peterhead harbor on the east coast of Scotland toward the end of December, 1715, foundered badly in rough seas. High winds and towering waves had tossed it mercilessly up and down for a week in its crossing from Dunkirk, leaving the crew and the handful of passengers aboard ill and miserable. To be sure, the violent weather had helped to protect the ship and the men from being captured by one of the English men-of-war patrolling the Channel. But this single piece of good fortune hardly compensated for the overwhelming bad luck that seemed to follow the ship's most important passenger, James Francis Edward Stuart, wherever he went.

James was accustomed to meeting his misfortunes stoically, yet year by year they weighed him down more and more, turning the corners of his mouth downward and leaving his regal yet vapid features bereft of animation or enthusiasm. At twenty-seven his tall, thin figure seemed to be growing leaner instead of filling out; his black eyes were sad, even woeful; he sighed, and on occasion wept, for his lot in life, which was so far from being the destiny to which he was born.

James had no doubt that he, and not the short, popeyed Elector of Hanover, whom the English perversely recognized as King George I, was the rightful King of England. James was, as he phrased it, "the only born Englishman now left of the royal family." His father, James II, had been ousted from his throne in 1688 by a selfish clique of political opportunists. Since then England had been ruled by the ousted king's two daughters—first Mary, who had ruled jointly with her husband William, and then Anne, who had died without an heir in August of 1714. He, James, the only surviving legitimate son of James II, believed himself to be Anne's only true successor. The Elector of Hanover was a usurper, and it was James's duty to remove him and restore the Stuart dynasty.

This much was clear to James, as he prepared to go ashore at Peterhead and put himself at the head of the army that awaited him. What was not clear was why, so far, life had conspired to thwart his efforts to recover his throne.

He had always been unlucky. As an infant he had been weak and sickly, blue at the lips from lack of oxygen and covered with an unsightly rash. Severe colic nearly killed him, and the royal doctors who dosed him with concoctions made from herbs, dried vipers and the skull of a hanged criminal would surely have finished him off had his father not intervened. While still a tiny baby he had been taken to live at St.-Germain-en-Laye near Paris, where his father, deprived of his crown, maintained an embittered shadow court. James's childhood had been spent under the eye of his father's quarrelsome advisers, who thought of little else but how to restore their master to his throne. To them James had been "the Blackbird," the undersized and unnaturally quiet child whose black hair and eyes and dark complexion made him look like a gypsy. He had been sheltered, kept away from other children, his delicate health guarded by his hovering mother and his mind formed by choleric tutors. Few children would have flourished in such an environment; the grave young James was driven deeper inward and absorbed his father's mood of somber resignation in the face of adversity. He was dutiful but cheerless, and on reaching young manhood he appeared to observers to be utterly lacking in vigor and resilience.

By the time he was nineteen, in 1707, his father had died and James himself inherited the burden of kingship in exile. He called himself James III and VIII (his father had been James II of England and VII of Scotland), and he listened, gravely, to his father's advisers when they counseled him to invade his kingdoms and right the wrong that had been done in 1688. James believed, with some reason, that his subjects would abandon their loyalty to his half-sister Queen Anne and support their true king once he appeared before them in person. Reports reaching St.-Germain-en-Laye indicated that James's Scottish subjects were particularly eager to welcome him, for many Scots resented the recent union with England that had left Scotland deprived of sovereignty and underrepresented, so they argued, in the English Parliament. (Ever since James VI of Scotland became King of England as James I, in 1603, the two kingdoms had been ruled by the same monarch. In 1707, by a Treaty of Union ratified by both governments, the two kingdoms became one and Scotland lost its political autonomy.)

Encouraged by the state of affairs in Scotland, and by the fleet of ships and six thousand soldiers provided by Louis XIV—then at war with England, and eager to take a hand in stirring up civil war there—James set off for the coast early in 1708 to lead the invasion force. But even before he set foot on board his flagship things began to go wrong. The admiral in charge of the thirty privateers and five men-of-war, the Comte de Forbin, quarreled with the commander of the soldiers, the Comte de Gacé. The weather was forbidding. And James contracted measles, forcing the vast assemblage of ships and men to wait idly for days until he recovered sufficiently to be carried on board.

At last the expedition got under way, at James's tremulous insistence, only to be forced back by a gale which did damage to the fleet and to the general morale. A second attempt brought James and his soldiers safely to Scotland, but Forbin, who was convinced that the entire enterprise was ill-advised, could not be persuaded to land there and risk the lives of the French troops. The fleet was harried by an English force with thirty-eight men-of-war; beyond this, the thousands of faithful subjects James had expected to greet him once he came in sight of the coast were nowhere to be seen.

Dejected, James returned to France, mournfully blaming the failure of the mission on his own ill health, the foul weather, and mistakes in provisioning and navigation. (His ever-suspicious advisers murmured that Admiral Forbin had been acting under secret orders from King Louis not to land at all.)

"We saw the person called the Pretender land on the shore," wrote an English prisoner captured during the expedition, after seeing James come ashore at Dunkirk, "being a tall, slight young man, pale smooth face, with a blue feather in his hat, and a star on his cloak." There were no shouts of "Vive le Roi" to welcome him back, the Englishman noted.[1] Everyone was "very mute," and the pale young man with the blue-feathered hat most silent of all.

James had begun to call himself the Chevalier de St. George, a romantic appellation with crusading overtones, and for the next several years he devoted his energies to building a military reputation. He was a brave young man, his bravery all the more admirable in that he was unimposing physically and emotionally withdrawn. At the battle of Malplaquet in 1710 he fought with the elite French household cavalry, the Maison du Roi, charging the English enemy twelve times and retiring wounded from the field. Nor was it the French alone who admired his bravery; the enemy English, far from despising the chevalier for fighting against the men he aspired one day to rule, drank James's health in their camp and at times held their fire when he rode within range of their guns.

He was behaving like a king, but politics were against him. King Louis, heretofore his patron and supporter, bound himself by the Treaty of Utrecht in 1713 not to harbor James within his realm any longer. And so the Chevalier de St. George became a royal vagrant for a time, coming to rest at last in Lorraine, at the château of Bar-le-Duc. It was there that news reached him, in August of 1714, that Queen Anne was dead.

Now, if ever, was his opportunity. Parliament had determined that the Elector of Hanover should succeed Anne,* but the people were, to say the least, unenthusiastic about their new king. "Behold he comes to make thy people groan," one poem about him began.

---

*The Act of Settlement of 1701 provided that Sophia, Electress of Hanover (a granddaughter of James I) and her heirs should succeed Anne. Sophia died shortly before Anne, and the succession passed to her son George.

And with their curses to attend thy throne;
A clod-pate, base, inhuman, jealous Fool,
The jest of Europe, and the faction's tool.[2]

George was reputed to be dull, stupid and provincial—no fit ruler
for the English, whom he neither liked nor understood. Scurrilous
gossip condemned his barbarous manners and his immorality—it
was said that he kept his two Turkish servants, Mohamed and
Mustapha, "for abominable purposes"—and deplored his treatment
of his wife. (To punish her for infidelity he shut her away in a tower
and kept her there for years on end.) In Scotland the "wee German
lairdie" commanded little respect, and people told one another that
James would be over from France before long to end the Hanoverian
fiasco once and for all.

King George's coronation day was marred by riots in favor of
James, and as his reign went on the popular reaction against him
gathered force. In some towns James was proclaimed king. At Oxford students roamed through the colleges, parading their loyalty to
the Stuart dynasty and drinking James's health. Jacobites, or
"Jacks" (as the adherents of James were called from his Latin name
"Jacobus") in London "insulted those that were passing the streets
about their lawful occasions, robbing them of their hats, wigs, etc."
and threatening to do worse unless they gave a shout for the
Stuarts.[3] Week by week through the summer of 1715, the incidents
multiplied: rioting at Peterborough, Burton-on-Trent, Sheffield,
Lichfield, Wolverhampton and a dozen other towns; street brawling
at Manchester, where angry crowds got out of hand and troops had
to be called in; demonstrations and shouts of "A Stuart! A Stuart!"
and "No King George!" whenever officials of the crown appeared.

On June 10, James's birthday, church bells rang out in celebration and there were well attended birthday dinners in many parts
of the country. The wine flowed, people sang "drunken tumultuous
songs" and raised their glasses to their champion, and afterward
reeled out into the streets to bawl out "vile seditious words against
the King." Some of the Jacobites were arrested, but most were not,
for often the town magistrates shared their political sentiments and
were reluctant to interfere. At Bath, the first steps toward revolution
were taken when several cannon and chests of arms were collected

for the use of James's followers once he arrived to lead them.

That he would arrive, and ultimately succeed in his aim of wresting the crown from the Hanoverian, one man felt absolutely certain. This was the Earl of Mar, a high-hearted and rather high-strung Scots nobleman who was an experienced politician and who had served Queen Anne as secretary of state for Scotland. Mar would have gone on to serve King George—and would have used his considerable influence to promote loyalty to the new dynasty—but the king spurned his offer of fidelity and turned him out of office. So Mar had offered his talents and influence to James, and James had gladly accepted his service.

While the Jacobite ferment was at its height in England, Mar called together those Scots willing to declare themselves for James, who, Mar assured them, was about to set sail from France. In the first week of September, 1715, Mar proclaimed "our rightful and natural King James the 8th by the Grace of God" and displayed his blue and gold banner. Two ribbon pendants declared the mottoes "For Our Wronged King and Oppressed Country" and "For Our Lives and Liberties." The words "No Union" were spelled out on the banner itself below the Scottish thistle.

Twelve thousand men responded to Mar's call on behalf of James that "all his faithful and loving subjects and lovers of their country should, with all possible speed, put themselves into arms."[4] Mar marched them to Perth, seized the town, and by October was poised to attack Edinburgh.

It was time for James to act, and at the end of the month he left Bar-le-Duc disguised as one of his own servants. Agents of the British ambassador in Paris waited on the road to waylay and kill him, but he eluded them and rode on to St.-Malo, now dressed as a servant, now as a priest. James and his advisers expected that Mar and his Scots would capture Edinburgh and that soon the Stuart supporters in Northumbria and the Borders would rise as well. Meanwhile James would land at Plymouth and rally the West Country, where he believed his strongest support was to be found, and then march on London.

Once in St.-Malo, however, James discovered that the embryonic West Country revolt had been crushed. Government troops controlled Bristol and Bath; the Jacobite arsenal had been seized, and the key men he had counted on to serve as his lieutenants had been arrested. He thought of landing in Cornwall but that too, he was informed, was out of the question. This was not his first disappointment. Two months earlier the twelve ships, two thousand soldiers and substantial store of muskets, field guns and powder the French had promised him had been withdrawn. He had only two choices: to give up and return to Bar-le-Duc or to gamble everything on the Earl of Mar and his twelve thousand Scotsmen. On December 16 James embarked for Scotland.

Now, a week later, he watched the coastline about Peterhead emerge from the clouds, musing on his bad luck and shivering in the freezing cold. He looked pale and ill, and made a poor impression on the men who greeted him when he came ashore. His obvious dejection drained away what enthusiasm they felt about his arrival, and his habitual silence and morose detachment from the people around him made them mutter that he would have done better to send five thousand troops than to come in person.

James's mood darkened still further when he discovered that Mar's army had fought a costly battle with government troops at Sheriffmuir and, instead of advancing southward, had retreated to Perth. A disastrous Jacobite defeat at Preston made matters worse, as did the problem of desertions from Mar's army. From twelve thousand, James learned, it had dwindled down to five thousand, and more and more men were leaving every day. Many of those who remained were poorly armed or otherwise ineffective. And the government troops at Stirling, recently reinforced, now outnumbered the Jacobites three to one.

Another man, faced with such a disheartening situation, might have risen to the challenge, summoning the heart and will to surmount it. But James, expecting bad luck, bowed to it. He had no drive, and little determination. It was only out of a relentless sense of duty that he pursued his failing venture, and his joylessness and lack of spirit were infectious. The men lost hope. The Chevalier de St. George, the leader they had awaited, turned out to be a tragic figure, devoid of manly heartiness and kingly fire. He was correct, he spoke and acted with a heavy chivalry that made him at once noble and pathetic. The black eyes in his thin face were sad, constantly brimming over with tears as he learned of fresh disasters.

"For me," James remarked to his officers, "it is no new thing to be unfortunate, since my whole life from my cradle has been a constant series of misfortunes." There was more somber honor in the statement than self-pity, but to those who had risked their lives and goods, and the safety of their families, to follow him James's defeatist attitude was repellent.

Mar did what he could to reverse the general reaction to the chevalier. "People everywhere . . . are excessively glad to see him," he wrote in a circular letter put about early in January of the new year. "Set aside his being a prince, he is really the finest gentleman I ever knew. He has a very good presence, and resembles King Charles a great deal." Mar's effort to compare the lugubrious, scrupulous James to his sensual, rakehell uncle King Charles II convinced no one, nor did his insistence that James had "the sweetest temper in the world."[5] Those few men who were able to observe James at close range tended to agree with Mar, however. A groom who accompanied him on his hazardous flight to the coast in November, 1715, recorded that he "never knew any have better temper, be more familiar and good, always pleased and in good humor, notwithstanding all the crosses and accidents that happened during his journey; never the least disquieted, but with the greatest courage and firmness resolved to go through with what he had designed on." In James all the qualities of a great prince were combined with those of "a most honest private gentleman."[6]

There was truth in these assessments, for in his dedication and dogged idealism, and in the enervated rigor with which he pursued his quest, James was princely, even kingly. But the harsher truth was that James was tragically blind to the fact that the average soldier could neither perceive nor appreciate the depth of his character or his sensitive nature, and mistook his *triste* demeanor for weakness. James thought he was every inch a king, and could not seem to understand that his men needed him to be dashing, energetic and inspiring, to spark them on to overcome their limitations. In their eyes he failed utterly to measure up. They saw him—and they despaired.

For the next six weeks the Chevalier de St. George pursued his melancholy crusade, pale and at times so ill he could not ride, attacked by chills and fever. He met with a number of noblemen but few of the country folk. When pressed by Mar he stopped along the wayside to address a forlorn sentence or two to a handful of villagers, but such attempts at contact with his subjects were rare—and dangerous. For he was a hunted man, the government had offered a reward to anyone who arrested him on British soil. And there were spies and assassins stalking him, he felt sure.

With his entourage he hazarded the bone-chilling cold of an exceptionally severe Scots winter. The rivers froze, the dirt tracks that served as roads were so blocked by deep snow that workmen had to be hired to clear them. Hill tracks were buried under many feet of frozen snow, and were completely impassable; the harshness of the season, many felt, was enough to blunt the force of even the most impassioned rebellion. As the dark, short days succeeded one another the snow continued to fall, piling in drifts so deep they blanketed the villages and brought life to a standstill. Mounting a military campaign in such weather was unthinkable. Transport was hopeless, provisioning a nightmare. As it was, the frost kept the mills from turning, so that no grain could be ground and Perth quickly consumed its scant store of bread. Wood was extremely scarce, and coals unavailable, as the coalpits of Fife were in government hands.[7]

The season was one thing, Mar's organizational problems another. There was chaos in the camp at Perth, with no orderly billeting of troops and no reliable method of paying them. Mar had ordered the men to form regiments, but had neglected to determine their composition himself. The result was a hodgepodge of units of all sizes, with every petty leader insisting on having a regiment of his own and refusing to defer to any higher authority. No one looked after essentials: for want of powder horns the men's gunpowder was wet and useless, there was a shortage of flints, and the total supply of gunpowder, wet and dry, was pitifully small. Worst of all, the guns the soldiers possessed were many of them "old rusty broken pieces," more fit for ornament than use, and no one bothered to order replacements.

On January 9, James rode into Perth and settled into the old royal palace of Scone, from which he issued written orders "given at our court of Scone . . . in the fifteenth year of our reign, 1715–16." His pride was intact, but all else was virtually in ruins. Privately, his

CAROLLY ERICKSON

leading supporters had abandoned hope. In his journal, published some time later, Mar wrote that he had never believed he could hold Perth, with or without James's presence.[8] Pretenses were kept up, on the chance that by some miracle the cause might be revived. The citizens of Perth were informed that their monarch, James III and VIII, was to be formally crowned on January 23, and a number of aristocratic Jacobite ladies came forward to donate jewels to be set into his crown. But the rebels were living on borrowed time. The government army, commanded by the Duke of Argyll, was making its way slowly northward, hampered, to be sure, by the snowbound roads and by the need to send to Berwick for cannon and mortars. Reprisals had begun, and were certain to spread throughout every district where men had come forward to fight for James. Soon Argyll would reach Perth, and then all would be lost.

In a vain effort to hold off Argyll and his men James was persuaded to order the burning of six villages that lay between the government army and his own forces. Scrupulous to a fault and tenderhearted as he was, James disliked giving the order, but yielded to the argument that to deny Argyll's men the food and forage the villages could provide might make the difference between immediate surrender and rescue thanks to the last-minute arrival of reinforcements—a fiction born of desperation. So, to prevent the inevitable, the six villages were sacrificed.

The villagers were driven out of their homes and into the deep snow. Their houses and barns were set on fire, their horses taken for James's army, their provisions destroyed. The "mournful screeches and frightful cries" of the inhabitants, left foundering in the deep snow in freezing temperatures, were a pitiful epilogue to the failed rising. No exceptions were made for infants, the aged, or the feeble, all were left exposed to the weather, "it being in the midst of a terrible storm of frost and snow, such as was not in Scotland these many years bygone." Some died within hours in the snow-covered fields, others lingered on for a day or two. Most survived, destitute and distracted by their ordeal, and full of hatred for James III and VIII.

By the last day of January James realized that he had no choice but to abandon the city. "I am in despair at finding myself compelled to withdraw from Perth," he confided, "but to offer battle would be to expose brave men for no reason." He wished, he said, to preserve the lives of his men "for a more fitting occasion." He had some hope of joining his "friends in the north," but what friends he had had taken to their heels, and by the time he reached Montrose James saw that he too had to flee if he was to save himself. The remnant of his ragged army was melting away. A few drunken stragglers had remained in Perth, others deserted on the way northward. It was over.

A small ship, the *Maria Theresa* of St.-Malo, was pressed into service to take the Chevalier de St. George back to France. His leavetaking had to be secret; to announce it would have meant certain pursuit and capture. Yet it must have galled his sense of honor to sneak away on foot, hurrying down an alley to the waterside, looking over his shoulder like a common thief. He had had to lie to his men, assuring them that he would be with them in Aberdeen "where he assured them a considerable force would soon come from France."[9] He had failed them, not once but twice—for the fiasco of 1708 was still lively in his memory. Whether he would have a third opportunity was in the hands of fate—and fate inevitably served him badly.

The *Maria Theresa* remained anchored in the harbor from nine o'clock until well after two o'clock the next morning, waiting for the outgoing tide. Her eminent passenger, wrapped in his own somber thoughts, submitted stoically to this final delay. He was cold and weary, more sick at heart over the harm he had brought to others than over his own profound disappointment. "It is crushing to me," he was to write shortly afterward, "who would have thought myself to some degree content if I were alone in my misfortune but the death and misfortunes of others of which I am the innocent cause pierces my heart."

On his return to France James
found himself in an extremely uncomfortable position. He had nowhere to go, he had very little money, indeed the only thing he had
in abundance was the loyalty of the hungry followers who lived at
his court and looked to him to support them.

And now those followers were growing in numbers, as the leaders
of the Scots who had rebelled made their way via the Orkneys to
France to join their king in exile. By April of 1716 there were some
five hundred of them, uprooted and restless, waiting in quarrelsome
impatience for James to take the initiative and launch another
invasion. James was himself responsible for bringing quite a few of
these men across the Channel. He felt obligated to them and responsible for them, and sent ships to pick them up and transport them
to France where, he assumed, he would be able to offer them his
protection.

France had after all been the exiled Stuarts' haven for decades.

James had lived at St.-Germain-en-Laye most of his life; the opulent baroque palace with its hundreds of rooms, its elegant gardens and air of serene regality was still home to him. His father had died there, and was buried at the convent church of Chaillot. His mother still lived at St.-Germain—where James went to see her shortly after his return from Scotland—and fully expected to live out her life at the palace. Culturally, James was a Frenchman, albeit a Frenchman with an acquired nostalgia for England.

Yet his lifelong connection with France was about to be permanently severed. Louis XIV, who had always sheltered the Stuarts, had died the previous year. France was ruled by a regency, with the pragmatic, shrewd Duc d' Orléans at its head. Orléans was indifferent to the Stuarts, except for their potential value as a weapon to be used against King George of England. For the time being he had no use for James (though he allowed James's mother, Mary of Modena, to continue to live at St.-Germain), and had no intention of harboring him. On the contrary, James's presence in France was an embarrassment, for Orléans was just then favorably inclined toward the English and was negotiating a rapprochement with King George. So James had to leave, and immediately.

Where was he to take his ragged court? Sweden was one possibility. The Swedish king, Charles XII, was at odds with King George—in his role as Elector of Hanover—over some disputed territories on the continent. He was eager to assist any enemy of the elector's, and indeed had entertained the idea of supporting James with troops and money. But Sweden was remote, and the intrigues under way there on James's behalf were not yet ripe. Spain was another possibility, but though James wrote to King Philip V asking for support, he got no response. Hard-pressed, and with the regent uncompromising in his hostility, James took the easiest course and accepted the hospitality of Pope Clement XI at Avignon. Here he took up residence in April of 1716, trailed by his horde of servitors and hangers-on.

James's position was especially difficult in that his abortive invasion of Scotland had provoked a crisis among his chief supporters.

Until recently his principal supporter had been his half-brother James FitzJames, Duke of Berwick, bastard son of James II and Arabella Churchill. Berwick was, like his uncle the Duke of Marlborough, a military genius and had been created Marshal of France.

With his achievements on the battlefield and his bluff, unbuttoned personality he completely overshadowed his younger half-brother, but as a boy James, far from feeling jealous, looked up to Berwick and relied on him completely. Berwick carried weight, people were impressed by him—if not always favorably. (The Queen of Spain judged him to be "a great dry devil of an Englishman, who always goes his own way.")

Certainly Berwick impressed James, and was not at all hesitant about giving him advice. In Berwick's view, James ought to make a bold, all-out bid for the throne, ignoring the risk and gambling everything on a successful outcome. James was too timid, his half-brother maintained. He held back when he ought to press forward. He held back in his personal affairs too, Berwick insisted; he ought to get married, and above all he ought to ingratiate himself with influential people who could be helpful to his cause.

Some of Berwick's brotherly advice was useful, even though the implied criticism it contained irked James. The older he got the more it irked him, until in 1715 there occurred a serious rupture between the brothers. James expected Berwick to command the Jacobite forces, and was mortified when Berwick refused—citing his primary allegiance to Orléans as his reason. James was furious at Berwick's disloyalty, and on his return from Scotland the breach did not heal.

Berwick had let James down, but Bolingbroke, James's erstwhile secretary of state, was guilty of treason. Viscount Bolingbroke, the most colorful personality and the most able professional politician in James's entourage, had carelessly—or perhaps deliberately—revealed James's invasion plans to a Parisian courtesan, who had sold the information to the British government. James dismissed Bolingbroke, who insulted him and called him a poor judge of men—an accusation that may have stung, as it was quite near the mark. In truth, without Berwick and Bolingbroke James was much the poorer in astute advisers. Those he trusted, principally the ever optimistic Earl of Mar and the rather prosaic Duke of Ormonde, were well-meaning but lacked superior intelligence and personal force—as James himself did.

Sound, experienced advice was what James needed most if he was ever to hold his own amid the intricacies of politics and at the same time prepare to make himself master of Britain. From a military standpoint the challenge was great enough, but from a political standpoint it was even greater. James had somehow to learn the interests of each of the European sovereigns—interests that shifted constantly—and then to calculate how he might turn these interests to his advantage. He needed informants at each of the principal courts, a reliable way of getting and sending messages, seasoned diplomats to persuade and cajole and apply the right pressure at the right moment. He had none of these things, only haphazard information supplied with difficulty by mediocre agents. Still, the intriguing went on.

In the autumn of 1716 Jacobite hopes rose when Charles XII of Sweden renewed his offer of twelve thousand troops to help James conquer England, and Philip V of Spain guaranteed a large subsidy to finance and equip the army. For the moment, Sweden and Spain had a common interest in crippling England, and a full-scale Jacobite invasion seemed opportune. During the months that it took to organize the expedition, however, the British government became suspicious, and when in April of 1717 the residence of the Swedish minister in London was ransacked, the secret plot came to light and had to be abandoned.

By this time James was in Pesaro, even farther away from the center of continental affairs and too far from England to foment rebellion. King George had brought pressure to bear on Orléans, who in turn had forced James out of Avignon. Pope Clement XI had offered him asylum in Rome, and he had begun making his way there by stages, stopping for a time at Piacenza, Modena, Pesaro and several other towns along the way.

Italy agreed with James, and Modena, his mother's original home and where her great-uncle, Duke Rinaldo d'Este, still ruled charmed him utterly. For once the corners of his mouth turned upward. His cousin Benedetta, Duke Rinaldo's pale, dark-haired daughter, reminded James of his mother. He fell in love with her, with all the intensity of a man of twenty-nine who had never been in love before. His advisers had been urging him to marry. He would marry Benedetta, he decided, and hope that the Roman Catholic church, which under ordinary circumstances forbade marriage between cousins, would make an exception in this case. Perhaps, with Benedetta as

his wife, his luck would change. King James III and Queen Benedetta—an attractive combination, he thought. He wrote to his
mother at St.-Germain, stressing the fact that his intended bride
resembled her and asking for her blessing.

But for once James was overly optimistic. Whatever Benedetta
may have thought of him, Duke Rinaldo was wary of allying himself
with an outcast Stuart princeling. James might dream of becoming
King of England one day, but the reigning king, George I, was the
genuine power to be reckoned with. And King George was ac-
cumulating powerful allies. Within the last year or so England had
become allied with the emperor Charles VI, with the French regent
Orléans, and with the Dutch. Her navy made Britain a sought-after
partner in continental affairs, and King George, who seemed to take
the concerns of Hanover more seriously than those of England, was
spending a great deal of his time on the continent.

Duke Rinaldo gave a gracious but inconclusive reply when James
asked his permission to marry Benedetta, and eventually, some
months later, he said a final no. It was with a broken heart that
James went on to Rome, where he was received with elaborate
formality as "King of Great Britain and Ireland." The deference and
ceremony pleased him, and Rome itself overwhelmed him with the
grandeur of its baroque churches and palaces and its noble ruins,
but he continued to pine for his beloved.

Things were little better in Urbino, where James spent the next
fifteen months or so. He liked the town itself, and the people, who
referred to him respectfully as *il Re,* "the King," whenever he rode
out in his coach or appeared at public functions. The pension of
twelve thousand scudi which the pope bestowed on him took care
of his immediate financial needs—though not the cost of his carefully nurtured invasion plans—and the citizens of Urbino gave
concerts and put on plays to entertain him.

He accepted it all with wan smiles and bland murmurs of thanks,
his dignity and correctness never failing him. But the canker of
failure gnawed at him. He had been unsuccessful in two attempts
to invade Britain, and his most recent scheme to invade once again
with Swedish and Spanish help had been a fiasco. He had failed in
his attempt to wed Benedetta d'Este. He was thirty years old, neither
old nor young; but time was passing and he was being left behind,

playing at being king in a tiny, remote mountaintop town in Italy, while life and opportunity passed him by.

One thing he could do: marry and beget an heir to continue the Stuart line. It was, some thought, his most pressing obligation, more pressing than raising funds and finding soldiers for another invasion attempt.

The choice of a wife was important, not only because she might be Queen of England one day but because her parentage, nationality and religion would influence the world's view of her husband. There was also the fundamental question of her appeal to James, of course, for if he disliked her there might be no heir.

Jacobite agents throughout Europe were asked to propose potential brides and to comment on their appearance and personality. The responses came in. Emperor Charles VI had a sister young enough for James, and several nieces, but either they were already spoken for or their dowries were small or the emperor would be likely to withhold his consent until James secured the English throne. The Tsar of Russia, Peter the Great, had a twelve-year-old daughter who might do, but she might offend James, it was thought, as Russians were (in the view of the English) uncouth and barbaric in their personal habits. The search went on. James wrote to his agents giving them wide latitude. He didn't insist on a beautiful woman, or an intelligent one; as long as she was fit for childbearing, "not horrible" to look at, and did not have "stinking breath," he would approve.

But every candidate he heard of seemed to have some drawback. The Princess of Hesse had rotten teeth. The Princess of Baden was a dwarf. Of the two Princesses of Fürstenberg, one was too thin in the hips and the other pockmarked and pimply. Then James heard from one of his scouts about the eldest daughter of Prince John Sobieski of Poland. Clementina Sobieski was sixteen, reasonably pretty, "sweet, amiable, of an even temper, gay only in season." Her teeth and breath were entirely acceptable. Clementina stood out in admirable contrast to her two sisters, one of whom frowned and "bristled with etiquette" while the other was giddy and lacking in dignity. Clementina was slight and delicate, with dark eyes and long light brown hair that fell far below her waist. Her portraits show a placid, almost bovine girl with a large, long face, wide-set eyes and heavy brows. Her features were strong, her nose large and her lips wide and well-shaped. She seemed ideally suited for James, for if she lacked beauty she had grace and an aristocratic appearance. She was said to be fluent in five languages—Polish, German, French, Italian and English—and to be "imbued with such deep piety that her life is truly that of a saint." What was more, her lineage was impeccable, for she was the granddaughter of King John III of Poland, heroic defender of Europe who had held Vienna against the Turks in 1683.

There were two drawbacks to a union between James and Clementina, one immediate, the other long-term. The immediate difficulty was that the Sobieskis were subjects of Emperor Charles VI, whose obligations to his ally King George of England might lead him to interfere and to try to prevent the marriage. The other difficulty concerned religion.

James was Catholic, but there were those who thought that, to enhance his chances of ruling the English, he ought to become a Protestant. His father's intolerant Catholicism had after all led to his removal from the throne. Most of the English were Protestant, with a deep-seated horror of "popery" and everything it implied; they would accept James much more readily if he joined the Church of England. So far James had refused to do this, but he could indicate his religious tolerance by marrying a Protestant. Clementina, whatever her virtues, had the disadvantage of coming from a family with an exceptionally close and longstanding association with the papacy. She was herself the godchild and namesake of Pope Clement, named after him at his request. Her grandmother, Maria Casimir, had come to Rome to live after the death of her husband King John, and the monuments she erected in the city's churches were prominent and conspicuous. Earlier generations of Sobieskis had lived in Rome from time to time, and were all but clients of the popes.

So in marrying Clementina James would be making a calculated political statement—or political blunder, depending on one's point of view. He would be underscoring both his Catholicism and his already strong ties to the pope, who was providing him with money, housing and protection. The fact that James sent one of his Protestant supporters, James Murray, to make a formal proposal of marriage to Clementina's father did not alter the case. In choosing Clementina as his preferred bride James was doing just what King George and the British government wanted him to do—making himself look more and more like a tool of the pope and of Catholic interests and less and less like a suitable king for Protestant England.

James was unable to be there to meet Clementina when she entered Rome in May of 1719, but a huge concourse of people turned out to cheer her and to watch her cavalcade pass. The liveried soldiers of the papal guard, the grand coaches of the Roman nobles and the cardinals, horsemen and mounted servants all formed a spontaneous procession to escort the Polish princess to the convent of Ursuline nuns in the Via Vittoria where she was to stay until James was able to join her. Cardinals Aquaviva and Gualtieri took her to the convent door and announced that "Mme. de St. Georges" had arrived, and the sisters took her inside. Clementina was no sooner across the threshold of the convent than she caught sight of a chapel dedicated to the Madonna of Loreto. At once she went in and "threw herself on her knees to worship the Holy Mary," causing the nuns to smile and nod to one another and remark how devout she was.[1]

The next day the pope sent an envoy to the convent to welcome Clementina—who brought with him a hundred baskets of sweets for her to distribute—and soon all the principal figures in the city were sending her messages of welcome and paying calls on her. The charming sixteen-year-old princess who had come such a long way to become the bride of the unfortunate James Stuart became the darling of fashionable Roman society. The Ursuline sisters had to keep the convent doors open until midnight each night to accommodate her visitors, and she was talked of in every street and at every social gathering.

What absorbed Clementina's attention, however, was not her hordes of visitors but Rome's churches and the brilliant pageantry of worship in the papal city. With her entourage she went to Santa Maria Maggiore to adore the relics there, which included, so the devout believed, Christ's cradle. She went to St. Peter's and immediately took off her shoes and stockings so that she could walk around the church as a barefoot pilgrim—until her father confessor dissuaded her from this and made her put them on again. She prayed in dozens of churches, sometimes spending all day and evening in her tireless peregrinations and forgetting to eat until past midnight. On the feast of Corpus Christi she watched the candlelit procession of two thousand wind past her window, the children singing motets, the patriarchs, bishops and cardinals in their variety of precious vestments, the pope in his triple crown and miter. At the climax of the ceremony she knelt and wept, moved by the glory and majesty of it all, her devotion heartfelt and, so those who witnessed it said, quite indescribable.

Pope Clement was gratified by his goddaughter's piety, and impressed too with her quick mind and understanding. When she visited him at the Quirinal Palace, she "surprised him with her intelligence, which he considered superior to that of her sex in general, and remarkable owing to her extreme youth."[2] He encouraged her to seek audiences as often as she liked, and insisted on treating her as a queen despite her preference for the modest title Mme. de St. Georges.

The fervor quickened in her by the wonders of Rome's churches, the excitement of being the center of attention so intoxicated Clementina that she seemed not to mind the absence of her future husband. The weeks passed and she attended more great festivals, her friendship with the Ursulines deepening. The convent was becoming home to her; the comfortable, well furnished rooms suited her perfectly while allowing her to indulge her religious passions to the full. The sisters called her "Mother Superior" at her request, treating her with as much fondness as deference. She gave a banquet at the convent to celebrate James's birthday in June, and another in July to celebrate her own, dining with the sisters and seated under a royal canopy. No doubt Clementina had seen portraits or miniatures of James, but all she really knew of him was that he was nearly twice her age, and that so far he had been unable to attain his dream of conquering England. Whether or not she looked forward to becoming his wife we don't know. But then, the honor was so great that everyone expected her to be overjoyed—and perhaps she was.

For his part, James was once again in the throes of disappointment. Yet another invasion scheme had proved abortive, this time launched from Spain.

Philip V had provided thirty ships and five thousand men. This force was to land at Bristol and proceed eastward toward London, while at the same time a diversionary force of three hundred men would land in Scotland. James left for Spain shortly before Clementina arrived in Rome, and planned to follow the main fleet a few days after it left Cadiz. He was on his way to the coast from Madrid when word reached him that the fleet had encountered a violent storm off Cape Finisterre and was so scattered that it could not possibly proceed. The small diversionary force managed to arrive safely in Scotland but was shortly afterward defeated at Glenshiel by government troops. To add insult to injury the battle at Glenshiel took place on James's birthday, June 10—while Clementina was banqueting with her nuns.

When James returned to Italy and met Clementina he was suffering all the pangs of disillusionment and must have looked it. He was aging rapidly, the lines on either side of his mouth and nose were deepening and his pale face was growing more gaunt. An admirer described him as "over-pensive and over-serious"; hostile witnesses thought he was ridiculously mournful, a tall, looming melancholic who never laughed and had the effect of squelching merriment in others.

James was anything but an eager, hopeful bridegroom, and Clementina must have been disappointed when she met him. They were married in the cathedral of Montefiascone, near Viterbo, in a ceremony of regal splendor. James wore an expression of paternal benevolence as he and his seventeen-year-old bride knelt before the bishop to recite their vows. Afterward there were formal receptions with all the local dignitaries and some of the Roman clergy coming to offer congratulations, and then a prolonged stay in Montefiascone before the couple journeyed back to Rome to start their married life together.

"She has surpassed all my expectations," James declared in praising his wife. "Had I asked God to give me a wife with all the qualities I could desire, I could not have hoped for another than the one He has been pleased to choose for me." He was more than content with her, he was completely satisfied. Clementina resumed

her regimen of visiting Rome's churches and of calling at the Ursuline convent three or four times a week. She had her preoccupations,
he had his; they got on without outward strain.

They lived in the Palazzo Muti, rented for them by Pope Clement.
The four-story palazzo, built of golden brown stone and ornamented
with columns and balustrades, was squeezed into a narrow street
just off the Corso, Rome's broad, busy triumphal avenue. At the far
end of the street was the Church of the Apostles, and the architect
of the Muti, in deference to the nearby church, had crowned the
palace roof with twelve stone figures of the twelve apostles. They
stood guard over the dim alleyway like holy sentinels, watching the
procession of servants, visitors and petitioners who entered and left
the tiny courtyard of the palace in a steady stream.

To the hundreds of Scots and English exiles who had followed
James to Rome and now lived from hand to mouth in squalid
circumstances, the Muti Palace was a lodestar. They went there as
often as the post reached the city, and waited for the latest news
from England and elsewhere to be announced before returning to
their tiny dark rooms and inadequate suppers. They watched for
glimpses of King James and Queen Clementina coming and going
in their coach, accompanied by a papal guard of troops, headed for
an audience with the pope or a religious service. And they observed
the arrivals and departures at the palace of the cardinals, noblemen
and political envoys, speculating about what the visits might mean
for the future of the Stuart cause.

By the summer of 1720 the exiles were delighted to learn that
Clementina was expecting her first child. A Stuart prince was just
what they needed to give them heart, and they looked forward to
his birth with all the eagerness of men with too little to do and far
too little to spend. Clementina was in good health; neither the
sweltering heat nor the disease-ridden air of the city affected her.
She often rode to the town of Albano in the hills to spend the
afternoon in the cool gardens of Cardinal Aquaviva's palace, or she
went with James to one of Rome's water carnivals, gaudy affairs at
which the crowds were doused with jets of water while fashionable
society paraded in finery around a flooded piazza.

By mid-December Clementina had grown "as big as a house,"
according to James, and her principal attendant Marjory Hay was

becoming apprehensive about the approaching delivery. She thought the baby would not be born before January, and at the rate the diminutive mother was swelling, the birth was likely to be difficult and the labor prolonged.[3]

On December 26 Clementina went into false labor, and at once all the clergy and magistrates of the city and several dozen of the nobility were informed and invited to attend the birth. They arrived at the palace, only to be told that the queen was not in labor after all and sent home. Four days later messengers were dispatched to the same notables again, "at a very late hour," to request their presence in the birth chamber. This time Clementina was truly in labor, and her pains continued all night and most of the next day.[4]

James was determined to make certain there would be no controversy over the legitimacy of his child. (His own birth in 1688 had been attended by doubts and accusations of fraud; his father's enemies had claimed that he, James, was not the queen's child but another infant smuggled into the royal apartments in secret.) With so many witnesses present, he reasoned, no one could claim afterward that this baby was not Clementina's child. Cardinal Aquaviva, the papal secretary of state Cardinal Albani, the English cardinal of St. Peter's, brother of the Duke of Norfolk, and a great many other cardinals mingled with the princes, dukes and duchesses of the Roman nobility in the birth chamber and surrounding rooms, aware of Clementina's gasps and cries and impatient for the extended vigil to end. They waited all morning and afternoon, refreshing themselves with wine and food and distracting themselves with gossip. At about sunset Clementina reached the final stage of her labor. The crowd became subdued, the anguished noises from the birth chamber grew louder. Finally the baby was born. It was a boy, a prince to inherit all the rights, hopes and destiny of the Stuarts.

James announced that the tiny infant would be baptized at once with the names Charles Edward Louis John Casimir Silvester Maria.[5] Charles and Edward were English royal names, Louis the name of the Stuart benefactor Louis XIV. John and Casimir recalled the baby's Polish grandparents, while Silvester and Maria were his Catholic baptismal names.

In the church of the Gesù a special mass was sung at the command of the pope to give thanks for the child's birth, and the cannon of Castel Sant' Angelo boomed out a salute. New Year's Day being by tradition a day of giving gifts, Pope Clement himself celebrated mass the next morning "for the gift granted to two such exemplary sovereigns, through whom the royal descent over three kingdoms is thus maintained."

3

The heir to three kingdoms was a vigorous, hardy infant, fair like his mother and with her liveliness and animation. His hardihood was a good thing, for within hours of his birth he was taken from Clementina and propped up on a couch, wrapped in gorgeous embroidered robes and subjected to the scrutiny of the hundreds of notables who had been waiting throughout Clementina's long labor for a glimpse of him.

Tiny, red and squirming, all but lost in the folds of his robes, he was nonetheless Prince of Wales, and deserved royal honors. A royal canopy of state was stretched above his head, while at his feet knelt well-wishers in an endless procession: his father's devoted followers, who now became his followers as well; the members of the household; diplomats and courtiers; Roman aristocrats and, one by one, the powerful members of the College of Cardinals. The cardinals, magisterial in their sweeping crimson robes, gold crosses and heavily ringed hands, symbolized not only the power of the Church but that of the European states as well. Cardinal Gualtieri was protector of England, Cardinal Sacripanti protector of Scotland. The Spanish minister Cardinal Aquaviva, liaison between the Jacobites in Rome and the Spanish court, represented his master King Philip V, while Cardinal Paolucci, prime minister, secretary of state and Great Penitentiary to Pope Clement XI, represented the Holy See itself.

Had he been born the son of a reigning monarch instead of the son of a defeated exile, Prince Charles could hardly have received more attention. As it was, crowds gathered at the Palazzo Muti to watch the parade of dignitaries, visitors thronged the courtyard, gifts poured in. There were chests of doubloons from Spain, thousands of gold scudi from the cardinals and from Pope Clement, who also sent relics and consecrated garments for the prince's christening. Cardinal Ottoboni, protector of France, sent the proud father a kingly gift that had once belonged to the Tsar of Russia—a long velvet pelisse bordered in solid gold.

To the Jacobites, this child was "Britain's hope," and the motto *Spes Britanniae* appeared on a medal struck to commemorate his birth. The more credulous among them swore that the heavens themselves bore witness to the importance of the event. A new star had appeared, they said, never before seen. And a great storm had suddenly arisen to ravage the kingdom of Hanover, home of King George who wrongfully occupied the English throne, as if to presage his destruction at the hands of the rejuvenated Stuart line.

It had been rejuvenated, they liked to add, by the Sobieski blood. For if the Stuarts had, until then at least, been notably unlucky, the Sobieskis had produced, in the little prince's great-grandfather, a hero of godlike proportions.

The exploits of King John III of Poland were legendary. Not content to be, by all accounts, the handsomest, most energetic and strongest ruler of his day, widely read and renowned for his cultural patronage, he had been seized by a sense of destiny. He had determined to beat back the advancing Turks whose armies were threatening Vienna. Calling his undertaking a holy war, and taking on himself the mantle of the medieval crusading kings, he led his Poles and the army of the Holy Roman Empire to the gates of Vienna, where he succeeded in relieving the city just as the starving inhabitants were about to surrender themselves into Turkish hands. It was a remarkable victory, for the Ottoman force was vast and powerful and King John was handicapped by the loss of tens of thousands of men en route to the battle. He emerged not only victorious but practically deified, with the grateful Viennese bowing down to kiss his feet and fighting one another for the privilege of touching the hem of his garment. Savior of Europe, vanquisher of the infidel hordes, King John was a resplendent hero and now, nearly forty years after the event, his name was more venerated than ever.

In his earliest months Prince Charles flourished. An English nobleman, the Marquis of Blandford, who spent some time in Rome in 1721, went to the Palazzo Muti where James and Clementina welcomed him, the latter insisting that he visit her son. "He is really a fine promising child," the marquis observed, adding that the prince was attended by his own household of English servants. Two of these, both Londoners, "kept such a racket about us to make us kiss the young Pretender's hand, that to get clear of them as soon as we could we were forced to comply." At this Clementina "laughed very heartily, and told us she did not question but that a day would come that we should not be sorry to have made so early an acquaintance with her son."[1]

Blandford turned the comment aside with a gallant reply, but it irked him that he had been coerced into acknowledging the baby's regality. He was a Whig, a loyal subject of King George, with an "inbred dislike" for the pretensions of the Stuarts. Yet he had to confess that he was favorably impressed by James and Clementina, and in particular, by their degree of religious tolerance. Clementina told Blandford that Charles's attendants were mostly Protestants, for as "he was to live and die amongst Protestants she thought fit to have him bred up by their hands." In Poland, she added, there were no distinctions of religion, only of "honest and dishonest." James went even further, the marquis thought, in arranging for Protestant services to be performed at the palace for the benefit of his servants, courtiers and travelers. This, according to Blandford, was "amongst the greatest wonders of Rome."

Another wonder was James's undeniable kingliness. His "air of greatness" and majesty, the power of his glance, which lesser mortals found unbearable, the "fire in his eyes" when he lamented the sorry state of England, his "air of sincerity," lack of bigotry and evident highmindedness all combined to overawe the marquis and threatened to make him "half a Jacobite." On first seeing James he was "perfectly stunned and not aware of himself," he confessed, and when James smiled on him the force of his "graceful countenance" was quite astonishing.

Possibly the arrival of a son temporarily inspired James as much as it did his followers, putting fire in his eyes and sparking his rather damp spirits with new hope. The news from England was particularly heartening in the spring of 1721, what with widespread bank failures creating havoc and turning more and more people against their Hanoverian ruler and his unpopular ministers. Jacobites in Britain and France began once again to plot and plan, and every post day brought fresh letters of encouragement to the Palazzo Muti.

Agents of the English government in Rome became concerned about the reviving hopes of the Stuarts. The most colorful of these agents was Baron Philip von Stosch, a thoroughly dissolute intriguer and sometime dealer in shoddy antiquities. In his dispatches to London Von Stosch tried to alleviate apprehension by claiming that the infant prince was sickly, that he "would not live very long." Even if he did live, Von Stosch said, he was likely to be a cripple, for his legs were reported to be "so turned inwards and distorted that it is very much in doubt if he will ever be able to walk."

The infant prince did have difficulty learning to walk, and his nurse had to help him, holding him with reins as his knees were too weak to permit him to walk unaided. When he was older, his weak knees were strengthened by a series of jumping exercises and by dancing. Apparently the exercises were effective, for another observer, more reliable than Von Stosch, reported that the youngest Stuart was soon "running about from morning till night," healthy and strong as could be.

Strength and stamina, coupled with strong-willed high spirits, were the young prince's earliest characteristics. As he grew older he added to these a far rarer and more valuable quality in a future ruler: charisma.

The Duke of Liria, Berwick's son, who encountered Charles when he was about six and a half, thought him "the most ideal prince he had ever seen, a marvel of beauty, dexterity, grave, and almost supernatural address." His manner and conversation were "bewitching," his charm infectious. There was none of his father's stiff correctness about him, no artificial politeness, no sense that he was playing a role he had been carefully coached to play by his elders. He was, quite simply, a naturally engaging young person whom those around him could not help but adore. That they were meant to adore him, to kiss his hand and bow when entering his presence, because of his rank among Jacobites as Prince of Wales, was almost an irrelevance. They were moved to pay him homage because of something far more compelling than rank, a force of personality that was ill-defined but unmistakable.

That unusual gifts and accomplishments should accompany this force of personality seemed perfectly appropriate. The prince grew into a precocious athlete and huntsman, with his own stable of little horses, his own crossbows and pistols, his own ceremonial armor. He was an excellent shot, his aim true enough to shoot birds off the roof and to "split a rolling ball with a bolt three times in succession." He was proficient at tennis and shuttlecock, was a skilled dancer and an apt pupil at fencing. "No porter's child in the country," wrote one of his tutors, "has stronger legs and arms."

By the age of six or seven he was speaking Italian, French, and English—the latter with a noticeable accent—and was reading and learning to write. He had a quick mind, but little aptitude for study, preferring riding and shooting and resisting his tutors' attempts at discipline. No doubt they were as susceptible to his charm as everyone else, and in any case the most important accomplishments in a future king were military, not intellectual.

The prince's earliest letter, written in a large Italian hand and showing a less than perfect mastery of the handling of pen and ink, was composed in 1727. "Dear Papa," it began,

I thank you mightily for your kind letter. I shall strive to obey you in all things. I will be very dutifull to Mama, and not jump too near her. I shall be much obliged to the Cardinal for his animals. I long to see you soon and in good health. I am, dear Papa,

Your most dutifull and
affectionate son,
Charles P[rince].[2]

When this letter was written, James was in France, attempting to rally the scattered Jacobite forces and to gather the backing, political and financial, for another invasion attempt. George I had died in June of 1727, and James, now nearly forty, was dutifully upholding the family honor by protesting the accession of his successor George II and championing the Stuart claim.

But his heart was no longer in it, and, brave though he undeniably was, he was gradually succumbing to continual frustration. He disliked having to keep his court in Italy, far from the kingdom he desired to regain. He was weary of having to be constantly on the alert for fleeting opportunities, constantly having to rally his dispirited followers when they lost heart and fell to bickering among themselves, constantly having to keep one step ahead of the continental rulers on whom he relied for support. He had the unenviable task of making his cause appear to be theirs, of convincing them that it was in their interest to back him even though that would mean alienating the English government. And this he had to do, day after day, while situations changed and uncertainty mounted.

It was hard work, an uphill battle that he must have feared he was doomed to lose. In 1727 and 1728, he met with failure everywhere. The French court had turned its back on him. There was no way he could get to Scotland with a sizable force of arms and men. In Lorraine pressure from England forced the duke to expel him. In Avignon, where the pope ruled, more English pressure was brought to bear in the form of military threats and threats against English Catholics. In the end, the pope, Benedict XII, recommended that James return to Italy. By this time George II was secure on his throne and the prospect of James III ever ascending that throne was remote indeed.

James's failure was all the more bitter in that his cause had been weakened by an ugly personal scandal.

Clementina, unstable, asthmatic and more than a little childish, had decided that she had had enough of marriage. She and James had produced two sons—a second son, Prince Henry, had been born in 1725—but motherhood had not brought her sufficient compensation for a joyless union with a man she had come to despise. To her James was ponderous, dull, overly conscientious; in short, unendurable. Everything about him—his heaviness of spirit, his lackluster leadership, his close alliance with Protestants—galled her. Her dissatisfaction gave intriguers their opportunity, and she allowed herself to be persuaded that James was being manipulated by un-principled advisers, chiefly John Hay, James's secretary of state, his wife Marjory Hay, one of her own waitingwomen (and formerly a close friend), and James Murray, Marjory Hay's brother and Charles's principal tutor. When James dismissed her friend and confidante Mrs. Shelton, Clementina was enraged. Impulsively she moved out of the palace and went to live among the Ursuline sisters at the Convent of St. Cecilia.

The principal difficulty in the marriage was simple incompatibil-ity, for which neither party was to blame. But other issues arose to cloud and complicate the breach between husband and wife. Despite her initial acquiescence in James's decision to surround Prince Charles with Protestant attendants, Clementina had come to distrust them and to accuse them of subverting her son's faith. She also accused James of treating her badly, and of infidelity with Marjory Hay. Given James's scrupulous gentlemanliness, both charges seem far-fetched, and there is no surviving evidence to support either of them. Still, there was a great deal of gossip, and it made James look ineffectual and farcical, while drawing attention away from his in-creasingly desperate political undertakings.

Worse still, the marital scandal created strain between James and the pope and certain of the cardinals. There were angry confronta-tions at the Palazzo Muti, reproachful letters, tensions that drained James of time and energy.

"See, Madam, to what difficulties you expose me!" James wrote in exasperation to Clementina. "What honorable man will venture to serve me after the scenes you have publicly exhibited?"[3] His lofty regality had been tarnished, his pride wounded, his very income affected—for the pope informed James that his pension would be cut in half and he himself denied any further papal audiences until he agreed "to give satisfaction to his wife, and remove scandal from his house."

Eventually Clementina and James became reconciled and she returned to the Palazzo Muti. But the reconciliation was largely a matter of form, the damage had been done. No wonder James was a king without a country, people said. How did he expect to govern a kingdom when he could not keep order in his own household?

James and his family were in fact living on the margins of reality. He acted the role of king when in public, appearing at civic fêtes under a canopy of state, wearing his Star and Garter, surrounding himself with those who addressed him as king and doing his best to maintain the appearance of royal surroundings. He entertained the Roman nobility and as many visiting English as possible, serving them bountifully with fine food and wine (though he himself ate roast beef and called for English beer) and diverting them with music and polite conversation. He drank healths to the English ladies, discussed English laws and customs with impressive familiarity, even displayed a knowledge of the names and histories of the English aristocracy. Yet it was all a feat of imagination, for James had no real experience of England and very little of Scotland, and had met few of the English. His preference for roast beef and English beer was an acquired taste, a cultivated eccentricity that fooled no one into actually thinking he was an Englishman.

The pretense extended to everyone and everything around him. His followers might call him king to his face, but they informed on him behind his back, their loyalty easily compromised by promises of money or glory elsewhere. His guests might eat his food and drink his wine with affability but were privately skeptical of his claims. His lodgings, both the Roman palazzo and the summer palazzo at Albano, were spacious but empty, for James could not afford to furnish them grandly and what money he had went to pay his servants and rescue his fellow exiles from their own humiliating poverty. His carriages, the guardsmen of his retinue, his horses, his very clothing came from the generosity of others. He had nothing of his own, except the anxieties that lack engendered.

And there were other anxieties, created by the unsettling presence of spies. In the employ of the duplicitous Baron von Stosch were dozens of James's servants, who gave the baron regular and detailed accounts of what went on at the Palazzo Muti. Nothing, it seemed, escaped the baron's notice—not what was whispered in the servants' quarters, not which baths Clementina visited in order to promote fertility, not what punishments were meted out to the little princes when they were disobedient. Even the oldest and apparently most faithful of the servants might be recruited as paid informers, and this led James, his wife and sons to be constantly wary.

Among James's close acquaintances was Cardinal Alessandro Albani, a wealthy, worldly and discriminating man who was the pope's nephew and whose other relatives were frequent guests at the Stuart palace. Albani, like his colleague, Von Stosch, was in the habit of letting the British government know everything he could discover about James, his family and his plans.

No one could be completely trusted. Hence the need for constant circumspection, secrecy, the presumption that unfriendly ears were always listening. Letters and messages had to be written in code, and messengers watched. People and places were referred to by cryptic references known only to an elite few. False information had to be spread in order to throw the hounds off the scent.

And where there were spies, there might well be poisoners, assassins, gangs of thugs paid to harass and do harm. Italy had a long tradition of intrigue and violence, in some circles it was a way of life. No one was immune from its menace, no matter how powerful. Indeed, power was a magnet for violence, as James well knew. The dark, narrow alleyways of Rome were hiding places for colonies of thieves and brigands, men who waited their chance to rob prosperous tourists, murder priests and rape nuns. Such characters would not scruple to assassinate a Pretender to the English throne, or his sons. Not when every street had chapels and oratories offering sanctuary to criminals, where they could be neither pursued nor punished.

Rome was, in a sense, a fitting setting for the court of a Pretender, its antique pretense hiding a shabby reality. In the early eighteenth century Rome was a grandiose shell of ruins and parkland inhabited by a small population catering to hordes of tourists, most of them English. Immensely broad avenues stretched away across long distances, flanked by magnificent churches, villas and public buildings. Wide piazzas adorned by opulent fountains and towering antique statues drew crowds of sightseers, beggars, peasants driving heavily laden donkeys and idlers resting from the midday heat. The Forum, then known as the Cow Field, or Campo Vaccino, was a jumble of half-submerged arches, towers and columns through which livestock wandered. Weeds sprouted from the ruins, bits of fluted marble and carved capitals jutted from the dirt and mud underfoot. Tumbledown huts and cottages, some built from the ruins, leaned against monuments, their occupants lounging in the shade of patches of trees. Animals were tethered in the Colosseum, which was little more than a dilapidated dunghill.

Yet despite its dilapidation, the sheer scale of the city overwhelmed the visitor and lent grandeur to ordinary events. Buildings were outsize, monuments huge and imposing, as if built to accommodate giants. The stairways that led up the steep hillsides were wide enough for twenty people to walk abreast. Thousands could crowd into the enormous squares. The vast porticoes of the basilicas alone provided shade and a communal gathering place for hundreds, while the extensive gardens and fields swallowed up hundreds more. Rome was not only grand, it was solemn, the gravity of the ancient ruins compounded by the weighty majesty of the baroque. Across the grand piazzas, tall antique columns faced massive neoclassical façades, heroic statues looked out on monumental domes and scenic balustrades. Over all floated wide skies and, for much of the year, a mercilessly hot sun.

Part of Rome's drama lay in her climate, the heat, dust and flies of summer alternating with the frigid winter when the marshes froze and the wind swept cruelly down the wide avenues. Mortality from malaria and plague was always high in the hot season, and in the cold, beggars died of exposure and the weak, the very old and the very young succumbed to chills and tuberculosis. Pilgrims avoided the city in the pestilence-ridden summer months, and residents who could afford it left for the countryside until cooler weather set in.

The everpresent risk of disease was made worse by the filth which was piled up against the houses and then left to rot there in malodorous mounds. Streets were never swept, and the narrow alleys of the poor quarters reeked with the mingled scents of garbage, sewage and garlic. Street vendors who offered fish, chicken and vegetables threw their scraps on the ground wherever they happened to be; housewives and servants too threw every sort of waste into the gutter. Fastidious visitors to Rome were appalled at the casual way the Romans relieved themselves against the venerable arches and columns that adorned their city, and did not hesitate to turn courtyards and hotel porches into public conveniences. It was no wonder, the visitors remarked, that the richer residents avoided going about on foot and used sedan chairs or carriages even when traveling very short distances.

Such squalor was not unique to Rome among eighteenth-century European cities, but the sharpness of the contrast between rich and poor, grandeur and wretchedness was unusually marked there. Hovels straggled in untidy rows alongside marble palaces. Ragged children howled and held out their dirty hands to beg coins from passing gentlemen in black silk stockings, silken capes and perfectly powdered wigs. Goatherds jostled aristocrats in embroidered waistcoats flashing with diamond buttons. Except in the worst weather the poor gathered, bedraggled and unwashed, in the piazzas, where they enjoyed the spectacle provided by the prosperous riding by in their painted and gilded litters or on their beautifully groomed horses, gleaming with silver bits and harness and gold saddlecloths. Most impressive of all were the carriages of the princes of the Church, carved and ornamented works of art inlaid with jewels.

If the contrast between wealth and poverty was unusually evident, that between spiritual and sensual was even more so. Rome was a city of clergy, their numbers so great that at times they appeared to form the largest element in the population. Yet in some quarters, streetwalkers and courtesans seemed to be even more numerous, parading aggressively along streets where religious processions were an equally common sight. And the greatest clerics were not infrequently the most worldly, using their vast wealth to subsidize very earthy recreations. The city's shrines to the Virgin and the saints, her chapels and oratories, her magnificent churches all invited the contemplation of divine mysteries. At the same time, the ruins of Rome's secular glory, the rich and pungent odors of her cuisine, even the fragrance of orange blossom and narcissus and jasmine rising from her gardens tugged visitors in the opposite direction, toward the voluptuous enjoyment of earthly pleasures.

The contrast between spiritual and sensual was at its most inescapable during the eight days of the Roman Carnival, just before the beginning of Lent on Ash Wednesday, when in a noisy outburst of exuberance the populace surged en masse up and down the Corso, disguised as Harlequins, Punchinellos, pirates, gods and goddesses, sultans, artists and buffoons. Their disguises making them daring, they danced and shouted their way along, throwing confetti and paper streamers and handfuls of flour at one another and at the spectators who sat in benches along the periphery of the avenue. The maskers wove in and out between carriages filled with more revelers, among them the city authorities and other prominent notables, and escorted large triumphal floats on which oriental potentates and exotic horsemen and mythological figures posed amid antique pillars and woodland scenes and artificial hills.

The spectacle went on throughout the day and evening, becoming wilder, more violent and lascivious as the day wore on. Toward the end of the afternoon the centerpiece of the Carnival day, the race of the Barbary horses, was staged. Soldiers rode down the length of the Corso, clearing it of carriages and merrymakers. A layer of sand was laid down over the pavingstones to prevent the horses from losing their footing, and the crowd, pressed back against the walls of the buildings, waited for the race to begin. The horses, bred from Berber stock, were swift and high-strung, and were goaded to a bleeding frenzy by sharp barbs that cut into their backs and made them run crazily through the street as the crowd roared and cheered. The brutality of the spectacle only added to the pleasure it gave, and the owner of the winning horse became a local hero.

Every night there were comedies and dances in the great houses, and on Sundays the Carnival was brought into the churches. Musicians played, worshipers sang and the holy statues were garlanded with flowers. For eight days restraint and inhibition were forgotten, excess ruled. Then suddenly, when a signal was given signifying the beginning of Ash Wednesday, the tumult came to an end, and for the forty days of Lent Rome was quiet. Easter brought a return to noise and celebration, however, with the dancing, shouting and merrymaking resumed.

Rome was, in fact, in a near-constant state of celebration. There were some one hundred and fifty holidays during the year—church feasts, saints' days and other festivals. Beyond this, individual neighborhoods had their own celebrations and fairs, whose disruptive jollity discouraged people in adjacent neighborhoods from working. Seasonal celebrations too were observed, some of them pre-Christian in origin. And on days when there was no official holiday, the Romans looked forward to the constant entertainment offered by the pageantry of the papal court.

Every time a new pope was installed, he went through the streets in a gorgeous procession, escorted by a glittering retinue of prelates, nobles, papal troops on foot and on horseback. Ceremonies hundreds of years old were periodically reenacted by the pope and cardinals, or by other high-ranking members of the court. Foreign ambassadors on their way to and from the papal palace were accompanied by soldiers, guardsmen and escorts of pages and valets, and because the spectacle was too elaborate to miss the populace customarily turned out to watch. Splendid religious processions added to the list of public events. And on the greatest occasions, the palaces of the aristocracy might be opened to the public, along with their spacious gardens, and for several hours the denizens of the street could wander through the grand rooms, lit with brilliant candelabra, tasting delicate morsels offered them on silver trays by liveried servants.

Grand, dramatic, ultimately artificial, Rome provided the showy backdrop to Prince Charles's childhood. It was an environment which fostered fantasies and grandiose dreams of glory, extravagant living and bold bids for acclaim. Everything was theatrical, nothing mundane. Realism, intellectual rigor, even common sense were assaulted on every side by imagination and illusion, by the sense of timelessness and limitlessness. Such was the vivid, flamboyant urban stage which formed the young prince's conception of the grander stage of the world.

4

In the portraits painted during his boyhood, Charles Stuart holds his head at a proud, confident angle, and his eyes—variously painted as warm brown or hazel—are alert and full of spirit. He looks like a healthy young animal, brimming over with vitality, bright and eager. To judge from these portraits, he possessed what his older contemporary Lord Chesterfield called "that living force of soul which spurs and excites young men to please, to shine, to excel." In his heavily embroidered velvet jacket, the Star and blue ribbon of the Garter across his chest, his curling bag-wig perfectly coiffed and powdered, he looks supremely self-assured—and without a trace of hauteur or arrogance.

Charles resembled his mother more than he did his father, and the similarity extended to personality as well as physiognomy. Clementina was mercurial and charming, though in the years following her formal reconciliation with James her mercurial charm was gradually transmuted into an eccentricity so pronounced that it must have left its mark on both her sons. She was by all accounts the sort of woman who compelled attention and attracted either intense love—as she seems to have done in her children and, overall, in her husband—or intense dislike. The pious poor of Rome, who were the frequent objects of her charity, looked on her as a living saint, and only the most irreverent of them suggested that her close relationship to the pope had anything other than religious devotion behind it.

Both his brooding, self-absorbed father and his increasingly reclusive, increasingly religious mother were proud of their elder son, but his radiant normality was out of key with their troubled psyches. James called him "Carluccio," Clementina's name for him was "Carlusu." Others in the household referred to him as the Prince of Wales, and visitors knelt when they met him and kissed his hand. He was accustomed to receiving deference wherever he went, even being granted the extraordinary privilege of sitting in an armchair during his audiences with the pope.

His brother Henry, who was just over four years his junior, was no real rival for Charles, though he too was a fair, good-looking child, lively and personable. The Italians called him "the little Duke of York," and his father was especially delighted with him, recording with pleasure how at the age of six Henry was a good shot and sometimes "took the air on horseback at night after a day's strong fatigue."[1] "I am really in love with the little duke," he confided, "for he is the finest child that can be seen."

A second son was essential to ensure the continuity of the Stuart line in case something should happen to Charles, and no doubt more children would have been welcome. But Clementina, who weakened herself by excessive fasting and whose health was deteriorating year by year, produced no more sons. So the two boys kept one another company, Henry no doubt admiring and emulating Charles, dressed like his brother in velvet jacket and small curling wig, though accorded less reverence and involved in less ritual.

As heir to the English throne—which all true Jacobites believed him to be—Charles required an exceptional education. Surprisingly, he did not receive one. His principal teachers were the Scot Andrew Ramsay, a man of letters; the aging Irishman Thomas Sheridan, a relative of the Stuarts (he was James's half-nephew), and the Abbé Legoux, a French cleric from the University of Paris. All were Catholics, and were under the supervision of the Protestant chief tutor, or "Governor," James Murray, Earl of Dunbar. None was able to instill discipline or develop concentration in the lively Charles, and Baron von Stosch, always on the lookout for stories of turmoil and conflict within the Stuart household, wrote to London that Charles was so unruly he threatened to kill Murray and had to be locked in his room—with his weapons taken away.

The boy had a quick mind, but a short attention span, and as a result he reached adolescence without acquiring that familiarity with the Greek and Latin classics which marked a cultivated man, without any apparent knowledge of mathematics—essential to soldiering—and without any knowledge of the history or governance of England. His heavily accented English did not improve as he grew older, and given his father's assiduous efforts to make himself appear to be an Englishman, Charles's deficiency in English speech and culture is remarkable. It is all the more remarkable in that he was exposed to the company of the English Jacobite exiles, and of the English tourists sojourning in Rome.

When Charles was nine years old, in the spring of 1729, Clementina wrote several letters to her "dear Carlusu," telling him she hoped he would continue to be "civil and good" and urging him to "remember well my lessons, which you know is the only proof you can give me of your love."[2] "Be certain of my constant and just love I always will have for my dear Carlusu," she went on, "for whom I have prayed with all my heart to day, and put you [sic] under the protection of the Blessed Virgin."[3]

James wrote Clementina that "Carluccio was mightily pleased with your Letter and to Sir Thomas's and my great surprise, read it almost current [i.e., almost without hesitation] without much help." That the reading of a relatively simple letter should surprise both James and Sheridan implies that Charles was no prodigy, but at least he could read reasonably well, and his own surviving letters show that, with the help of his tutors, he could compose a well-turned brief letter in either English or French.[4] Outdoor activity continued to be his forte, however. As James told Clementina, "I saw him ride yesterday much to my satisfaction, and on the whole I am very much pleased with him." Riding, hunting, playing games:

these were what mattered to Charles. He had taken to setting harder challenges for himself, such as staying out after dark with a shotgun, taking aim at flying bats.

The cultivation of Charles's mind and physique were one thing, the cultivation of his manners another. The training of a young aristocrat in the arts of civility required many hours of sophisticated instruction, and one wonders which of the four tutors was responsible for this dimension of Charles's education. There were music teachers to teach him to play the viol—precursor of the cello—and dancing masters to teach him the steps of the current courtly dances, at the same time showing him how to walk with elegance, how to stand and sit gracefully, how to carry himself with regal distinction in any situation. But the subtler lessons of good breeding and gentility must have been left to Murray and his colleagues—and perhaps to Clementina and James as well.

There is no better guide to these principles of aristocratic civility in the earlier eighteenth century than the letters Lord Chesterfield wrote to his errant son. Chesterfield was an English peer, active in politics from the 1720s on and an astute observer of court life. His models of polished manners and wise conduct were the French, and his instruction was as applicable to continental society as to that of England. His purpose in writing letters of advice to his son Philip was to make the young man capable of holding his own in the most urbane company anywhere in Europe, and to prepare him to enter the world of politics and to succeed in it.

Every well-bred man should cultivate politeness, Chesterfield wrote, avoiding the English propensity to be either shamefaced or impudent and behaving in an easy and natural way, attempting to please yet never pressing himself on others in an irritating fashion. The politeness of an elegant man puts others at their ease, is comfortable rather than tense, and is above all unobtrusive.

Indeed unobtrusiveness is a primary virtue in a genuinely polite man, according to Chesterfield. He ought never to call attention to his own social superiority, particularly with servants, and he ought to avoid talking about himself as much as possible. In fact, he ought not to talk very much at all, for to be reserved while appearing candid is the first lesson of diplomacy.

On the potentially treacherous arena of politics, Chesterfield had a good deal to say. It would be naïve, he counseled, not to assume that every man involved in politics is out to gain his own ends; indeed one ought to be suspicious of anyone who feigns disinterest. It would be equally naïve to expect logic and rationality to prevail over irrationality and subjectivity in the dealings of power-seeking men; they are fallible, emotional, excitable, and can often be swayed by judicious flattery or by the influence of their mistresses. Flattery is particularly effective, though it requires tact, for the more important the personage you wish to flatter, the more careful and indirect your flattery has to be.

Chesterfield's advice about sex was worldly and practical. He advised the polished young man to seek out the erotic company of well mannered women, for they could be useful to him in advancing himself as they often had the ear of important men. Seduction, like dancing and music, was a necessary accomplishment for a man of the world. Chesterfield's view of women in general, though, was unflattering. He thought them weak-minded and inconstant, like overgrown children, incapable of solid reasoning or good sense.

One wonders just what instruction Charles was given in manners and conversation, and on the subtler points of manipulating and influencing others without becoming manipulated by them. He had ample opportunity to learn by doing, for when still a child he was taken to Carnival balls where reportedly he "bore his part . . . as if he were already a man."[5] He met the guests at the Palazzo Muti with a graciousness that greatly impressed them, and showed no awkwardness as he approached adolescence. His childish prettiness became youthful princeliness, and his strong arms and legs were becoming manly. Portrait painters now portrayed him as a self-possessed, statesmanlike youth, determined and ready to carry on his father's cause and to make it his own.

If he was to begin to do this, he needed to make a military reputation, for as Murray pointed out, he "had no fortune in the world but what he must gain by the point of his sword." His opportunity came in the summer of 1734, when he was thirteen.

The army of Spain, accompanied by the nineteen-year-old Don Carlos, heir to the Spanish throne, was besieging the fortified town of Gaeta on the coast midway between Naples and Rome. The siege was an episode in the prolonged confrontation between the forces of the emperor Charles VI, who ruled Naples and Sicily, and Philip V of Spain, Don Carlos's stepfather, who sought to seize the territories. With the help of the French, the Spanish armies under the command of the Duke of Montemar were slowly winning over the imperialists, and by July of 1734 they were advancing toward Naples. Calling himself "King of Naples," Don Carlos anticipated victory and expected that the emperor's soldiers, who had taken their stand at Gaeta, would not be able to hold out for long.

One of those intending to take part in the siege was Charles's cousin the Duke of Liria, who had recently become Duke of Berwick on his father's death. He proposed to James that Charles be allowed to join the besieging forces and after some hesitation James agreed. Charles was eager to go—as was Henry, only nine years old but burning to be off on campaign with his brother, and mortified when James told him he would have to stay home. After a farewell visit to the pope, who blessed him and sent him on his way with a large coffer of coins, Charles left for the wars, taking Murray, Sheridan, a half-dozen servants and two friars with him. The day after his departure James wrote his son a letter, and sent it off together with a scabbard which, he said, "may be of use to you." "Remember and practice all I said to you yesterday," he reminded Charles, "and then you will I hope be one day both a great and a good man, which I pray God to make you, and that I may have good accounts of you, which will be the greatest comfort I can have during your absence."[6]

The group arrived at Gaeta to find that the siege was in its final stages. Nevertheless Berwick took Charles immediately to where Don Carlos was holding court and there Charles was greeted as Prince of Wales and shown every formal courtesy. According to Murray, who sent a detailed account of events in Gaeta to James in Rome, Charles was grateful for these honors but asked that he be shown no special distinction as he was under his father's orders to remain incognito. When the king arrived, Murray went on, Charles went to meet him and talked to him "very prettily" and without the least display of awkwardness or embarrassment. Indeed he talked to Don Carlos "with the same ease as he used to do to any of the Cardinals at Rome," introducing Murray and Sheridan to him and keeping up a gracious flow of conversation. It was noticeably more gracious than that of Don Carlos, who was, according to Murray, "of a bashful temper" and inclined to be brittle in his manner.[7]

The following morning Charles returned to the court and dined there, after which Don Carlos, who conferred on him the honorary rank of general of artillery, took him by boat to the vicinity of the military camp, to a house from which he was accustomed to watching the fighting. The king's advisers told him the house was the officers' command post, Murray wrote, but in fact officers only went there while Don Carlos was there, to lend credibility to this fiction. The house was of no significance whatever, and was perfectly safe from the enemy's guns. Everyone but Don Carlos himself seemed to know the truth, and the soldiers laughed at him behind his back, the thing being "a joke to the whole army."

If he were not to be laughed at, Charles would have to get a great deal closer to the action than this, yet, as Murray realized, the Spaniards would be "mortified extremely" if Charles were seen to display more courage than Don Carlos, who was six years his senior. Military etiquette too had to be considered, and permission given from the commander Montemar. These issues were apparently resolved, for Berwick took his young cousin into the trenches, where "he showed not the least concern at the enemy's fire, even when the balls were hissing about his ears."

The following day Berwick had suddenly to leave the house where he was staying, when five of the siege guns began firing on it at once, making gaping holes in the walls. The duke got out, but Charles, who arrived on the scene only moments later, insisted on going into the house despite the evident danger, and stayed there "a very considerable time with an undisturbed countenance."[8] Berwick, apprehensive not only for his cousin's safety but because he had promised James he would be responsible for the boy, tried to take Charles into the trenches only at times when the enemy guns were customarily silent, so that he would run "little or no risk." And Murray wrote, a little cynically, that by visiting the trenches at a safe hour Charles was gaining "in a few days a great reputation at a very cheap rate."[9] Still, Charles was obstreperous and eager to show how brave he was, and insisted on going back several times to the house where the cannon had breached the walls, enjoying the fact that he was tempting fate.

He must also have enjoyed the stir he was creating with his charm and liveliness. Possibly because he was such a contrast to the diffident Don Carlos, the Spaniards were delighted with him. He was "adored by the officers and soldiers," Berwick wrote, for "his manner and conversation are really bewitching."[10] He mingled with the men, asking each one how he carried out his particular duties, talking with sappers and engineers and experts in artillery as if exceptionally concerned with their individual branch of siegecraft. On one occasion he visited a group of men engaged in building earthworks, and began talking with them. "They were struck with wonder and astonishment," a witness wrote later, "when they heard this young Prince speaking to each of them in their own language. To the Walloon he spoke French, Spanish to the Spaniards, and to the Italians Italian, being perfect master of these three languages. The soldiers flocked about him and disputed among themselves who should have the honor of speaking a word to him."[11]

Word of Charles's bravery went out via the Spaniards to Spain, and via the French to French diplomats throughout Europe. Unfortunately, it was also widely publicized that he had brought two friars along in his retinue—a faux pas which was certain to be published to his detriment in the newspapers in Protestant Holland and England. It was "one of those minor things which could lose a kingdom," Murray was told by Don Carlos's Italian physician, a cultivated man who had the Stuarts' interests at heart.

To counterbalance this there were the reports of Charles's winning manners, his success in gaining the genuine liking of Don Carlos, and his evident civility. He dined frequently with the king and with the officers, and spent time conversing with "some pretty gentlemen" Berwick knew. He never went to court, according to Murray, without saying something memorable while there; people remarked "that he was already a man," though still a boy in years. "Today at court," Murray wrote, "his cockade fell from his hat and Mr. de St. Estevan took it up and the hat in order to put it on, but was placing it wrong, upon which the King put it right." Charles immediately remarked "that he would keep that cockade as long as he lived because His Majesty had done him the honor to touch it."[12] It was flattery of the kind Chesterfield would have commended.

The Gaeta campaign whetted Charles's appetite for the military life, and after the capitulation of the fortress he went on to Naples at the invitation of Don Carlos. He wanted to accompany the Spanish army into Sicily, but James ordered him home. Despite the good reports he had received, he was dissatisfied with Charles for writing him so infrequently and so perfunctorily. (One of Charles's letters to his father read, in its entirety, "I am very glad that you are contented with me. I have been very good and hope with the Grace of God to continue so and humbly ask your Blessing. Charles P[rince]."[13]) Beyond this, James was worried about his son's eating habits, even though Murray had written him that the boy ate twice as much at Gaeta as he did at home. "I earnestly recommend to you," James wrote to Charles, "to have a particular care of your diet, for it would be a foolish and vexatious thing should you fall sick there, by eating trash, and so not be able to do and see what is fit for you."[14] The food in Naples was bad enough, but that of Sicily would be impossible. Prince Charles must come home. So, laden with jewels, looking "rich and opulent," and no doubt shining with the praise and attention he had received, Charles returned to Rome with his retinue.

His reputation had preceded him. Von Stosch, who had dismissed the idea of sending a mere boy to the scene of fighting as a showy and meaningless gesture, was impressed with what he had heard about Charles. "Everybody says that he will be in time a far more dangerous enemy to the present establishment of the Government of England than ever his father was," he wrote. And while this was not saying much, given James's dismal record as a would-be conqueror, still it attested to the extent and degree of favorable comment that was making the rounds of the European courts.

While Charles was advancing his reputation Clementina, who had sent him off to Gaeta with her blessing and her prayers, was pursuing the austere regimen which had prematurely aged her. She was no longer, in her own mind, Mme. de St. Georges, she would never be Queen of England, nor would she survive to see her charming Carlusu become king. Her asthma prostrated her, her prolonged fasting weakened her and left her hollow-eyed and pasty-faced. Beyond her children, nothing gave her satisfaction but her endless devotions. She did not dine with James and his guests any longer, and was rarely seen outside the Palazzo Muti. She stayed secluded in her darkened apartments, growing weaker and yet continuing to

fast until her body was wasted and her gums bled from scurvy. Spies
in the household reported all this to the English agents, who drew
the unkind conclusion that Clementina was trying to mortify her
flesh past endurance so that through her early death she could earn
canonization. If she could not be Queen of England she could at
least be Saint Clementina, a martyr to her faith.

Charles and Henry were summoned to their dying mother's bedside. Her final wish was for them never to renounce their faith, no
matter what political pressure might be placed on them, not "for all
the kingdoms in the world, none of which could ever be compared
to the Kingdom of Heaven." With her sorrowful sons and husband
near her she died in January of 1735, and her thin embalmed body
was dressed in queenly purple for the funeral. Thousands of wax
tapers surrounded her bier in the Santi Apostoli church adjacent to
the Palazzo Muti where the funeral was held. James was so dis-
traught, Murray reported, that he nearly fainted, while the two boys
were "almost sick with weeping and want of sleep, and on all sides
there was nothing but lamentation." Huge crowds assembled to
watch as the funeral procession went on its way to St. Peter's.
Clementina was indeed venerated, and mourned. In accordance with
her wishes the purple robe was laid aside and she was buried in the
habit of a Dominican nun. Her heart was placed in an urn in the
Santi Apostoli church. It was not long before people began to claim
that miracles were being performed at her tomb.

Afterward, James developed the habit of praying for an hour each
morning in Santi Apostoli. It may have been a sort of penance for
his shortcomings as a husband, or it may have been a simple tribute
to Clementina's memory, performed by an exceptionally methodical
and conscientious man. Certainly James changed, no longer playing
the hearty Englishman but subsiding more and more into a semi-
reclusive life. He continued to hold court for visitors in the mornings, and invited them to stay to dinner afterward, but he did not
put forth the effort to be an effusive host, and he spoke little during
the meal. As soon as he sat down at the table his sons approached
him and knelt down, asking him to bless them. This ritual com-
pleted, the servants came in with the meal. There was a good deal
of strained silence as the food was served, and much consternation
was caused by the fact that, as James did not drink any wine, the

guests had to refuse it also, for to drink before their royal host did would have been the height of bad manners. To the relief of the thirsty company, James did not linger at the table but retired immediately after he finished his meal. In the evenings James occasionally went with his sons to social gatherings, but only stayed an hour or so. His health troubled him, his physicians sometimes prescribing goat's milk to improve his digestion along with "a course of steel."[15]

Life went on, but with marked differences. James was less visible, Charles and Henry much more so. They received all the attention now, with parties given in their honor where they mingled suavely with cardinals and princes and dignitaries from foreign courts. Once a week Charles and Henry held a musical soirée, where Charles played the viol and Henry sang, to the accompaniment of a small string ensemble. A visiting Frenchman, Charles Des Brosses, heard them. "Yesterday I entered the room as they were executing the celebrated composition of Corelli, the *Notte di natale*," he wrote, "and expressed my regret at not having heard the commencement. When it was over they were going to begin a new piece, when Prince Charles stopped them saying, 'Stop, I have just heard that Monsieur Des Brosses wishes to hear the last composition complete.' "[16] The Corelli was repeated, and Des Brosses took away an impression of Charles's considerateness and good manners.

He had not yet become the "great and good man" his father often urged him to be, but Charles was progressing well. The world had begun to notice him, to applaud his merits, and to speculate about what chance he might have to succeed where his father had failed.

5

James was worried about his elder
son. He was growing up, yet he remained, in James's view, "very
innocent, and extreme backward in some respects for his age." He
was old enough to shave, yet not old enough, it seemed, to take an
interest in women, not even the beautiful women of Rome. He was
also "wonderfully thoughtless for one of his age," and would not
apply his mind to anything. In personality he was more a bright,
accomplished child than a young man. He clung to childish pastimes
instead of, in his father's words, "endeavoring to cultivate the
Talents which Providence had given him." He had not developed
the depths and moods of adolescence; he remained a sunny, irrepressible boy, infectiously blithe yet without the dignity and weight
of burgeoning maturity.

No doubt James missed in his son the qualities which he himself
had in abundance: gravity, excessive seriousness, dutiful religiosity.
His younger son Henry was developing all these traits. What was

wrong with Charles? How was he ever to muster the sense of responsibility that James felt so keenly and without which he could never hope to accomplish the great task James would one day pass on to him?

Von Stosch reported that James and Charles often went walking together amid the ruins of Rome, talking and planning. Though it seemed to the baron that they were scheming to invade England, the truth may have been that James was trying to impress on his ebullient son just how significant and challenging an undertaking the invasion of England was, and how in order to encompass it Charles would have to develop self-discipline and sober concentration.

Though Charles could not be expected to understand it, there was something weighing on James, and it added poignancy to his efforts to shape his son into a future king.

For the past decade and more the Jacobite cause had been disintegrating. One by one the men who had fought with and for James were dying, and there were few younger men as yet to take their places. The last spark of English resistance to the Hanoverians had come in 1722, when a barrister named Christopher Layer had gathered a small force of men and plotted to capture King George and seize the Tower and St. James's Palace. Layer had been discovered, imprisoned and ultimately hanged, and though the incident had frightened the Whig government it had also strengthened it, by presenting a specter of revolution to be raised whenever the opposition became restive.

There was a Jacobite bloc in the House of Commons, led by William Shippen, but it represented too modest a voting strength to carry much weight, even when on occasion it was joined by discontented Whigs. Shippen declared stoutly that he received his voting instructions from James in Rome, though this was at best a generalization; Rome was too far away, and communication with London too perilous and too difficult to permit James any but the broadest influence over the Jacobite M.P.'s. In the course of the 1730s even James's parliamentary support dwindled, and the prevailing peace between Britain and the continental states allowed the Jacobites no opportunity to offer themselves as allies to Britain's enemies.

Marooned in Italy, forced to endure the dwindling away of his supporters and helpless to change the course of events, James must have felt keenly the weight of his years and the intense frustration of having produced an immature if vigorous son. An unkind fate still pursued him, having made havoc of his once-promising marriage and left him a widower, and having given him at best a marginally satisfactory heir.

Hoping that a broadening of Charles's experience might improve him, James decided in the spring of 1737 to send him on a tour of the principal Italian cities. For more than two months Charles and his traveling companions—including Murray, Sheridan, another tutor called Strickland, five liveried servants and six others—traveled from city to city, with Charles presenting himself as "Count of Albany" though in fact representing the Stuart monarchy.

He began his tour in Bologna, where a troupe of guardsmen escorted him to his palatial lodgings and a great ball was held in his honor. At Parma, where he went next, the dowager duchess presented him with a gold snuffbox and, on his departure, a costly diamond ring. Here he was the guest of honor at a state dinner— hardly an appropriate welcome for a mere Count of Albany—and even inspected the troops as a visiting monarch might be expected to do. At Genoa Charles received the Spanish envoy and was the guest of Cardinal Spinola, while at Milan every prominent person in the city sought to pay his respects to him—except for the representatives of Emperor Charles, who were ordered to ignore him.

The tour was proving to be even more of a success than James had anticipated. Charles was "the fashionable idol at the moment," the central attraction at dances and receptions, the object of attention wherever he went. Tall, fair, bright-eyed and smooth-skinned, he was enviably princely as he moved gracefully over the dance floor, enviably noble as he toured the sights of the cities and received the gifts, compliments and honors that were showered upon him. He wore his blue Garter ribbon and star, and may have worn— as he did in some portraits—tartan dress, which became his fair skin and light hair. His manner, as usual, captivated his public, especially when he spoke of his ambitions. "Had I soldiers," he reportedly said, "I would not be here now but wherever I could serve my friends."[1]

In Venice Charles was given a kingly reception, sitting on the

Bench of Princes at the Assembly of the Grand Council and later conversing with the doge as ruler to ruler—or at least ruler to heir apparent. He rode through the canals in the splendidly appointed gondola of the French ambassador, and was allowed to use one of the gondolas of the Venetian Republic as well.

By this time Charles had been on tour for two months, garnering praise, arousing gossip, his royal and near-royal receptions an insult to the Hanoverian monarchy. Every time Charles Stuart was honored, George II was snubbed, and the English decided that the repeated insults had gone on long enough. The Venetian ambassador in London, Businiello, was expelled from the capital and ordered to leave England within three days. And the English envoy in Florence—where Charles was expected soon—made it known to the grand duke that he and his government hoped the Florentines would not indulge in any unseemly celebrating when the young man arrived.

But despite assurances by the grand duke's secretary that Charles would receive no "improper mark of distinction," the ducal coaches were sent to meet him on his way into the city, and the grand duke himself, heedless of the disapproving British, expressed a strong desire to meet with Charles. The English envoy insisted that such a meeting would be viewed with severe displeasure.

"But you know how curious his Highness is!" burst out one of the Florentine officials to the adamant Englishman. "Surely it cannot be considered a grave political offence to permit a brief interview to take place!"

The envoy at last relented, agreeing not to protest if the grand duke received Charles as a mere private person, and at a time when few people were present to take notice. In the end the grand duke's illness prevented the meeting, averting a possible diplomatic contretemps. Shortly afterward, having been fêted at the customary round of dinners and balls, Charles left Florence and made his way via Lucca, Pisa and Livorno back to Rome.

"I understand that you have behaved very well in all respects on this journey," James wrote Charles on May 19. "I hope you will continue to do so, and that I shall find you quite a man on your return to me."[2] He was not yet quite a man, though soon after his tour Charles was fitted out for an adult wig, and not long after that he began to be shaved regularly. In private his bad temper had shown itself, especially to Murray, who wrote James that Charles "gives us rather more uneasiness when he travels." Fortunately, though, Charles was "only a trouble to his own people," and not to strangers. To strangers, in fact, he seemed mature enough to be thinking of marrying, and one result of his Italian tour was a series of rumors about possible brides for him.

The summer passed, and then the fall, and nothing came of these rumors. Charles had very little to do, apart from boating on Lago Albano with his brother and attending water fêtes in the Piazza Navona, throwing coins into the water for the street boys to fish out. There was riding, and dancing, and incessant practice at shooting— but no real enemy to shoot at. Charles was beside himself with impatience to take part, however briefly or peripherally, in another siege or battle. But no army would have him now, not even that of Spain, in which he had already shown his valor. The French turned him down, as did the emperor, who was preparing an expedition to fight the Turks. To have the Stuart heir among one's forces was a provocation to King George in England, and in the late 1730s no ruler or minister wanted to present such a provocation—at least for the time being.

Obsessively energetic, Charles turned his full attention, during the summer and fall at least, to hunting. There was no moderation in him, it seemed; he threw himself into the hunt with the same eagerness and persistence he had shown in the trenches at Gaeta. He craved the stimulation of challenge, of constant change. He felt his powers, and was constantly being reminded of them by his admirers. Yet he had no scope to develop them, no arena in which to prove himself. At the same time, he felt the goad of his father's dissatisfaction, and the annoyance of being held back, overly protected, stifled in his growing desire for independence and bold action. At birth he had inherited a mission—the mission of restoring the Stuart dynasty. By temperament he felt himself ideally suited to fulfilling that mission, as he understood it. He was not troubled by self-doubt. On the contrary, he gained confidence when imperiled, rising to the occasion when confronted with risk and danger as if risk and danger were his natural element. The dull, safe and stagnant world of his father's court was becoming ever harder for him to bear.

In 1742, when Charles was twenty-one, James wrote that Charles was "quite wearied of this country," adding "I don't wonder at it, for his sole amusement here is to go out shooting, to which he has gone every other day during all this season before daybreak, whether fair or foul." James's secretary James Edgar described how impatient the young man was for his sport, sleeping in a chair in his clothes, "with his riding-coat thrown over him, all gartered and ready," so that he could be away at one or two in the morning with his huntsmen. He had far more stamina than they did. He wore them out, hunting tirelessly and "killing a great deal of game," keeping up a pace which no one could equal and refusing to turn back even when it rained or when the ground was hard with frost. Returning from these expeditions, Charles would sit down and attack the viol with the same vigor he had shown in attacking the game birds and rabbits, "diverting himself with music for an hour or two, as if he had not been abroad."

It was a shame to see such energy dissipated in the insignificant pursuit of hunting. "What a pleasure it would be," Edgar wrote, "to see better game than the shooting of quails."

Charles's capacity for singleness of purpose was remarkable. Apparently he had no vices to distract him. No one, not even Von Stosch, hinted that he was overly fond of gambling, or drinking, or of the other pleasures common to aristocratic young men. He had no cohort of companions his own age, no particular favorite or favorites. He chose solitary pastimes, and though he was convivial he seems to have had no intimate friends at this time. It is tempting to think that in these fallow years he was nurturing his aspirations, brooding inwardly on what he was later to refer to as that which he was "put in this world for," namely to serve his father and Britain as effectually as possible.[3] But to presume this one would have to discount the comments James and others made about how Charles lacked depth and seriousness. The observant Englishwoman Mary Wortley Montagu, who saw him at a masque in 1741, wrote that he appeared to be "thoughtless enough."

At the same masque she observed his brother Henry, and was more impressed with him. Henry, she wrote, "is very well made, dances finely, and has an ingenious countenance." Certainly he was more thoughtful, or inward-turned, than the extroverted Charles, though to some he seemed a "warlike young prince," full of the Sobieski fire.[4]

The "little Duke of York" was growing into a handsome, well-built young man, with "a certain agreeable robustness in his mien, and a more than common sparkle in his eyes." He was noticeably shorter than Charles, and did not have the latter's magnetism. Nor was he passing breezily through adolescence as his brother had. When he was about seventeen, Henry went through a phase in which he became obsessed with religious devotions and "in constant inquietude for fear of not having time for all he ought to do." He began scheduling his time so tightly that there was not a minute to spare, and he consulted his watch constantly in order to make certain not a minute was wasted.

From the time he got up in the morning, at five forty-five, until he went to bed at night—still thinking guiltily about all that he had left undone that day—Henry was governed by his unforgiving regimen. He alloted himself fifteen minutes to pray in bed, then time to dress, then an hour to pray in his bedroom, his prayers said so loudly that his attendants outside could hear him through the closed door. He allowed only seven to ten minutes for breakfast, after which his confessor, Father Ildefonso, arrived and heard his confession for another hour. Twice a week he had two confessors visit him, one after the other. Dancing and fencing lessons then intervened, but Henry hurried through these, watch in hand, so that he could get to mass in the chapel of the Palazzo Muti. Often one mass did not suffice; on Sundays and holy days he liked to hear three or four masses if he could, and when the last of these ended he remained in the chapel, on his knees in prayer.

He kept his eyes on his watch all through dinner, in order to have another forty-five minutes in which to pray before going out for the afternoon. His afternoon sojourns gave him no respite from his devotions, however, for he usually went to a church to pray for another half-hour there. By this time it was four o'clock, and now

CAROLLY ERICKSON

Henry spent another hour and a half in the chapel of the Palazzo Muti, reciting his rosary with such passion that he alarmed his governor.

"It deserves serious attention," wrote Murray, who recorded Henry's excessive behavior, "that he undergoes much greater application of mind than his delicate health can bear."[5] In reciting his prayers he "puts his mind in agitation, pronounces his words aloud, and crowds them with great precipitation one upon another." Murray often saw him in the middle of the day "with a blackness about his eyes, his head quite fatigued and his hands hot and the same thing when he comes from his prayers at night." Praying had become his only pleasure; in fact, the prospect of spending an evening at a social gathering instead of in chapel actually gave him pain. His whole "temper and inclination" had changed, Murray thought, and he was so fervently attached to his unhealthy way of life that were he to be deprived of his constant devotions "it would have a very violent effect on him." Furthermore, his devotions were interfering with his studies, and with his acquiring the habits of a gentleman.

The contrast between the brothers, the one outgoing and athletic, the other preoccupied with his rosary and his watch, must have been startling.[6] Yet they were on perfectly congenial terms, and were together often enough to elicit joint comment from visitors to the palazzo. "The elder is more worth while and has a sweeter disposition," Des Brosses commented. "He has a large heart and is full of courage." Both brothers, he added, were "of mediocre intelligence and less developed than princes of their age ought to be." And despite Henry's sudden aversion for society, both he and Charles continued to be the focus of attention for many Englishmen spending time in Rome. The English could not, without compromising their professed loyalty to George II, have any contact with James. But they could greet and admire his sons, and even show them a degree of "tenderness and compassion" which the English agents believed was damaging to the Hanoverians.

In the winter of 1740 a wellborn young Scotsman arrived in Rome, eager to see the man he had always called "King Jamie." He was Lord Elcho, the twenty-year-old son of the Earl of Wemyss, a

Jacobite partisan living in Paris. The earl was a strong enough Jacobite to have refused to take the oath of allegiance to King George, but he had not taken part in any of the risings, and was living in a kind of cosmopolitan limbo in France. Lord Elcho had been sent to Winchester for his education and there he had allied himself with the Stuart faction among the boys, taking "King Jamie's" part against the favorers of the "wee German lairdie" George II. It was natural enough that in leaving Winchester he should begin his Grand Tour by traveling to Rome to see the man he considered to be his rightful sovereign.

Once installed in the papal city he had no difficulty in arranging an audience with James, and the latter received him with his customary graciousness. James told young Elcho that he was aware of his father's loyalty, and that he hoped to show his appreciation in a concrete way once he became King of England. He then summoned Charles and Henry to meet the visitor.

Elcho took to Henry at once, recalling afterward that he was "very affable, well-informed and sensible," and that they conversed agreeably. With Charles he was put slightly on the defensive when James, observing that he and Charles were about the same age and nearly the same height, had them stand back to back to see which one was taller. Charles won the contest, but was too preoccupied with his favorite pastimes of shooting thrushes and blackbirds and playing golf in the Borghese gardens to care very much—or to pay very much attention to his guests. Despite this lukewarm beginning, however, Elcho attached himself to the Stuart court and was in constant attendance there.

Another young Scotsman, John Murray of Broughton, arrived at the Palazzo Muti at about the same time and was received more warmly than Elcho. Murray of Broughton, whose father was a minor laird, was handsome and personable and had been educated at Edinburgh and Leyden. He and Charles took to one another at once, and James too was so impressed with him that he appointed him secretary of state for Scotland. Murray of Broughton seems to have had the sort of personality that energized people and galvanized them to action, and his reactions were strong and his admiration easily engaged. He admired Charles enormously.

"Charles Edward, the eldest son of the Chevalier de St. George," he wrote in a letter to his sister, "is tall, above the common stature, his limbs are cast in the most exact mold, his complexion has in it somewhat of an uncommon delicacy; all his features are perfectly regular and well turned, and his eyes the finest I ever saw. But that which shines most in him," the young Scotsman went on, "and renders him without exception the most surprisingly handsome person of the age, is the dignity that accompanies his every gesture; there is indeed such an unspeakable majesty diffused through his whole mien as it is impossible to have any idea without seeing, and strikes those that do with such an awe as will not suffer them to look upon him for any time, unless he emboldens them to it by his excessive amiability."[7]

The panegyric did not end there, but went on to praise Charles's well-balanced nature, which made him "equally qualified to preside in peace and war," his courage, and—contrary to the opinions of most others—his "extensive learning." According to Murray of Broughton, Charles had a mastery of Latin and Greek, was "not altogether ignorant of Hebrew," and was well versed in history and philosophy. "What he is ordained for we must leave to the Almighty," he concluded, "who alone disposes all; but he appears to be born and endowed for something extraordinary."

Elcho and Murray of Broughton were, in their youth and idealistic adherence to the Stuart cause, typical of a new generation of Jacobites. They were too young to have experienced the failures of the past; to them James was not an unsuccessful would-be conqueror but a patriarch, a venerable and benign figure whose rights were to be upheld by a younger champion in the person of his peerless son. They had little in common with the quarrelsome, aging and penurious exiles who crowded James's court clamoring for money and attention. Nor had they known the frustrations these querulous and embittered men had endured, their hopes alternately raised and lowered by the on-again, off-again attitudes of the French and Spanish toward the Jacobite cause.

Besides, the situation was changing. In 1739 Britain went to war with Spain, once again raising hopes that the Spanish might finance a Jacobite invasion. The conflict arose over Britain's illicit trade with Spanish colonies—a trade that went on despite explicit prohibitions.

BONNIE PRINCE CHARLIE

Throughout the 1720s and 1730s British ships had continued to run the risk of capture by Spanish coast guards in order to pursue the enormous profits to be made in the colonial trade, but a great many of them were lost, leading to increased tension between the two countries. Sometimes atrocities were committed. One English captain, Robert Jenkins, claimed that a Spanish sailor had cut off his ear—and he caused a sensation when he brought the severed ear, pickled in a bottle, into the chamber of the House of Commons. Negotiations over compensation to the injured British broke down, and war ensued.

The outbreak of war was symptomatic of broader changes in Britain, where the leadership of the peace-loving Whig prime minister Robert Walpole was being eroded. The Englishmen who were coming to maturity in the 1730s and early 1740s had never lived through a major war. They associated warfare with heroism and glory, not with economic dislocation, political strains and social unrest, and they welcomed the conflict with Spain. Walpole's government was discredited by an incident in Edinburgh, where a crowd of some four thousand people broke into the prison and executed a captain of the city guard who had ordered his troops to fire on a crowd of demonstrators. The government could not keep order, it seemed, nor could Walpole keep his majority in the Commons—which depended in part on its ability to control the votes of the Scottish Members. Early in 1742 Walpole resigned.

By this time most of Europe was embroiled in warfare. In 1740 Emperor Charles VI had died, leaving to his daughter Maria Theresa sovereignty over his immense and lucrative domain. Almost at once Prussia, Bavaria, Poland and France moved against Austria, and Britain, where sympathy for the hapless Maria Theresa was strong, prepared to go to Austria's aid. A joint British and Hanoverian force was put into the field, under the command of George II, and a British fleet was sent into the Mediterranean to prevent the King of Naples from supporting the Spanish.

The turmoil delighted the Jacobites, who believed that it could only work to their advantage. James's agents were everywhere, holding clandestine meetings with supporters in England and Scotland, talking with ministers in Madrid and Versailles, intriguing to obtain money and troops, arms and transport.

Though Britain and France were not yet at war, it could not be long before France's close alliance with Spain drew her into the conflict—or so the Jacobites hoped. They approached Cardinal Fleury, chief minister of Louis XV, proposing that seven or eight thousand French troops be landed in Scotland, where, they assured him, twenty thousand Highland clansmen would be waiting to join in an invasion. The cardinal, while recognizing that even a small Jacobite force might cause enough havoc in Britain to tip the balance against the English on the continent, was reluctant to lend any support to James and his men beyond money and arms. To do more would be to invite open warfare with Britain, which he was not yet prepared to undertake. It was not the first rebuff Fleury had given the Jacobites, nor would it be the last. But in the current climate of excitement and uncertainty, even the skeptical cardinal might be persuaded to change his mind.

Hopes were beginning to run high, especially in Scotland, where if the raising of twenty thousand troops was not yet practicable, a number of influential men thought it soon might be. A group of these men had come together to form a "Concert" or "Association," pledged to further the Stuart cause. Among them were the young and daring Duke of Perth, his uncle John Drummond, Simon Fraser, Lord Lovat, chief of Clan Fraser, and Donald Cameron the younger of Lochiel, chief of Clan Cameron and a minor Highland magnate greatly admired for his loyalty and courage. Not all the members of the Association were equally sanguine about the potential for a successful rising—Lochiel in particular was dubious, and with good reason—but the very existence of the group was encouraging. The secretary of the Association, William Macgregor of Balhaldie, spent many months traveling from Scotland to Rome to Madrid to Versailles to London and back to Scotland, meeting with James, Fleury, and most of the prominent Jacobites in London and abroad.

Balhaldie was a colorful, aggressive figure, with something of Shakespeare's "poor, decayed, ingenious, foolish, rascally knave" about him if the accusations of his fellow conspirators are to be believed. That James trusted him indicates that he was more rogue than criminal, but one of his colleagues complained that he was "always in a passion, a mere bully, the most forbidding air imaginable, and master of as much bad French as to procure himself a whore and a dinner."[8] He was clearly unreliable when it came to money. It was rumored that he had had to leave Scotland because of a dispute over a note for fifty pounds, and that he had embezzled Jacobite funds set aside for buying arms.

Clearly Balhaldie was not the sort of man to understand or manipulate government ministers, who saw through his boastfulness and became more skeptical than ever about the actual numbers of Jacobites in Scotland committed to fight under the Stuart banner.

This skepticism had always been the Jacobites' problem. Ministers as capable as Fleury were too hardheaded not to realize how precarious any Pretender's support must be. James's supposed adherents might promise to stand with him in the event of an invasion, but loyal words were one thing, bellicose action quite another. Rebel armies were slow to coalesce and quick to melt away when threatened by firm and well equipped authority. And even under the best circumstances, with a sizable Jacobite force at his disposal, James could do relatively little to advance French interests, apart from providing a distraction to draw Hanoverian troops away from other battlefronts.

No one knew this better than James himself, who for decades had had to swallow his humiliation and repeatedly entreat foreign courts for assistance, knowing that in all likelihood they would eventually disappoint him. "We have been now more than fifty years out of our Country," he wrote in a melancholy vein, "we have been bred and lived in the School of Adversity . . . long experience teaches us how little we can depend on the friendship of foreign Powers." Still, as long as there was a chance that one of the powers might, for reasons of its own, actually provide troops and money, the entreaties had to be made. And so the Jacobite representatives continued to make the rounds of Europe, hoping that the widening warfare would throw opportunity their way.

Late in June of 1743, the Anglo-Hanoverian force under George II's command—the so-called Pragmatic Army—left its camp at Aschaffenburg on the Main and marched out to engage the French.

King George had some thirty thousand men, while the French army of Marshal Noailles, marching parallel to the British force on the other side of the river and watching its every move, was some fifty thousand strong. Ahead of the British was a low area of marshy ground, and beyond it the village of Dettingen. Thirty thousand of the French crossed the river and occupied the village, where they waited for the British to attack. Instead, King George brought his troops to a halt and waited patiently for several hours. Eventually the French commander, discontent with the stalemate, ordered his men to abandon their advantageous position and advance across the marsh, where the waiting English routed the French cavalry and faced the oncoming infantry bravely. George, on foot and "sword in hand," led his men so resolutely that they drove the French back across the marsh into the river, where many of them drowned. In all the French lost nearly five thousand men, the British barely half that number.

The British victory of Dettingen infuriated Louis XV. The British had already provoked him by giving Maria Theresa 500,000 pounds to finance her defense against his armies; now King George himself was waging war on her behalf. He wanted revenge. And he no longer had Cardinal Fleury at hand to restrain him in that desire and to counsel peace, for Fleury had died the previous January. Cardinal Tencin, who replaced Fleury, was less pacific. Moreover, Tencin had close ties to the Stuarts, owing his advancement to the cardinalate in part to James's influence. And a number of Jacobite agents, including not only Balhaldie but the more solid and reliable Murray of Broughton, were on hand in Paris when the news of the British victory at Dettingen arrived. They pressed their case, and King Louis was more than ready to listen.

In August he sent an agent of his own, his equerry James Butler, to London, ostensibly to buy horses for the royal stables but in fact to discover at first hand how many of the English were likely to come out for James in the event of a rising. Butler was impressed by what he found, and came back to his master with a report that a great majority of the most influential Londoners were for James, including the lord mayor and ten aldermen. Outside the capital, there were hundreds of reliable Jacobites, Butler said, and he had a partial list of them which included more than three hundred names.

Had Louis realized how gullible his envoy Butler was, and how indiscreet (he talked so freely while on his mission in London that he revealed its true purpose to more than one government spy), he might have hesitated before going ahead with a plan to aid the Stuarts. He might have changed his mind entirely had he realized just how divided and mutually suspicious the Stuart conspirators were, with Murray of Broughton contemptuous of Balhaldie, many of the Scottish Jacobites highly critical of one another, and the English Jacobites at cross purposes from the rest, and too self-protective to commit their pledges of support to writing.

But these handicaps were not immediately apparent, and so an invasion plan was drawn up, designed to be carried out in the following year of 1744.

The plan called for nothing short of a French invasion of England, with a Jacobite rising timed to coincide with it and to cause chaos while the government troops tried to deal with the invading army. Marshal Saxe, France's most brilliant general, was to command the main body of troops—twelve thousand men—who were to land at Maldon in Essex, not far from London. Three thousand more troops were to land in Scotland, half at Inverness and half on the western coast. It was expected that a number of the Highland clans would come out in force to augment the French armies, but their numbers would be relatively insignificant compared with Marshal Saxe's very sizable body of men.

The moment James had hoped for for so many years was finally drawing closer. Troops were beginning to gather at the Channel ports, and an invasion fleet was being assembled at Brest and Rochefort. This time there would be no equivocation on the part of the French, for the king was committed to the undertaking. And this time the Jacobites would rally behind a new leader, whose youth and energy would inspire and vitalize them. Charles had been summoned to France to sail with the fleet, and he could not wait to be on his way. For years he had "felt his situation acutely," trapped in the narrow confines of the pope's domains. He was as confident as his friend Murray of Broughton that he had been born for

CAROLLY ERICKSON

something extraordinary, and now it appeared that his extraordinary endowments were not to be wasted. His dynamic vitality had
a focus; he had a definite purpose at last. "If he does not come to
the fore," wrote the admiring Des Brosses, "it will not be owing to
lack of energy."

6

"I am not at all ashamed to say I am in fear of the Pretender," Robert Walpole declared frequently during his twenty-one years as principal minister of George I and George II. "It is a danger I shall never be ashamed to say I am afraid of, because it is a danger we shall always be more or less exposed to."

Walpole was deeply and sincerely fearful that Britain might be invaded by a foreign power acting on behalf of James, and he never let his countrymen forget how alarmingly easy it would be for a well equipped force to land, gather local support, and eventually take over.

"Five or six thousand men may be embarked in such a small number of ships, and so speedily, that it is impossible to guard against it by means of our fleet," he told the House of Commons in the late 1730s. "Such a number may be landed in some part of the island, with the Pretender at their head, there is no question that they would meet with many, especially the meaner sort, to join them."[1]

Walpole was almost as worried about the "meaner sort" as he was about the invaders. In the event of a landing, he conjectured, the government could not afford to send the entire army against the foreigners, lest some counties be left without any troops at all; without troops to guard them, "the disaffected would rise" and turn against the forces of order. As long as there was a Pretender, the Protestant monarchy was potentially in peril. Only "peace and tranquillity" could assure its secure continuation.

For two decades Walpole had been warning his countrymen about the Pretender and his secret followers. They were everywhere, spinning out their intrigues behind locked doors, in cellars, at clandestine midnight meetings. They were plotting to assassinate the king, to destroy the Protestant religion and install Catholicism, just as Bloody Queen Mary had done two hundred years earlier, to make all English men and women worship the pope. They were winning over the weak and the discontented, claiming to be champions of liberty when in truth they wanted a return to enslavement under Stuart rule.

"Your right Jacobite, Sir," Walpole maintained, "disguises his true sentiments. He roars out for revolution principles, he pretends to be a great friend to liberty, and a great admirer of our ancient constitution, and under this pretense there are numbers who every day endeavor to sow discontents among the people by persuading them that the constitution is in danger, and that they are unnecessarily loaded with many and heavy taxes."[2] Of course, no Jacobite in his right mind would call himself such; that would do injury to the cause. Therefore no one could be trusted, and the more vehement a man might be in his expression of loyalty to the nation, the more suspect he ought to be.

No large-scale Jacobite plot had been unearthed since the early 1720s, but Walpole was certain that conspiracies were constantly being carried on and that only his vigilance and that of his colleagues and his informers stood between Britain and disaster. "These lower sorts of Jacobites appear at this time more busy than they have for a great while," he wrote in 1736. "They are very industrious, and taking advantage of every thing that offers, to raise tumult and disorders among the people." When Westminster Hall was damaged by a gunpowder explosion he was sure he knew who was behind the "vile transaction." "There is no reason to doubt but the whole was projected and executed by a set of low Jacobites," he insisted. One of his agents had brought him word concerning it, and he trusted in his intelligence system.

Walpole's view of the precarious situation of the Hanoverian monarchy was widely shared. People recognized the possibility that Spain or France—or perhaps even Russia or Sweden—might supply money, arms and men to the Stuarts and realized too that, given how slowly news traveled, a small landing force might have a chance to conquer the country. Britain's army was relatively small, and scattered, and the militia could not be expected to stand for long against foreign soldiery. A good many people remembered what had happened in 1715, when in response to James's landing in Scotland the government had set up a military camp in Hyde Park and had brought down the heavy guns from the Tower, expecting to have to use them to defend the capital. No one had put much faith in the army then, especially when it was discovered that there were Jacobites serving in the Horse Guards and that at least one officer in the Foot Guards had a commission from James as colonel of a cavalry regiment and was busily enlisting men to serve under him in the Stuart army. The ministers, meeting in an emergency session, had come to unanimous agreement that, if James or one of his generals attacked London, the army could not be relied on to defend the king. He would have to flee to Holland.

Nor was the military threat the only thing to be feared. Once word reached London that a rebellion had begun or an invasion force had landed, there was certain to be a financial panic. There would be a run on the National Bank, stocks would fall until they became virtually worthless. Gold would be the only asset worth having, and with public credit collapsed, the government itself would soon come to a halt.

It was a horrifying prospect, particularly to the substantial Whigs who owed their wealth to investment. And as Walpole hoped, the more he increased the public's fear of plots and plotters, the more they would tend to forget how much they disliked the aloof, prosaic kings from Hanover. Anything was better, they were inclined to think, than the "popish Pretender." The constant fear of a "wicked Jacobite conspiracy" also had the effect of turning public opinion toward the government, which kept them informed about and protected against the danger from abroad. The City, which had been a center of opposition to Walpole, became loyal to him; the London crowd, which had been known to storm the lobby and corridors of the House of Commons, tearing the coats of officials and threatening M.P.'s, turned its fury against the Jacobites instead.

Walpole used the situation to make a profit for the government. He taxed the estates of Roman Catholics, taking in a hundred thousand pounds which otherwise, he claimed, would have been used to finance rebellion. According to Walpole, English Catholics were in the habit of making "ill use" of their savings, laying out money "in maintaining the Pretender and his adherents abroad, and fomenting discord and rebellion at home."[3] It was far better that the money go into government coffers.

And in fact James did ask his supporters in England to send as much money as they could spare to help his cause, soliciting twenty or thirty thousand pounds apiece from the wealthiest of them. He supplied his agents with signed receipts, with the amount of the contribution and the interest to be paid on it left blank, to be given out in return for cash.

The government's first line of defense against having large sums of money leave the country was to search the mails, and warrants were issued to postmasters telling them to open all "suspected treasonable correspondence," read it, copy it and then reseal it so that the tampering could not be detected. Copies of all diplomatic correspondence, all letters in the French and Flanders mails, anything going to or from a suspicious person were to be transmitted immediately to the authorities for evaluation. Boxes, packages and chests were opened—even coffins were not spared. When the body of the Bishop of Rochester, Francis Atterbury, exiled for his role in the 1722 Jacobite conspiracy, was returned to England from France for burial in Westminster Abbey, the government ordered the coffin opened. Only the bishop's corpse was found in it, but as an extra precaution the body was slit open and searched to make certain no important documents had been slipped inside.

Suspect correspondence was forwarded to the Deciphering

Branch, where a highly paid chief decipherer and four assistants combed through it, breaking codes that were at times intricate and complex. One foreign minister sent his dispatches abroad from London written in a code employing at least two thousand different characters—and even the simpler codes were challenging, especially as they were altered frequently. The Jacobites had a private nomenclature, referring in their documents to "N" (Lord Lovat), or "T" (Lord Nairne), "Lord of the Manor" (the Earl of Strathmore) and "Mr. Piercy" (the Duke of Argyll). The decipherers were kept busy scratching their heads over who "Mr. Acorn" was, or "The Sexton," or "Jack Caesar," and when symbols were used in lieu of false names their puzzlement deepened.

In *Gulliver's Travels,* published at the height of the anxiety over "wicked Jacobite conspiracies" in 1726, Jonathan Swift made fun of the Deciphering Branch, calling the decipherers "a set of Artists, very dextrous in finding out the mysterious Meanings of Words, Syllables and Letters." They recognized in "a Flock of Geese, a Senate; a lame Dog, an Invader; the Plague, a standing Army; a Buzzard, a Minister; . . . a bottomless Pit, the Treasury; a running Sore, the Administration," and so on.[4] In fact the experts were skilled at what they did, with the result that the government was kept well informed about what its opponents were planning, with reports reaching the Deciphering Branch from post offices throughout Europe, from Danzig to Hamburg to Brussels to Calais.

The cornerstone of the government's intelligence system was its network of paid informers. Several of these had held positions of trust in Jacobite households, or belonged to an inner circle surrounding an important Jacobite personage. John Sempill (not to be confused with the Jacobite agent Lord Francis Sempill), Walpole's principal agent, was at the heart of the exile community in Paris, and conveyed news of the comings and goings of the principal conspirators there. Also in Paris were two Sicilian abbots, Carracciolo and Platania, who had been privy to James's dealings with the Spanish court until sent into exile by the queen, Elizabeth Farnese. The colorful antiquarian Baron von Stosch, who had given the English court so much information about what went on at the Palazzo Muti, became less useful after 1731, when his carriage was attacked by masked brigands who told him to leave Rome and

CAROLLY ERICKSON

frightened him so thoroughly that he moved to Florence. From there he continued to send weekly dispatches to London—based in part on the reports of informers who worked for him in Rome—but because he no longer had personal access to highly placed individuals, his information was not of much value—except, as Walpole remarked, to amuse King George.[5] To be sure, Cardinal Alessandro Albani, nephew of Clement XI, continued to be a useful source of news, and there were others, particularly British connoisseurs traveling to Rome to collect antiquities, who were willing to collect information as well.

Still, Walpole was always eager to recruit new agents, and preferred to meet with them face to face, sometimes going incognito to an out-of-the-way tavern for a rendezvous. There was no shortage of candidates wanting to be hired as agents. Letters arrived frequently from all sorts of people—doctors, businessmen, practitioners of the psychic arts—offering to reveal Jacobite secrets for a price. These people claimed to know when and where James and his army would strike, how many men he had recruited to his cause, and what their names were, what Catholic priests were lurking in the suburbs of the capital, waiting to take over the Church when the Pretender landed. None of these offers could be dismissed lightly, every one had to be investigated, no matter how unlikely. Walpole paid a good deal out of the treasury to bring potential informers from the continent to London just to hear what they had to say.

Had the Hanoverian kings been popular their hold over the throne would not have seemed so precarious. But they had never been popular—merely tolerated because of what they represented: Protestantism and the parliamentary "revolution" of 1688.

George I, who was fifty-four when he became King of England as well as Elector of Hanover, was and remained a mild, dull-witted, unadventuresome German nobleman throughout his thirteen-year reign. He did not bother to learn English, less from snobbery than from an expectation that he probably would not keep his English throne long. He knew the English did not like him, and he was not reticent in saying—though not in English—that he did not like them very much either. (His German courtiers were downright insulting to the English. One of them, Baron Schutz, was overheard to say that "nothing could make him believe that there was one handsome woman in England," while another, Countess Bucke-burgh, was said to believe that "English women did not look like women of quality.") George distrusted his English ministers, with whom he carried on thoroughly unsatisfactory and blessedly brief conversations in French. With Walpole his relationship was margin-ally better; they both spoke a little Latin, and managed to stumble through a dialogue from time to time, though with a considerable sacrifice in clarity and mutual understanding.

Personally the first King George was stodgy and lumpish. "The King's character," wrote Lady Mary Wortley Montagu, "may be comprised in very few words. In private life he would have been called an honest blockhead." He had no ambition, no boldness, no desire to get ahead at anyone else's expense. "He was more properly dull than lazy," thought Lady Mary, "and would have been so well contented to have remained in his little town of Hanover, that if the ambition of those about him had not been greater than his own, we should never have seen him in England." In a pathetic way, she believed, the king was ashamed of his rank in England. His natural honesty, and his genuine lack of understanding of how a foreign nation such as Britain should desire him as a ruler, led him to "look upon his acceptance of the crown as an act of usurpation, which was always uneasy to him."[6]

It may have been this uneasiness, coupled with a native shyness, that made King George reclusive. His subjects rarely saw him, save when he passed them on his way to morning service at St. James's chapel or when, infrequently, he appeared at the opera—choosing not to sit in the royal box but in a less visible place, where he was half hidden by his looming mistress the Duchess of Kendal. He had a private theater built in the great hall of Hampton Court where he could enjoy watching plays without the distraction caused by his own celebrity. His favorite plays were said to be *Hamlet* and *Henry VIII*—the latter appealing to him, perhaps, not only because of King Henry's repudiation of the pope but because like Henry with his six wives, George knew what it was to have trouble with women.

Before coming to England he had had trouble with his wife. She was Sophia Dorothea of Celle, an unfortunate woman who unwisely became involved in a liaison with Count Philip von Königsmark when her marriage to George became tedious. Although George was himself an adulterer, he could not pardon his wife's transgression. Her lover, Count Philip, disappeared under mysterious circumstances and his body was never found. George divorced Sophia Dorothea and imprisoned her in a castle for the rest of her life, turning a deaf ear to her entreaties for mercy and refusing to allow her so much as a glimpse of her children.

When he arrived in England, it was with two mistresses—the tall, emaciated, sixtyish Ehrengard Melusina von Schulenburg (who became Duchess of Kendal) and the "corpulent and ample" Charlotte Sophia Kielmannsegge (who became Countess of Darlington).* To English eyes at least, they were figures out of farce, the one dwarfing the short king by her height, the other eclipsing him with her girth. The countess was particularly memorable, having "two fierce black eyes, large and rolling beneath two lofty arched eyebrows, two acres of cheeks spread with crimson, an ocean of neck that overflowed and was not distinguished from the lower parts of her body, and no part restrained by stays." The duchess lacked charm, but the countess was lively and warm, and the unkind courtiers who referred to them as "old ugly trulls" and "the Maypole and the Elephant and Castle" did them an injustice. Toward the end of his life the king took another mistress, an Englishwoman named Anne Brett, but the two German women remained his preferred companions and the portals to royal favor. Bribes paid to Kendal and Darlington worked wonders for petitioners and ambitious men seeking advancement at court, and they served incidentally to protect the shy King George from harrassment.

Quiet, passive and uneasy on his throne, living in two rooms at St. James's Palace, King George escaped frequently to Hanover, where he died in 1727.

Much was hoped for from his son, who as Prince of Wales had gone out of his way to ingratiate himself with his future subjects and, in contrast to his father, had announced that he thought the English were "the best, the handsomest, the best shaped, the best natured, and lovingest People in the World." The new king was

---

*Because the countess was a daughter of the Countess of Platen, who had been a mistress of George I's father, some historians have asserted that she could not have been King George's mistress. She may or may not have been his illegitimate half-sister (her paternity being indeterminate) but there was no doubt in any of the courtiers' minds that she was his mistress.

crowned in October of 1727, amid lavish and highly public display. He was no more physically attractive than his father had been, but his wife, Caroline of Anspach, was a handsome woman, fair and blond and with a powerful feminine charm, and she added a good deal to the occasion in her diamond-studded gown—the diamonds having been hired from the London jewelers.

This promising beginning to the reign of George II was short-lived, however, and it was not long before the king was revealing his "bilious temper" and referring to his kingdom as "this mean dull island." The honeymoon was over.

The problem was that England simply did not measure up to Hanover, and the oftener the king visited his electoral domain the more he returned convinced that "no English or even French cook could dress a dinner, no English confectioner set out a dessert, no English player could act, no English coachman could drive, or English jockey ride, nor were any English horses fit to be driven or fit to be ridden."[7] The list of English inadequacies was endless. English manners lacked polish, English clothes were ugly, English recreations insipid. Conversation in England was not to be borne— the men talked of nothing but "dull politics," the women of their unbecoming fashions.

At Hanover, naturally, all was perfection. According to King George, "the men were patterns of politeness, bravery, and gallantry; the women of beauty, wit and entertainment; his troops there were the bravest in the world, his counsellors the wisest, his manufacturers the most ingenious, his subjects the happiest," and so on.[8]

Queen Caroline, normally calm and controlled, was vexed when her husband returned from Hanover to pour out his venom on his English subjects.

"I see no reason that made your coming to England necessary," she told him once in an unusual display of sharpness. "You might have continued there." Whereupon the king, trembling and beside himself with anger, left the room without saying a word.

His silent rage was unusual. Normally he was loud and brash and full of bluster. He shouted at the queen, insulting her rudely and often in public, and nearly became apoplectic when angered by his ministers. James Waldegrave, lord of the bedchamber to the king and his close friend, described him fairly candidly as moderately

intelligent, capable of affability, knowledgeable about foreign affairs, and polite to women, especially good-looking ones. He was
also, Waldegrave pointed out, personally brave, an admirable if
somewhat anachronistic quality in a monarch. He liked to dress up
in the old battleworn hat and coat he had worn as a courageous
young soldier in the battles of Oudenarde and Malplaquet, and
every Saturday he rode to Richmond in a coach-and-six escorted by
his uniformed Horse Guards. Leading his men at the battle of
Dettingen was an obligation he welcomed and would gladly have
repeated.

"He has a restless mind," Waldegrave wrote about King George,
"which requires constant exercise." "He becomes fretful and uneasy, merely from want of employment." The king's restless mind
fed on trifles, looking for petty excuses to let loose his bilious
temper. He liked his household to be run according to a precise and
unvarying schedule, and if anyone or anything interfered with that
schedule, he flew into a towering rage. The court wintered at St.
James's, spent the spring and summer at Kensington, and the autumn at Hampton Court. Day in and day out, week in and week out,
King George followed his exacting routine. Once a year, on his
birthday, he put on a scarlet velvet suit and presided, with his family
and household officials, over a reception and ball. Usually his evenings were quiet, however. At nine o'clock the tables were put up
for card playing, and the queen, her ladies, and some of the royal
children sat down to play. While the others were playing, the king
liked to slip away to the apartments of his daughters Emily and
Caroline, whose governess, Lady Deloraine, was to take her place
in his sequence of mistresses.

Queen Caroline, herself a woman of healthy sexual appetites, was
resigned to her husband's infidelities and urged him, on her deathbed, to marry again.

"No," he protested in a burst of loyalty, "I shall have mistresses."

He was as good as his word, and did not remarry. Before long
he brought Mme. Walmoden, who had been his mistress during his
stays in Hanover, to London, and installed her at St. James's Palace.
But he grieved for the late queen, and dreamed about her. One night
he awakened out of a dream "very uneasy," and had himself carried

in a great hurry to Westminster Abbey, where he ordered Caroline's burial vault opened. In his anxiety he even had the coffin itself opened—perhaps to reassure himself that she was still inside—before returning to the palace and going back to bed.

George II was tolerated by his subjects because he was preferable to the Catholic James Stuart. But he was intensely disliked nonetheless. His quarrels with his son Frederick, Prince of Wales, put him in a bad light, and he was the subject of endless bawdy lampoons and rhymes, which ridiculed his lechery in earthy language. People spread stories about how he liked to visit masquerades and pleasure gardens where he could attempt to seduce young girls. "His Majesty's character with all ranks of people," a well informed contemporary wrote, had "fallen so low that the disregard with which everybody spoke of him, and the open manner in which they expressed their contempt and dislike, is hardly to be credited."

It was no wonder Walpole did his best to stir up fear of the Pretender and the wicked Jacobites. There had to be a counterforce to the general contempt for the king.

Clearly the army could not be relied on to any great extent in the event of a popular uprising. The standing army, consisting of some eighteen thousand men (plus another twelve thousand serving in Ireland), was a poorly trained, rough and unsavory collection of recruits. They volunteered for the sake of the pay—which, after deductions were made for billeting, food, clothing, medicine, and other charges, came to only about 6d. a week for a private in the infantry—or to escape unemployment or personal entanglements. Criminals and debtors were routinely offered their freedom from prison if they joined the army. Ill-fed, ill-housed and underpaid, the soldiers had little incentive to do their job well, and many deserted. Those who remained varied in effectiveness, sometimes fighting courageously, sometimes proving to be all but useless.

Had they been at their peak of efficiency thirty thousand soldiers were not enough to defend the realm, particularly a realm that lacked an organized police force and had to rely on its army to put down riots and deal with other local emergencies. More men were needed, yet Parliament resisted authorizing recruitment, preferring to leave the government no alternative but to hire troops from Hanover or Holland in case of need. Parliament also resisted pro-

CAROLLY ERICKSON

posals to build barracks, preferring to have the soldiers billeted in inns scattered over the countryside.

The haphazard nature of these arrangements arose in part from the lack of a central administrative focus. The secretaries of state, on the king's command, determined general strategy and troop movements, but the actual marching orders came from the secretary at war, who also issued orders for recruitment and arranged billeting. Pay for the soldiers came from yet another source, the paymaster of the forces, while clothing was under the jurisdiction of the Board of General Officers. Arms and stores came from the Board of Ordnance. Coordination among these agencies was the exception rather than the rule, and George II's close supervision of military affairs made things generally worse from an administrative standpoint.

There had been improvement since 1715, when the exasperated Foot Guards demonstrated in front of St. James's, lighting bonfires and throwing their shabby uniforms into the palace gardens shouting "Look at our Hanover shirts!" But the army was still small, its recruits badly trained and their morale very low. It was an unreliable bulwark standing between the monarchy and the combined forces of invasion and rebellion.

7

Long before dawn on the cold winter morning of January 9, 1744, the household was astir. It was another of those mornings when Charles, eager to be out and shooting game, awakened in his riding coat and boots and was up and ready to be off before the huntsmen had finished preparing themselves.

The members of the hunting party began to assemble in the courtyard, the breath of men and horses condensing in the chill air. The day's destination was the Pontine Marshes near the town of Cisterna, and Charles, who had just celebrated his twenty-third birthday, and eighteen-year-old Henry were both to take part, along with Charles's tutor Murray and various others. They were to hunt wild boar, a dangerous sport, and as usual Charles was impatient to be after his quarry.

He was so impatient that he did not wait for Henry, but dashed off ahead with only the postilions and servants, Murray, and one or two others accompanying him. Henry and the remainder of the party would catch up with them at Albano, Charles said, and they rode on. Suddenly, a few miles along, there was another change of plan. Charles and two servants pulled ahead of the rest of the riders, and Murray, to distract attention from what was really going on, pretended to hurt himself in a fall, necessitating a delay. While the others lingered behind to attend to him, Charles and his servants widened their lead, but instead of going to Albano as announced, they turned northeast toward the Tuscan border. A brief stop along the way was all that Charles needed to transform his appearance. He changed his wig and put on the coat and ensign of a Neapolitan courier. Farther on, he and his companions mounted fresh horses and he acquired a passport identifying him as Don Biagio, an Italian officer in the service of Spain.

Charles dared not stop, though the winding, snowbound roads made the going treacherous and there was always the chance that he might be recognized and seized. Tuscany was a stronghold of British intelligence, and British spies abounded in Florence. Jacobite spies were often sent from Rome to attack them in an attempt to prevent the transmission of intelligence to England. In one such incident, not long before the events of early 1744, a British agent named Dixon was set upon by one of James's men, Chamberlayne, and left for dead. Dixon survived the attack, but was so wounded and scarred that he no longer had any value to the British.[1] The clandestine battles went on, and in the intelligence underworld the capture of James's son as he attempted to flee northward would have been the supreme coup.

The British envoy at Florence, Horace Mann, sent out a description of Charles, accurate save for the erroneous detail that his eyes were blue instead of brown. "The young man is above the middle height," Mann wrote, "and very thin. He wears a light bag-wig; his face is rather long, the complexion clear, but borders on paleness; the forehead very broad, the eyes fairly large, blue, but without sparkle, the mouth large with the lips slightly curled; and the chin more sharp than rounded."[2]

It had been suspected for some time that Charles would try to make his way to France, though exactly when, and exactly how, the British could not predict. It was difficult for him to go anywhere without being observed, for the activities of James's household were public knowledge and neither of James's sons went anywhere without servants in attendance. The boar-hunting party that provided Charles's opportunity to escape had been announced for January 12, then had been rescheduled for the ninth at short notice, and even then a series of swift and sudden maneuvers had been required to detach Charles from his retinue once the hunt was under way. Complete secrecy was not possible; the only chance Charles had to outsmart the British and their Italian colleagues was to outrun them, and this he was determined to do.

With his fatigued servants in tow, he rode for five days and nights with only a minimum of rest and no halting for changes of clothes. The horses slithered across frost-covered tracks and stumbled through snowdrifts, their riders' faces and hands blistered by freezing winds and pelted by snow and sleet. Charles seemed indefatigable, but his companions were completely exhausted. "I gave them little or no rest," Charles wrote later to his father. "The two servants suffered by my impatience to arrive at the end of my journey. . . . If I had been to go [sic] much further I should have been obliged to get them tied behind the chaise with my portmantle, for they were quite *rendu*. "[3] The suffering paid off, for Charles was able to get to Massa, and from thence by boat to Genoa, where he finally allowed himself a brief respite from travel.

After a day and a half he went on to Savona, where an obstacle of some sort presented itself—possibly a quarantine. He was delayed in Savona for some six days, but then managed to get aboard a small fishing craft which took him, through waters patrolled by the British fleet, to Antibes.

It was essential to maintain the fiction that Charles was continuing his boar hunt at Cisterna all this time, and to this end Henry, who was always willing to play the loyal second to his brother, went on with the hunt and helped to keep up pretenses. He sent loads of boar meat to the pope, to Cardinal Aquaviva and to other friends. He professed himself willing, for Charles's sake, to do anything at all, and did not complain about the fact that he had been told nothing of the plan in advance. He acted as if his brother were with him, hiding his anxiety for Charles's welfare from everyone but his father, to whom he wrote of his impatience "to hear news of our

Dear Traveller, which news I doubt not will be but good, for the hand of God seems to be remarkably upon him on this occasion." The others in the hunting party played their parts equally well, and when the entire entourage returned to Rome on January 17 they took with them a tall, fair young man who resembled Charles—a double who apparently succeeded in convincing the Romans that he was indeed Charles Stuart.

The last leg of Charles's journey was accomplished without incident, though while he was at Antibes rumors of his presence spread and he could have been endangered had he lingered. From Antibes he rode toward Lyons, still keeping up a fast pace, and finally arrived in Paris at the end of January.

By this time the secret of his flight was known, and James was receiving the congratulations of the French and Spanish ministers in Rome. It was James, of course, who had carefully planned and arranged the entire dramatic episode. Believing, as he wrote to his agent in Paris Lord Sempill, that it was "to be now or never in relation to France," he had decided to send his son northward to join the expedition to England. Earlier he had sent Balhaldie along the route Charles was to take, to prepare the way, and had made arrangements with Cardinal Aquaviva to supply Charles with post-horses and with his false passport. James knew that he could rely on Charles to unleash his pent-up energies to their fullest once he was given a chance to act. He believed that if anyone could run the gauntlet of bad weather, miserable roads and British spies it would be Charles. He seems to have believed that the invasion attempt would be a success, for he ordered new liveries for the members of his household, liveries to be put on when word arrived that Charles had ridden into London in triumph and proclaimed his father king.

Charles arrived in Paris, went directly to the lodging of Lord Sempill, and waited. Sempill was optimistic, confident that once the invasion force landed Londoners would rise up and overthrow King George. Charles too was optimistic, writing to his father that he had "met with all that could be expected from the King of France." King Louis, he said, was expressing "great tenderness," and was evidently prepared to support the Stuarts to the hilt. It may be that Louis sent Charles messages through intermediaries, but he did not meet with him face to face, and this filled James with "no small astonishment and concern." After all the assurances he had received that Charles would be put ashore in England with the invasion fleet, after all the trouble he had gone to and the risk Charles had taken, the French king's "negligent and indifferent behavior" toward Charles was dismaying.

It was difficult for the Jacobites to know how to interpret the behavior of the French, for neither Charles nor James nor any of their agents had a broad enough perspective to arrive at judicious conclusions. James, who relied heavily on his then preferred informant Daniel O'Brien, believed that Cardinal Tencin was the principal friend of the Jacobites at the court of Louis XV. Yet Tencin was only one member of King Louis's council of state, and was in fact the last member to be informed of the king's decisions regarding the invasion plan. Tencin was also embroiled in a bitter rivalry with the foreign minister Amelot—who was Sempill's principal court contact—and it was Amelot, along with the navy minister Maurepas, who were the moving forces behind the whole expedition. The fact that the utmost secrecy about the invasion plan was preserved, even in the highest government circles, led at times to poor communication, confusion and misunderstandings between French officials and the Jacobites. Yet there can be no doubt that the king and his ministers had every intention of launching an invasion, and were at no point merely pretending to do so.[4]

After two weeks in Paris Charles moved to the Channel port of Gravelines, where he could be at the heart of the rapidly forming invasion army. Soldiers were gathering there in large numbers, and at St.-Omer and Bergues as well, waiting for the final order to go to Dunkirk and board the transport ships. It would have been easy for Charles to leave his rooms and walk through the narrow streets of Gravelines, disguised as a soldier himself or as a serving man, all but lost—save for his height and handsome face—amid the crowds and noise. After all that he had been through the sight of so much activity, all of it evidently military, must have been reassuring. The harbor was full of packet boats and cargo ships laden with timber and coal and stores, soldiers thronged the streets and taverns and the marketplace, laborers loaded sacks of grain, casks of water, beer and wine and other provisions for an army of ten thousand men.

"Little intrigues are going on for Mr. Fisher's amusement," Charles wrote cheerfully if cryptically to his father, referring to himself as "Mr. Fisher." Because of a last-minute decision to change the landing site from Maldon in Essex to Blackwall in the Thames estuary, the launching date for the invasion had been set back, but clearly the delay was only temporary. Within days the final phase would begin, the men would mass at Dunkirk, the transports would be launched and the French fleet would sail up the Channel to engage the English.

The British were preparing for the worst. They knew, through informants and through the observations of their own seamen, that an invasion force was soon to be launched. They knew that Charles was in Paris, or not far away. They made diplomatic protests, reminding the French of guarantees they had given not to allow any of the exiled Stuarts to enter French territory, though realizing that these protests were only a matter of form. Toward the end of February the English fleet, commanded by Sir John Norris, was at Spithead and the government was concerned for the safety of the capital. All Roman Catholics in London were commanded to take an oath of allegiance to the sovereign; those who refused to do so were to be sent at least ten miles outside the city, their horses and arms taken from them. Unauthorized arms were seized, and suspected Jacobites put in custody. Everything that could be done, was done, but the inescapable fact remained that Britain could muster practically no defending troops, for her army was on the continent supporting Hanoverian interests.

The French knew this, and it made them eager to strike. Because of the delay in embarkation they had lost the advantage of surprise, yet they expected to be able to hold the English navy at bay long enough to effect a landing. Once they were safely inside the Thames estuary, the rest would go smoothly.

The French admiral, Roquefeuille, led his squadron up the Channel from Brest and did not at first sight any British warships. Norris, with twenty ships of the line, was in the Downs, but Roquefeuille assumed that the British had not yet left Portsmouth and sent a signal ahead to indicate that the army should embark from Dunkirk as soon as possible. Shortly after this the French fleet encountered the British near Dungeness, but it was late in the afternoon, and both the hour and the state of the tide were wrong for an engagement. Roquefeuille, sobered by the strength of Norris's fleet, and with a storm coming on, made for the French coast. The storm blew harder, sudden winds churning the water into giant peaks and troughs in which many of the French vessels foundered. It was an omen of worse to come. Early in March fierce winds drove on across the Channel, striking at the unwieldy transport vessels where they were massed in the harbor at Dunkirk. Many were swept onto the rocks, where their valuable cargoes of men, animals and provisions were smashed to bits. Charles and Marshal Saxe had already embarked when the storm arose, and were lucky to return to port with their lives.

Hardly had the surviving men and ships had time to regroup and consider what to do next when bad weather struck once again, sending more ships and men to the bottom. By this time the French could no longer delay declaring war on Britain. It was understood that the battles of this newly declared war would be fought in Flanders, and so no troops could be spared for an invasion headed by a Stuart claimant to the British throne. The logic of the situation was relentless; Charles, who had always been at best a useful ancillary to French ambitions, now found that he was expendable. It was not that the French were fickle, merely that circumstances now forced them to alter the deployment of their forces. King Louis made provision for Charles to receive a pension of five thousand livres a month, and then turned his attention elsewhere. Marshal Saxe left Dunkirk to lead the French army in Flanders.

It was characteristic of Charles that, having survived the dangers of drowning and shipwreck, having watched his opportunity to become the conqueror of England melt away overnight, and having lost King Louis's attention, he impulsively declared that he would sail to England by himself. He would go "in an open boat," risking all on the hope that "his presence could be of service in England." The French prudently advised him to stay out of sight, suggesting that he take refuge with his cousin the Bishop of Soissons. But Charles was reluctant to leave the coast, and lingered on at Gravelines, made irritable by the constant advice of George Keith, Earl of Marischal. Unlike the fiery Balhaldie, the earl was possessed of a cool head, and good sense rooted in decades of military experi-

CAROLLY ERICKSON

ence. He had sheltered James in Scotland in 1715, had played a major role in the abortive invasion attempt four years later, and had served Frederick the Great as well as James. He had been prepared to play his part in the invasion, but was resigned to accepting its failure. He knew folly when he saw it, and he saw Charles courting disaster with his rash talk of setting off for England alone.

"To go single, unless you are invited by the principal peers both for credit and good sense, would be for ever the destruction of the Cause," Marischal told Charles. To Charles the advice sounded like an insult, and he complained, in letters to his father, of the earl's pessimism and deliberate undermining of French support. He had "discouraged" the French "to the last degree," Charles claimed. He had even gone behind Charles's back and talked the French out of letting him serve in the army in Flanders. The earl "tells them," Charles wrote, "that my serving in the army in Flanders, it [sic] would disgust entirely the English, by serving in the same army that is to fight against them, and so forth. He has done all this without telling me anything of the matter or consulting me about it."[5]

If he could not fight with the French in Flanders, perhaps he could go to Scotland with the Scots and Irish serving in the French army, Charles suggested, but no one at the French court heeded the suggestion. The days passed, the soldiers left the Channel ports. Charles could not help but be disheartened, though he tried to maintain a stoic detachment. "I have learned from you," he wrote to his father on March 26, "to bear with disappointments, and I see it is the only way, which is to submit oneself entirely to the will of God, and never to be discouraged."

He was in limbo, caught between the temptation to give in to despair and his own ever resilient hopes. His physical energy demanded an outlet, yet everyone around him seemed to be conspiring to prevent him from acting.

"The situation I am in," he wrote to James on April 3, "is very particular, for nobody knows where I am or what is become of me, so that I am entirely buried as to the public, and can't but say but [sic] that it is a very great constraint upon me, for I am obliged very often not to stir out of my room, for fear of somebody's knowing my face. I very often think," he went on, "that you would laugh very heartily if you saw me going about with a single servant buying fish and other things and squabbling for a penny more or less."[6]

At times even this harmless diversion was impossible, and Charles stayed in his room, reading, writing letters, no doubt brooding on his future. He was learning to discipline himself, to force himself to do disagreeable things. In the past the task of writing even one letter had been almost unendurable for him; now he forced himself to write for hours at a time. "I have every day large packets to answer," he told James, "without anybody to help me but Malloch [i.e., Balhaldie, one of whose code names was Malloch]. Yesterday I had one that cost me seven hours and a half." Marischal wrote him very long letters—they seemed to Charles to be "almost books"— and he dutifully answered them point for point. He was taking on the role James had played for so many years in Rome, that of being chief secretary to the Stuart cause. He was receiving letters of advice, letters of encouragement, letters counseling caution and others urging him to undertake wild adventures. Information came to him from many sources, information that required sifting and thoughtful consideration. The burden of acknowledging the letters alone was a sizable one, and beyond this their contents had to be weighed mentally. Each new letter meant more hours of confinement, more entrapment in the sticky web of intrigue and less action.

In April, desperate for "company and diversions" and apparently convinced that there was no point in remaining at Gravelines any longer, Charles moved to Paris. There he found lodging in a charming small house near Montmartre with a good view of the city. Compared with the Palazzo Muti, these were cramped quarters, but Charles's household was very small—and, for the moment, very modest. (He had "but twelve forks, spoons and knives," and the furnishings must have been correspondingly spare.) In Paris he was joined by his old tutor Sheridan, whom he had sent for earlier in the year. Sheridan was by this time well over seventy, and so frail and ill that he was frequently subject to slight strokes. On his way from Rome to Paris he suffered another of these strokes, and soon after he joined Charles's household he began to complain of another of his chronic ailments: deep depression.[7] Sheridan's health problems ranged from fainting fits to headaches to digestive troubles which kept him on a strict diet. "Poor Sheridan," James wrote, "is not fit to exert himself very greatly."

Still, he was fit enough to send James news of a personal nature about his son. "I found him in very good health," Sheridan wrote early in June of 1744, "and he seemed to me both taller and broader than when I saw him last. He is certainly increased in bulk, but for his height, when I seemed surprised at it, he let me into the secret. He showed me the heels of his shoes which he wears now of the usual size, whereas before he wore them remarkably lower than other people. In fine," he concluded, "he has altogether a much more manly air than he had when he began his travels."[8]

A stouter, taller, and more manly young man who had begun to wear the high heels then in fashion: this was Charles in the summer of 1744. He was away from his father for the first time, and feeling his own strength. His political fortunes might be uncertain, but his faith in himself was glowing more brightly than ever, and this despite a host of major and minor annoyances.

Chief among these was a lack of funds. The promised French pension was not paid, and the fragile Sheridan had to be dispatched to Flanders to make a personal appeal to King Louis. This proved unsuccessful, and Charles had no recourse but to go to moneylenders. The rent on the little house had to be paid, there were tradesmen's bills and servants' wages and the usual expenses of princely largesse, albeit on a small scale. The moneylenders were assured that they would be repaid once King Louis's minister of finance made good on what was owed to Charles, but while they waited they added interest at high rates, making the total owed mount astonishingly month by month.

Nearly as plaguing as the lack of funds was the lack of harmony among those pledged to the Stuart cause. Most of the prominent Jacobites were locked in conflict with each other, Sempill criticizing Sheridan, Murray of Broughton accusing Balhaldie and Sempill of petty crimes and general irresponsibility, Balhaldie attacking Murray. Faction fought faction, with Charles in the middle trying to keep his supporters united while feeling the seduction of faction more and more himself. The attempt to keep the peace left him weary, as did the constant effort to discover where the truth lay in all the petty squabbling. It was difficult at times to remember the common goal, that of organizing military resistance to George II. Of all the men in Charles's circle in 1744, only Murray of Broughton seemed to be vigorously pursuing that goal.

Murray came to Paris in July, and met with Charles in secret "at the great stables in the Tuileries." He was full of news from Scotland, where as he told Charles, the Scots were doubtful that any French help would ever be forthcoming. Though Charles insisted that he had "the strongest assurances" from King Louis and his ministers that the invasion would eventually take place, no later than harvest-time, Murray was equally adamant. According to Murray, Charles listened calmly, "acting with as much coolness, caution and circumspection, as the most experienced statesman." Yet beneath this judicious exterior Charles was much affected. Murray's arguments impressed him with their force. Instead of allowing himself to be taken in by the continual ruses of the French, Murray was actively enrolling Scottish Jacobites, persuading them to sign documents promising to fight for Charles should he come to Scotland, even if he came without French support. The course Murray was advocating seemed the one most likely to succeed.

Yet it was precisely the course James was warning him against. "Avoid precipitate and dangerous measures," James cautioned him sternly in his letters, "some rash or ill-conceived project, which would end in your ruin, and that of all those who would join with you in it." James, having resigned himself to the French abandonment of the invasion attempt, no longer dreamed of an imminent military opportunity for his son. The royal liveries he had ordered for his servants had long since been put away. It seemed to James, in fact, that Charles might as well return to Rome, so slim were his chances in Paris. Besides, Charles would soon be needed to take over James's own work there, for his energies were flagging. At fifty-six he was finding it harder and harder to concentrate for any length of time; when he attempted to read or write he was overcome by vertigo and the room began to spin around him. He referred to himself as "a useless old father," whose ills, though not mortal, were growing worse every day.[9] He needed to be able to pass on his responsibilities to his elder son.

In mid-November of 1744, Charles wrote to James in a tone of extreme exasperation. It was a private letter, intended for James's eyes alone and expressive of Charles's candid feelings. After assuring James that he was well aware of his obligations "before God and men," that he was attending to his public and private devotions and conducting himself dutifully, he began a *cri de coeur.*

"You may well imagine how out of humor I am, when for comfort I am plagued out of my life with *tracasseries* [petty bickering] from our own people, who as it would seem would rather sacrifice me and my affairs than fail in any private view." The quarrels were endless, and it did no good for Charles to remind the individuals involved that "whatever is said of our own people, though never so well grounded, was cutting our own throats." The bickering seemed to be getting worse as time passed, fomented by idleness and the increasing sense of futility that threatened to destroy the Jacobite party entirely. "The more I dwell on these matters, the more it makes me melancholy," Charles concluded.[10]

It was a pessimistic letter, yet it held one bright sentence. "As long as there is life there is hope!" Charles exclaimed in the midst of his ill humor, and in fact he had begun to form one specific private hope, one that he did not share with his father. Murray of Broughton's assurances about the faithful Scots sworn to aid him once he landed in Scotland had strengthened his resolve and helped to sustain him amid his current troubles. Whatever else might happen, whether the French kept or broke their promises, whether or not the Jacobites in Paris destroyed themselves with infighting, Charles had a plan of his own. As Murray wrote later, Charles swore to him that "at all events, he was determined to come the following summer to Scotland, though with a single footman."

8

Charles was finding his life in Paris intolerable. He felt stifled there, "imprisoned," as he put it, by the strong hand of the French court, prevented from living as he chose and forced to endure inaction. He tried to escape his quarrelsome advisers by going to the opera, but James forbade this. He could not go hunting, as the weather was too severe. He tried to tell himself that, sooner or later, the French invasion plan would be revived, but as winter closed in with its gales and frosts he recalled the bitter experience of the previous February and March and realized that no invasion would be launched until spring at the earliest.

He tried to be patient. "Whatever I may suffer," he wrote to James early in the new year 1745, "I shall not regret in the least as long as I think it of service for our great object. I would put myself in a tub, like Diogenes, if necessary."[1] He nourished his dream of journeying to Scotland, but did not yet see how it could be done.

He had just written to the French foreign minister complaining that he had been living in Paris for eight months, waiting for the government to fulfill its promise that within six months at most a new invasion would be launched. This promise had not been honored, nor had his modest pension been augmented as he had been told it would be. He had been forced to borrow between thirty and thirty-five thousand écus and was having to borrow more each month. He was about to leave Paris for the château of FitzJames, a house which had been lent to him by his cousin the Duke of FitzJames, younger brother of the Duke of Berwick. The house was in Picardy, situated along the Paris-Calais road, and the grounds offered excellent hunting—which he hoped to take advantage of if the weather improved. The prospect of leaving the stifling environment of Paris was exhilarating, but he could not leave until his debts were paid. It was an emergency.

Charles's remonstrances were noted in a minute at the French foreign office, where he had by no means been forgotten. To judge from what happened over the next few months, the French ministers had every intention of profiting from Charles's presence in France and from his pent-up energies and boundless ambition, but they intended to do this in their own time and in their own way. The war minister Argenson authorized payment of Charles's debts up to a limit of thirty thousand crowns—which in fact fell short of the total—and informed the controller general that no further sums were to be given to him.[2]

Housing in Paris had become an acute problem. The stay in the house in Montmartre had not lasted long. From there, to save money, Charles had gone to stay for a time with a Scots banker, Aeneas MacDonald, assuring MacDonald that he would not be a guest for very long as the finance minister Orry had promised to secure a house for him. Orry had disappointed him, however, and so he had decided to rent the least expensive lodgings he could find. "I was forced to take a few rooms in town," he wrote, "which is but a hole, for to be less suspected, and also for want of money."[3] He was still living in this "hole," with only Sheridan and another companion, George Kelly, for company when he decided to leave Paris for the château.

In contrast to the frail, fatherly Sheridan Kelly was a tough and doughty warrior, a man of immense willpower and determination who had spent his life in the service of the Stuarts. No one had made greater personal sacrifices than Kelly for the sake of restoring the Stuarts to the British throne. An active Jacobite plotter in the 1720s, he had been captured by the English—holding his captors off just long enough to destroy important papers which would have jeopardized others. Imprisoned in the Tower of London, he managed to survive its disease and damp for fourteen years, and finally escaped. He made his way to the continent, where he served as secretary to the Duke of Ormonde at Avignon. From there he came to Paris and Charles, who no doubt admired Kelly's toughness and indomitability, drew him into his circle. (Kelly, a Protestant and a parson, was a relative of Charles's Catholic confessor, a bibulous man also named Kelly.) Wit, courage, intelligence and discretion—all qualities Kelly had in abundance—were in short supply among the Jacobites of Paris, and it was no wonder Charles made a particular friend of Kelly.

Then too, Kelly was Irish, and Charles was coming more and more to feel a kinship of spirit and personality with the Irish he met.

There was a large Irish contingent in France, made up of soldiers in the French army, merchants, down-at-heels adventurers and Gallicized Irish, some of whom came from families that had been living in France for several generations, and had prospered greatly there. Charles met the soldiers first, through the good offices of Lord Clare, commander of the Irish brigade in the service of Louis XV. Clare introduced him to Lord Tyrconnel, Colonel Dillon, and others who impressed him with their daring and boldness. Among these men was John William O'Sullivan, a Kerryman who had had a long and distinguished military career. O'Sullivan had been sent to Rome to study for the priesthood as a boy of fifteen, and later, after entering holy orders, he had become a tutor in a French military family. His employer, Marshal Maillebois, had glimpsed his military promise and had taken him along on campaign in Corsica. It was a harsh baptism in the science of war, for Maillebois drank heavily and increasingly left strategic decisions to his young protégé. By the time the Corsican campaign ended O'Sullivan had laid aside his priestly identity permanently and gone on to serve as an officer in Italy and elsewhere. He was an expert, his colleague said, "in the irregular art of war," and was not inferior to seasoned generals in commanding troops.

Men such as Kelly and O'Sullivan were as different as could be from Balhaldie, Sempill, and the slippery French. When he left for the château of FitzJames, Charles took O'Sullivan with him.

Charles gravitated toward the Irish soldiers because they told him what he wanted to hear: that he ought to make a bold bid for success on his own, without waiting any longer for French military support. To his father he might write that he felt keenly his "want of experience" and that, being "very young," it was hard for him to keep his perspective, but in truth he knew his intentions and was working to fulfill them.

Some time in the early months of 1745 he composed a list of tasks for Murray to carry out, a list which reveals that he was doing a good deal of detailed planning toward what he called his "resolution of going to Scotland without forces."[4] He required of Murray, first, that he endeavor to procure "a considerable sum of money for arms and in as short a time as possible," and that he send a reliable person to Holland to buy them. Next he was to gather more funds for use on Charles's arrival, contacting an English Jacobite agent in London, Dr. Barry, for this purpose. Next he relied on Murray to recommend the most advantageous landing site for Charles and his party. Murray was to send Lord Traquair to "concert with the English," but his most urgent task, apart from raising money, was to rouse the Highland Scots to gather broadswords and kilts and the Lowland Scots to "provide as many horses as they can without suspicion."

Money, arms, and horses: without these there would be no semblance of a Stuart army. Charles was doing his best to raise money himself. In the first week of March he informed James that he had taken it upon himself to borrow forty thousand livres from James's Paris banker Waters, to be used to buy broadswords for the Scots. The money, he told James, was "the only comfort" he could give them, and rather than deny them this comfort he "would have pawned his shirt." He asked his father to pawn his jewels—part of his Sobieski inheritance—and to forward the proceeds to him to repay the loan, assuring James that he would use the money for nothing but arms and ammunition, "or other things that tend to what I am come about in this country." "In an urgent necessity," he added, the money might come in handy "for the cause."[5]

James disapproved. "I cannot but tell you freely that I am sorry you have given the money in question," he replied, and he did not pawn the jewels—though he did repay Waters. James was disturbed by letters he was receiving from Paris, letters that revealed how bitterly his supporters were divided. He hated to see his people all in pieces," he said, and he was particularly concerned about the changes Charles had made in his own inner circle. A letter from an opinionated Englishwoman, Lady Clifford, informed James that Charles had surrounded himself with "unknown, low-born" men, "of no credit or weight, and so useless." These unknowns were keeping others away who might benefit the cause. "Don't you see plainly," she wrote to James, "that till the Prince has proper people about him, he may go on years and ages in the same fruitless way he has passed days and months, since he has been in France." Without "people of quality" around him he would never be able to rally the English to his support. As it was, Lady Clifford went on, Charles's behavior was attracting ridicule. English Jacobites had recently had to suppress a pamphlet titled "The conduct of a young Hero, his Court, and amusements" which made fun of Charles's unprincely behavior.[6]

Back in Paris after his stay in Picardy, Charles was faced once more with the familiar problems of finding lodging, raising loans and setting up housekeeping. Tradesmen were unwilling to deliver groceries to the rooms of "Baron Renfrew"—Charles's current pseudonym—and for a time this caused a minor crisis.[7] Yet he was able to rise above these nuisances because, thanks to Lord Clare, a major element in his plan of going to Scotland was falling into place.

Besides money, arms and horses, Charles needed transport, and for this he looked to the Irish privateers who operated out of Nantes and St.-Malo.

Many of these privateers were Jacobites, and all of them were eager to play a role in a Stuart restoration, not only because they stood to profit from backing the victors, but because as licensed marauders assaulting British ships they were in effect in the employ of France. Rather than mount a costly and elaborate military invasion, the French had decided to give Charles indirect support. Maurepas, the navy minister, authorized the gathering of arms and ammunition, the recruitment of marines, and the use of a French warship by Antoine Walsh, a former French naval officer operating as a privateer. Charles had approached Walsh through an intermediary, Walter Ruttledge, a Dunkirk banker and shipowner who had been born in the shadow of James II's exile court at St.-Germain and had never lost his Jacobite loyalty. Ruttledge told Walsh what Charles had in mind—to sail to Scotland and land where he could assure himself of raising an army.

The negotiations went well. "My zeal for your cause has no limits," Walsh wrote to Charles in March, "and I am prepared to undertake anything where the service of your Royal Highness is concerned." Walsh's father Philip had been captain of the ship that had taken James II to France after the Battle of the Boyne in 1690. There would be a strong historical symmetry in operation if his son Antoine delivered James's grandson Charles to Britain to begin his conquest. To be sure, the undertaking would be very dangerous, and Walsh was in the best possible position to realize the dangers. Still, as he told Charles, he was willing to do his part. "If, after my representations, your Royal Highness persists in wishing to undertake the passage, I will willingly give him a little frigate, a good sailer, which I will cause to be ready as soon as possible but on condition your Royal Highness will allow me to accompany him and share all the perils to which he may wish to expose himself."[8]

In addition to the little frigate, the *Du Teillay*—named for the French naval commissary at Nantes, M. Du Teillay—the expedition would require a fighting escort, a gunship to protect her in the event of a British attack. Here Maurepas's cooperation was crucial. He allowed Walsh to charter a sixty-four-gun line-of-battle ship, the *Elisabeth,* and to man her with sixty officers and at least several hundred men. (One volunteer company of French cadets aboard was called the "Compagnie Maurepas.")[9]

The *Elisabeth* was well over thirty years old, though still sturdy.

She was in origin an English ship, christened the *Elizabeth,* and she had been captured by the French in the reign of Queen Anne and refitted to serve in the French navy. In 1745 she was one of many ships leased to privateers attacking British merchant fleets. Her diversion to Scotland would indirectly benefit both the French and the privateers, for if Charles succeeded in raising a rebellion in Scotland, the British would have to respond by ordering naval ships northward, weakening their convoys and patrols, and thus making their merchant shipping more vulnerable to attack.

The war was not going well for the British. During 1744 the Pragmatic Army, which had distinguished itself under George II at Dettingen, was commanded by the gouty septuagenarian Marshall Wade, whose health was so poor he could barely sit his horse for more than a few hours at a time. The English, Dutch, Austrian and Hanoverian soldiers who made up Wade's heterogeneous fighting force quarreled among themselves and barely held their own in the Low Countries while Britain's ally Austria challenged the French in Alsace. In the spring of 1745, as campaign season began again, command of the Pragmatic Army passed to King George's twenty-four-year-old second son William, Duke of Cumberland. But Cumberland and his motley army were overmatched by the French forces of Marshal Saxe, all picked men and with twice the numerical strength of the British. At Fontenoy the two armies met on May 11, and though the British infantry made a remarkable stand in the end they were forced to give way and Saxe's men were victorious. Fontenoy was merely the first of a string of French victories in Flanders, culminating in the taking of the British base at Nieuport.

From Charles's point of view all this was to the good, for the weaker the British became on the continent the more reinforcements would have to be sent there, leaving Britain denuded of troops. Even before he received word of the British defeats he had written to Murray of Broughton in Scotland telling him that he expected to arrive there in July, and would probably land on Mull or one of the other islands off the western coast. "I venture myself," Charles had written, "and hope to find friends enough among you to do the same and I am persuaded if we can make ourselves masters of the Highlands, and of both or even one of the castles you mention, we shall be able to make such a stand as will encourage those abroad to give us the succours we want."[10]

Once they made a stand, both foreign support and money—specifically, the money from his pawned jewels and another "large sum which has been ready these many years past for such an occasion" in Rome—would be forthcoming. He had had to act quickly, and secretly, for to do otherwise would have meant gossip, delays, and eventual inaction. He asked Murray to "prepare for his reception" and to have copies printed of the Commission of Regency James had given him to be published "the moment hostilities are begun."

The timing of the adventure he was about to undertake was crucial, for although the French victories in Flanders were welcome, they threatened to shorten or even to end the war—which would mean a peace treaty between France and England, and no further chance of French help for the Stuarts. Charles had to sail before the British were utterly defeated, but not before his own preparations were complete and his Scots supporters were in readiness for his landing.

At the same time he had to choose carefully when to reveal his plan to his father, who had to be kept in the dark until it was too late for him to interfere. Charles wrote to James in June, but did not dispatch his courier with the letter until the eve of his embarkation in July. "I have, above six months ago, been invited by our friends to go to Scotland," he began, "and to carry what money and arms I could conveniently get; this being, they are fully persuaded, the only way of restoring you to the crown, and them to their liberties."[11] He explained that, having found his situation in Paris unendurable, honor demanded that he either return to Rome, "which would be just giving up all hopes," or "fling himself into the arms of his friends, and die with them." The time had come to show his mettle, to take daring action or risk losing the respect of all those who looked to him for leadership. "If a horse which is to be sold if spurred does not skip, nobody would care to have him, even for nothing; just so my friends would care very little to have me, if after such usage as all the world is sensible of, I should not show I have life in me."

He was like a young, spirited horse impatient to slip its reins and be off. His enthusiasm was unbounded. He was doing what James himself had done thirty years earlier, only now, as he told James, "circumstances are indeed very different by being much more encouraging, there being a certainty of succeeding with the least help." He advised James to come at once to Avignon, in order to be nearer to England when the hour arrived for him to enter London as king.

"Let what will happen," he wrote confidently, "the stroke is struck, and I have taken a firm resolution to conquer or to die, and stand my ground as long as I shall have a man remaining with me."

There was less bravado, and more detail, in the letter Charles wrote to his father's secretary James Edgar at the same time. In it he asked for immediate repayment of the loans he had taken—a total of a hundred and eighty thousand livres—and described the arms he had bought with the money: fifteen hundred muskets, eighteen hundred broadswords, powder, balls and flints, dirks, brandy and twenty small field pieces ("two of which a mule may carry") and four thousand gold *louis* in cash.[12]

There were hundreds of last-minute arrangements to be made. Besides coordinating the embarkation, and keeping Murray in Scotland abreast of all that was happening, Charles had to decide on his precise landing point, ensure that pilots would be available to guide the large ships through the dangerous Hebridean coasts, keep up with his mail—packets still arrived for him frequently, and had to be read and answered—and send out last-minute appeals for aid from all his continental supporters. He wrote to the King and Queen of Spain asking for arms, munitions, and money. Through Antoine Walsh he arranged for money and goods to be sent to Scotland via business firms in Hamburg and Amsterdam, and through Ruttledge's bank in Dunkirk. He made certain new ciphers were issued. And he decided which of his personal companions to take with him, along with the sixty specially chosen, brightly uniformed cadets of the "Compagnie Maurepas" who would form his personal guard once he landed.

That he would take George Kelly and O'Sullivan was certain, for their experience and military expertise would be greatly needed. Sheridan, he decided, would come along as well, despite his frailty. The banker Aeneas MacDonald, who happened to have business in

Scotland and who had useful clan connections in the Highlands, would also accompany the expedition. Another old soldier, John MacDonnell, was included, presumably because having spent many years serving in the Spanish cavalry he could be expected to help command whatever mounted men came to Charles's aid. And there were two others, both of whom could be expected to be liabilities. The first was Francis Strickland, an Englishman who had held various posts in James's household in Rome, including that of tutor to James's sons, but who after a falling out with James had come to Paris. ("I have no scruple to say he is an ill man," James told Charles about Strickland, "and conjure of you to forget if possible whatever he may have said to you on any subject.")[13] The second was the Marquess of Tullibardine, yet another semi-invalid who was nearly sixty and could barely walk without an attendant on either side to help him. Charles had been afraid that Tullibardine would find out what was going on and could not be trusted to keep what he knew to himself; "for the sake of secrecy," he told Murray, he intended to take the old man along.

Besides these seven ill-assorted traveling companions Charles took a chaplain, the Abbé Butler, Aeneas MacDonald's clerk Duncan Buchanan, who had served as a useful courier in the recent past, and his own Italian valet Michele Vezzosi, who had made a dramatic escape from Scotland nearly thirty years earlier. A Barra man, Donald Cameron, came along as pilot. Antoine Walsh commanded the *Du Teillay*, while one Captain d'Eau was to command the *Elisabeth*.

Charles and the others converged on Nantes, traveling separately to avert suspicion. Charles had been staying at the château of the Duc de Bouillon at Évreux in Normandy, and when he left the château he hid his real destination by saying that he was going on a brief tour of the Norman countryside. On the way to Nantes he assumed yet another incognito, as Mr. Douglas, a student at the Scots College in Paris. Dressed in the plain cloth of a student, with a cheap wig and an unshaven chin, he looked innocuous. Sheridan posed as his father. No doubt Walsh made the arrangements for all the travelers in Nantes. There they waited while contrary winds delayed them until at last the *Du Teillay* was ready to sail, and

BONNIE PRINCE CHARLIE

Charles and the others went on board. They sailed to Belle-Isle and there waited a week, taking on provisions, for the *Elisabeth* to join them from Brest. On July 15 she appeared, and on the morning of the sixteenth both ships set sail for Scotland.*

The voyage began uneventfully. The trim little frigate made good speed toward the Cornish coast, the gunship staying within sight. Only Charles and the few who were in his confidence knew the purpose of the expedition. The seamen and soldiers were told nothing, they knew only that France was at war with England and that they had to remain alert for English ships. As for the little cluster of passengers aboard the *Du Teillay*, they appeared to be just an ordinary group of travelers, thrown together by the chance of a common destination—two elderly men and the student son of one of them, three Irish soldiers, a down-at-heels English gentleman, and a Scots man of affairs.

The July sun was hot. The ships rode the Channel swells, out of sight of land, adrift in the monotony of the vast green water. The tall blond student, Mr. Douglas, was probably tempted to shoot at the sea birds that followed the *Du Teillay* but, having learned prudence, restrained himself. It did not suit the persona of a sober scholar of humble birth to recreate himself in the manner of a sporting young lord. In any case the mild rolling of the ship made him unwell, and most likely he kept to his cabin much of the time.

"We have nothing to do now but to hope in the Almighty's favoring us," he had written to his father just before embarking. God was with them, of that he felt certain. Through his father he had asked for the pope's blessing; Catholic Europe wished him well. There were thousands in Scotland and England, both Catholic and Protestant, who would welcome his arrival. He was bringing his own arms and the strong core of a fighting force with him. His uniformed guard, the hundreds of soldiers Walsh had hired, the chests of swords and muskets, the cannon—all would allow him to establish a beachhead and then begin seizing strongholds, one by one. The Highland Scots would join him and then, once King Louis saw how

---

*Once they were at sea, they adjusted their time reckoning from the New Style Gregorian calendar in use on the continent to the Old Style then still in use in England; Old Style dates, in the eighteenth century, lagged behind New Style dates by eleven days. Thus July 16 became July 5.

he was prospering, there would be French troops to swell the Stuart ranks. The army would grow, would surmount opposition, would be invincible.

About a week out from Belle-Isle, just at dusk, the crew of the *Du Teillay* sighted a shadowy vessel in the distance. They were about a hundred miles off the Lizard, on their way to round Cornwall and sail up the west coast of Ireland. The phantom ship drew closer, then withdrew out of sight. The next morning she appeared again, and this time came close enough to be recognized as the H.M.S. *Lyon,* carrying fifty-eight guns. The *Lyon,* newly refitted, was en route from Spithead to duty in the Bay of Biscay, and it was evident that she was swifter and more maneuverable than the larger *Elisabeth.*

Captain d'Eau and his officers went aboard the *Du Teillay* to confer with Walsh. The French captain was convinced that the *Lyon* was not alone. They should engage her now, he said, before her companion vessels appeared. The *Du Teillay* could draw her in, then the *Elisabeth* could close with her while both fired on her. These were sound, if obvious, tactics yet Walsh would not agree. He did not dare to take any chances with his royal passenger. There would be no engagement unless the *Lyon* attacked.

Drawing his sword, Captain d'Eau returned to the *Elisabeth* with his officers. The *Lyon* was coming closer. D'Eau ordered his gunners into position and hoisted French colors as the *Du Teillay* moved off to the west, out of range of the action. The *Lyon* came on until, at d'Eau's command, the *Elisabeth* fired a single gun. There was an answering shot. Then, obedient to Walsh's command, d'Eau made sail and attempted to outrun the British ship. But the *Lyon* was intent on combat, her captain ordering her longboat cut away to increase her speed.

By this time it was late afternoon. As the *Lyon* came alongside, the *Elisabeth* fired her sixty-four guns, breaching the *Lyon*'s hull, and received damaging fire in return. Thick black smoke surrounded the two ships, making it hard for the gunners to sight their targets, but they kept up their murderous fire. The French shot away the *Lyon*'s mizzen mast and tore her sails to ribbons; her rigging hung crazily. Yet she managed to cut ahead of the *Elisabeth* and rake her across the bows, inflicting heavy casualties on her crew and putting her in danger of sinking.

So evenly matched were the two vessels that they fought on, hour after hour, with the men of the *Du Teillay* watching and dodging wayward shot. Charles became agitated. Why couldn't the *Du Teillay*'s guns be fired on the *Lyon* to save the *Elisabeth*? Walsh refused, and kept his ship at a safe distance. Charles must hold his peace or be confined to his cabin.

Through the gray twilight the bursts of orange fire continued, less frequently now, the embattled ships only a few hundred yards apart. Both were taking on water. Aboard the *Elisabeth* more than two hundred men were killed or seriously wounded, and the *Lyon*'s crew was decimated as well. In the last exchange of fire, Captain d'Eau fell.

At about ten o'clock the *Lyon*, barely seaworthy, sheered off "like an old tub," and the *Elisabeth*, listing and leaking, was unable to pursue her. The *Elisabeth* had no choice but to try to return to Brest. Walsh decided not to accompany her in the *Du Teillay*. As the last light faded Charles was forced to watch the great French gunship wallow off into the darkness, taking with her most of the men, arms, and provisions with which he had hoped to conquer England.

9

Unescorted, her sails smoke-blackened and pitted by cannon shot, the *Du Teillay* crept northward up the coast. Crew and passengers alike were aware that should another English gunship appear the little frigate would have to surrender, and each time sails were sighted on the horizon they tensed and prayed for deliverance.

Day after day the odds grew greater that they would encounter an English patrol, and face capture. Even if their luck held and they managed to make a safe landfall in Scotland, they had next to nothing with which to make a rebellion. The hundreds of hired mercenaries, the uniformed guard, the cannon, the stores of arms and provisions: all were gone. Except for the *Du Teillay* herself, and the chests of gold *louis d'or,* there was nothing to prove that Charles had the backing of the French—and without this the Scots could not be expected to be sanguine about his chances for success. The fifteen hundred guns and eighteen hundred broadswords the *Du*

Teillay carried would not go far in any case, even if a respectable number of Scots presented themselves to fight for Charles.

Arguments broke out over whether to persist in the expedition or give it up and return to France. Charles, still disguised as a divinity student, his true identity and the purpose of his journey kept secret from the crew, was staunch for going on. In his sea chest was the declaration of regency his father had sent him when he left Italy for France.

"It will be absolutely impossible for Us to be in Person at the first setting up of our Royal Standard," James's declaration read. Because of this he designated "Our dearest son, Charles, Prince of Wales, to be sole Regent of Our Kingdoms of England, Scotland and Ireland, and of all Our other Dominions, during Our Absence." The document was dated "in the forty-third year of Our Reign."

If James were ever to reign in fact as well as in imagination, then his son dared not turn back. Not when it had cost him such trouble and expense to come this far. Not when he had raised such expectations in his supporters. Before leaving Paris he had received from these supporters a leather-covered shield embossed in silver with images of crossed swords, standards and a Medusa head. He would carry this into battle when he led his faithful Highlanders against the British army. Providence would protect him, he believed, and aid his cause.

About ten days after the fight with the *Lyon*, the *Du Teillay* approached the remote island of Barra in the Outer Hebrides. The weather was foul. A storm was whipping the waves to froth, the winds were high and the rain heavy. A party was sent out in a longboat, but while the others were waiting for their return, a British man-of-war was sighted and Captain Walsh decided to put Charles and his party ashore out of harm's way. With the man-of-war following closely, a local pilot guided the frigate to a shallow, sheltered bay on the smaller island of Eriskay. There, on "a very wet dirty night," they disembarked and set about looking for shelter.

They found it in a crude hut about a mile from the beach, where they huddled in their wet clothes around a smoky peat fire and attempted to roast some flounders for their evening meal. Charles sat in a corner, laughing at the Barra man, Duncan Cameron, when he burned the fish, ebullient despite the storm and the general danger in which he found himself. The dense smoke in the room irritated him, so that he got up frequently and went outside into the storm for fresh air. But it was not only the smoke that drove him to get up and sit down again a dozen times. He was restless with excitement, sanguine about what lay ahead for him. When on the following morning he received word that several of the local clan chiefs would not support him, in spite of their previous assurances to the contrary, he was undaunted. He listened while Alexander Macdonald of Boisdale insisted that no one would join him, and advised him to return home.

"I am come home, sir," he replied gravely, "and I will entertain no notion at all of returning to that place from whence I came, for that I am persuaded my faithful Highlanders will stand by me."

Charles repeated his sentiments to his companions aboard the *Du Teillay*—who were all in favor of going back to France—and added that "he would rather die" than turn back simply because Boisdale and a few others had disappointed him. He had friends remaining who would come to join him, he said. Their loyalty would be shown beyond question, once they reached the mainland.

This was problematical, as the warship they had sighted the day before was still cruising near them, though the bad weather prevented her from attempting to close with the *Du Teillay*. At sunset she was still in view, but when night fell the *Du Teillay* got under sail and made for the Scottish coast.[1]

In the morning the islands of Rum and Eigg were in view, and beyond them the rugged coastline, mountainous and desolate, penetrated by deep sea lochs. There was no sign of the man-of-war. Captain Walsh sailed up Loch nan Uamh, which divides Arisaig from Moidart, and anchored there.

No part of the Scottish Highlands was more remote than this. The steep rock faces of the mountains were forbidding, the stormswept coast a challenge to even the most experienced sailors. Few tracks wound through this inhospitable country, whose inhabitants were famous for their loyalty to the Stuarts and their bitter opposition to the government.

Several more Macdonald chiefs came to meet with Charles on shipboard in the following days. They found him in a large tent erected on the deck of the ship, "covered and well furnished with variety [sic] of wines and spirits." At first glance he looked like a clergyman, dressed in a plain black coat with a plain shirt in need of washing, a simple neckpiece with a silver buckle, and a round wig. But his elegant bow, his graciousness in toasting the chiefs with a glass of wine, his affability were aristocratic. He was unmistakably princely. "At his first appearance," one of the Macdonalds wrote, "I found my heart swell to my very throat."

Boisdale had warned Charles that news of his arrival was spreading rapidly—there had been rumors all summer that he would soon come to Scotland—and it would only be a matter of time before the government in Edinburgh dispatched its forces to meet the rebels. Once dispatched, they would not reach Charles and his men quickly—the difficult terrain ensured that—but they would come in strength, and before very long. He had to raise and organize his own forces, and supply them with arms, in as short a time as possible.

He moved from the *Du Teillay* into a farmhouse at Borrodale on the shore of Loch nan Uamh, taking with him his closest companions and some of the men from the ship. Here he busied himself overseeing the unloading of the ship and the distributing of guns and broadswords. Most of the weapons and the remaining men went to Kinlochmoidart some six miles to the south.

"I am joined here by brave people as I expected," Charles wrote to O'Brien on August 4. "As I have not yet set up the standard I cannot tell the number, but that will be in a few days as soon as the arms are distributed, at which we are working with all speed. I have not as yet got the return of the message sent to the Lowlands, but expect it very soon. If they all join or at least all those to whom I have sent commissions to at request, [sic] everything will go to a wish."[2]

These were optimistic words, for in fact only a few minor chieftains had as yet agreed to send men to Charles's camp, among them Alexander Macdonald of Keppoch and Alistair Macdonald of Glengarry.* As he wrote in his letter, nothing had been heard as yet from the Lowland Jacobite leaders, and it was clear that many Highland

---

*From this point on, to avoid the confusion of multiple surnames, the Scottish lords will be referred to wherever possible by their territorial titles.

chiefs were hesitating, wanting to lend their support but wary of being among the first to commit themselves. Beyond these, who were in a position to provide fighting men, there were other Jacobites who, if discreetly approached, might give money, either directly or through intermediaries. But they too had to be persuaded that they would be contributing to a successful rising and not merely a bold and ultimately futile adventure. What helped to sway them in these early days was Charles's own absolutely unshakable faith in the success of his undertaking. He would succeed or die in the attempt, he announced to skeptics. He was leaving himself no alternative. Unlike James in the 1715 rising, he did not provide himself with a convenient means of escape if things went badly; he sent the *Du Teillay* back to France, after rewarding Walsh with the grandiose title "Lord of Ireland."

Curiosity drew the local populace to the Borrodale farm, where "the whole neighborhood without distinction of age or sex crowded in . . . to see the Prince." He received them sitting in state, where everyone could see him, surrounded by his retinue and presiding over a table abundant with food and drink. He was toasted in the Highland tongue, with the words Deoch slainte an Righ—To the King's Health—and he did his best to repeat the unfamiliar words convincingly.

This was mere posturing—though Charles did it well. The loyalty of the Borrodale locals would count for nothing if none of the major clan chiefs took a stand. Yet Donald Cameron of Lochiel, head of the large and powerful Cameron clan, having been strongly opposed to Charles's undertaking at first, had begun to waver. Fifty years old, practical and hardheaded, he faced the bright-eyed, irrepressible Charles Stuart, and told him he ought to "be more temperate." There was no reason why he shouldn't go back to France, hire more soldiers and buy more weapons, and return in force. But Charles was more than a match for him.

"In a few days," he informed Lochiel, "with the few friends that I have, I will erect the Royal Standard, and proclaim to the people of Britain that Charles Stuart is come over to claim the crown of his ancestors, or die in the attempt."

Lochiel, who had almost certainly not been prepared to find such absolute toughness in a mere boy of twenty-four, was taken aback when Charles invited him to either join him or "stay at home, and learn from the newspapers the fate of his prince."

"I'll share the fate of my prince," Lochiel swore, having made up his mind in that instant to commit himself body and soul to Charles, "and so shall every man over whom nature or fortune hath given me any power."

The ringing promise was music to Charles's ears, for with Lochiel on his side it was easy for him to claim that the hesitation and outright disloyalty of other chiefs was only a pretense designed to test him, to see whether he had the fortitude to press on in the face of opposition. "The prince shows a vast deal of resolution and undauntedness," the Abbé Butler wrote in his account of the early days of the rising, "which prodigiously pleases the people." "As much as I can perceive things could not be in a more smiling attitude."[3]

This was hardly true, for although Lochiel's promise was heartening, it was only a beginning, and not all of those who pledged themselves to Charles's cause were satisfied. They complained that there was not enough money, that their weapons were too few and inadequate, and that there was no noteworthy commander to lead them into battle. The scant provisions Charles had brought along were running low, and the local harvest was late. Fortunately, the capture of two British grain ships made available extra supplies of oatmeal and barley just when they were most needed. Still, with "numbers crowding daily to offer themselves," the problems of weaponry, command and supply were certain to escalate.

It was with these problems very much in his thoughts that Charles made the journey from Kinlochmoidart to Glenfinnan to await the arrival of the men Lochiel and the other chiefs had promised to provide. He had written to the mainland clan chiefs asking them to join him at Glenfinnan on August 19, but he could not predict how many of them would come, or with how many supporters.

Charles arrived at the rendezvous point, conspicuous in scarlet breeches and waistcoat, to find that only about a hundred and fifty of Clanranald's men had come in response to his summons. He waited—an hour, two hours. After three hours, early in the afternoon, bagpipes could be heard in the distance, eerie and solemn. Then Lochiel and his piper came into view on a mountaintop, marching in slow cadence at the head of the Camerons, who snaked down the zigzag path to the valley floor in their hundreds. They came in lines two abreast, herding between them eighty or so British prisoners whom Keppoch's men had captured in an ambush several days earlier.

The procession of outsize, fearsome Highlanders, descending the mountain in full war regalia, overawed the spectators, some of whom reckoned their numbers as high as fourteen hundred.[4] When they were all assembled at the head of the loch, the elderly Tullibardine, as usual leaning on the arms of two younger men, came forward to stand before them and unfurl the red, white and blue banner of the house of Stuart. James was proclaimed king, his son Charles proclaimed regent. Immediately the men broke into loud huzzas and threw their bonnets up into the air in such numbers that it "appeared like a cloud."

When the cheering had died down, a proclamation was read which constituted a formal statement of the terms under which the new king would take his throne. In it King James, through his regent, declared that all those who had rebelled against the Stuart monarchy since 1688 would be pardoned, provided they now declared their allegiance to their rightful king and renounced their allegiance to the Hanoverian usurper. Soldiers serving in the usurper's army would also be pardoned, so long as they left their regiments and joined King James's army; as an added incentive they would receive any arrears of their pay and an entire year's pay in addition. Officers serving in the Hanoverian forces would, once they entered King James's army, receive commands with higher rank.

The government would continue as presently constituted, the proclamation assured. A free Parliament would be summoned, to function without any degree of duress from King James; officials and magistrates, revenue collectors and judges were all to remain in their offices, save that they were to acknowledge that they held their authority from King James and not from King George. Churchmen too were to carry out their duties unchanged, for King James utterly opposed any form of religious persecution. (In this sensitive area, care was already being taken to prevent giving offense to British Protestants; when Keppoch's Catholic clansmen were marching to Glenfinnan, they were told they could not be accompanied by a priest—an announcement which led some of them to desert their chief—who was himself Protestant.)

Finally, the proclamation ordered every subject between the ages of sixteen and sixty to present himself for service in the Stuart army, on penalty of royal punishment should he fail in his duty.

The clansmen listened to the words of the proclamation, though few of them understood it, speaking only Gaelic. Afterward Charles said a few words, complimenting his hearers on their adherence to his father's right and telling them that, with God's help, "he did not doubt of bringing the affair to a happy issue."

No doubt this was greeted with more huzzas, especially when Charles ordered casks of brandy opened for the men so that they could toast King James's health. Shouts of "Deoch slainte an Righ" floated out over the loch and echoed from the craggy mountainside. All in all, it was an inspiring afternoon and an auspicious new beginning to what had until then seemed a very fragile rebellion.

Slender though Charles's forces were, they might well prove sufficient to the task of conquering Scotland for King James, for Scotland's defenses, in the summer of 1745, were sadly inadequate.

The government officials in Edinburgh had fewer than four thousand troops at their disposal. There was only one tested, seasoned regiment of infantry. Two others were newly formed and untested, and another was only at half strength. A miscellany of "additional" companies had recently been raised, intended for use in combat on the continent, but these too were under strength and hardly constituted reliable troops. The two available dragoon regiments had been raised in Ireland, with ill-disciplined men and young horses untrained to gunfire. And though there were guns and mortar in Edinburgh Castle, there were no artillery officers or men to fire them.

Given the fact that for two decades, Walpole had raved about the Jacobite menace, and Britain's vulnerability to attack, the sorry defenses in Scotland were inexcusable. The current rumors of a Stuart landing ought to have resulted in increased preparedness, but the officials did not take the rumors seriously, and in London, Walpole's rather mediocre political heirs did not share his sense of urgency and vigilance. The Marquess of Tweeddale, secretary of state for Scotland, was preoccupied with saving money on Scottish defenses in order to enhance Britain's campaigning strength abroad, and could not be persuaded that a Highland rising was either dangerous or imminent. The king was away in Hanover, renewing his appreciation of the superiority of everything German to everything English, and was not expected to return in the immediate future.

Perhaps the only person in authority who was truly alarmed about what was happening in the Highlands was Lieutenant-General Sir John Cope, Commander-in-Chief for Scotland. Cope had fought at Dettingen, and had been in Scotland for a year and a half. Disliked by his political masters, he was described as "a dressy, finical little man" whose good breeding and fastidiousness were more striking than his military capabilities. Brilliant soldier or not, Cope at least had the sense to take very seriously the report that reached him on August 8 that Charles Stuart had landed and was raising an army.

Cope had been warned to keep "a strict eye on the Highlands," but he knew that this was meaningless. What was vital was to arm those Highlanders known—or believed, at least—to be loyal to the Hanoverian ruler so that they could join the existing infantry regiments and oppose the Stuart forces. In the aftermath of the Fifteen, Parliament had made it illegal for any Highland clansman to carry arms. That meant that the so-called "well affected" clans would be defenseless against the rebels, unless arms were brought to them from the Lowlands.

A thousand stands of arms were assembled at Stirling Castle, northwest of Edinburgh, for Cope to take northward. His troops gathered there, and waited vital days while bread was baked for them to carry on the march and a butcher with a drove of cattle was found to follow them. Though he had no artillerymen, Cope decided nonetheless to equip his troops with artillery, to frighten the rebels. The guns were brought, though the only men who could be found to handle them were an elderly gunner, long out of service, and three invalids from the Edinburgh Castle garrison.[5]

On August 20, the day after Charles exhorted his men at Glenfinnan, Cope started northward, intending to rendezvous with the "well affected" clansmen of the Duke of Atholl (that is, the Hanoverian duke, not his elder brother Tullibardine, whom the Jacobites recognized as Duke of Atholl) and Lord Glenorchy—both of whom had promised to provide him with men. Having armed them, he planned to proceed to Fort Augustus, where he would establish his headquarters. On the twenty-first he arrived at Crieff, only to discover that neither Atholl nor Glenorchy had been able to raise a single man to swell the ranks of the government troops. This was a shock, as Glenorchy's Campbells in particular had been counted on to be staunchly loyal.

Not only did the "well affected" Highlanders prove to be disaffected, they added injury to insult by raiding Cope's provisions and ambushing his troops. And what was worse, the Highlanders in his regiments began to desert, leaving him with fewer men than ever to face Charles and his growing army.

To these difficulties were added others. Rumors reached Cope that French troops had landed to support the rebels, and these rumors accelerated the desertions in his ranks. Then the deserters went over to the Jacobites, and told them everything they knew. The scouts and guides he had hoped would be forthcoming from Highlanders loyal to the government were not forthcoming. Rain spoiled food supplies, pack animals were stolen. The thousand unused stands of arms were a burden to already overburdened soldiers.

Then Cope learned that Charles, with three thousand men (in actuality he may have had as many as fifteen hundred, but no more) was waiting to confront him at the Pass of Corrieyairack. The boulder-strewn, nearly perpendicular mountain pass was approached, from the south, by a dangerously steep ascent with seventeen traverses—making it arduous enough in itself, but suicidal with an enemy waiting at the top. Cope changed his plans and decided, despite orders from Edinburgh to the contrary, to march his men to Fort George, at Inverness, instead of to Fort Augustus. Had he attempted Corrieyairack, he would have found the Stuart forces entrenched there, having placed their guns in position so as to enfilade the treacherous traverses and then waiting at both the top and bottom of the pass to capture the survivors.

Cope's decision left the Lowlands virtually unprotected. After chasing the Hanoverians for a day or two, with many of Charles's Highlanders furious at not being able to engage him, the Stuart forces marched southward, through Atholl country. Here where Cope had not been able to find a single fighting man to join him, Charles found hundreds of people running out of their houses to greet Tullibardine, whom they considered to be their rightful chief. The Hanoverian Duke of Atholl fled, and Tullibardine installed himself at Blair Castle.

Charles was elated. More and more men were turning out to follow him, some of them men who had supported his father thirty years earlier, bringing their sons and their tenants. People cheered him as he rode by, and cheered for King James, and wished the army well. Cope had been afraid to face him, and that was surely an encouraging sign. Even the weather, which had been lowering and stormy, had improved, and the sun shone on their southward progress.

On September 4, toward evening, Charles entered Perth. He rode into the ancient capital in triumph, dressed as a Highland prince in a suit of tartan cloth with gold lace trim, the Star and Garter on his chest, the Stuart white cockade in his bonnet. Cheers went up all around him as he made his way to the home of Viscount Stormont, where he was to stay for a week while his growing body of men drilled and trained and his officers made their plans.

Three decades earlier, James had ridden into Perth. Pale, austere, and defeated-looking, he had presided over the disintegration of his army and the dissolution of his hopes. In deep snow and bitter cold, his underfed men had marched with rusty guns until, overwhelmed by chaos and by their lack of faith in James, they had left him and gone back to their homes.

Now his son, handsome, sanguine and energetic, had arrived to redeem that sad defeat. Charles's men were well fed and reasonably well equipped, and what they lacked in organization they more than made up for in enthusiasm and battle-eagerness. Their numbers were growing: Charles Stewart of Ardshiel brought two hundred and fifty Stewarts of Appin, there were four hundred Glengarry Macdonalds, and the twenty-year-old Lord Ogilvy, whom Charles had known in France, arrived to pledge an entire regiment of six hundred men as soon as they could be brought from Angus.

Most important of all, the men were intensely committed to Charles. The chiefs had drawn up an association pledging themselves never to abandon him while he remained in Scotland, and never to surrender unless he ordered them to. The soldiers, Murray of Broughton recalled later, were so utterly devoted to him that "there was scarce a man among them that would not have readily run on certain death if by it his cause might have received any advantage."[6] They shouted their support "by huzzas and acclamations that even rent the sky whenever they saw him," and wrote songs to him, which they sang loudly and lustily in his presence.

The wintry melancholy that had hung over James's cause for thirty years had been dispelled forever; the Stuart sun had come out at last.

10

The English, in the middle of the eighteenth century, thought of Scotland as an impossibly remote, sparsely populated region with a boreal climate and a bleak, treeless landscape. Its mountains were "black and frightful," one traveler wrote, its hills bore "a most hideous aspect." "The huge naked rocks, being just above the heath," another visitor commented, "produce the disagreeable appearance of a scabbed head."[1]

"The face of the country is wild, rugged and desolate," wrote John Home in his contemporary history of the 1745 rising, "as is well expressed by the epithets given to the mountains, which are called the gray, the red, the black, and the yellow mountains, from the color of the stones of which in some places they seem to be wholly composed, or from the color of the moss, which, in other places, covers them like a mantle." (Another writer suggested a slightly different palette, describing Highland scenery as "of a dis-

BONNIE PRINCE CHARLIE

mal brown drawing upon a dirty purple, and most of all disagreeable when the heath is in bloom.")

To venture forth into this blighted wilderness was an act of reckless courage, for there were no roads in the usual sense, only narrow dirt tracks and the paths beaten out by cattle being driven to market. These deeply rutted, boulder-strewn pathways turned to swamps in wet weather, and in the long frigid winters the swamps froze over and were buried under deep snowdrifts. Horses could barely stumble their way along; for carriages the going was nearly impossible.

Before starting out, the intrepid travelers had to assure themselves that their carriage was in good repair, and some even took the precaution of carrying a wheelwright along with them so that when the axletree broke—as it almost invariably did—the driver did not have to leave them stranded while he searched the deserted countryside for a blacksmith. Often a footman rode ahead, armed with pistols and broadsword, to warn of obstructions in the path or to fend off highwaymen, while two more footmen rode alongside the carriage carrying long poles with which to extricate it from the mud. Delays for repairs normally added several days to the journey. While they were being made, the travelers took refuge in the nearest tumbledown inn while the wind howled and rain cascaded down the mountainsides in torrents. Or, where there was no inn, they simply waited in the open air, at the mercy of the elements, while repairs were made on the road. The horses were unhitched, and villagers were recruited to bring carts and lumber and heavy tools out to the site of the accident. Many hours later, the journey was resumed.

Conditions in the Lowlands were bad enough, but travel in the Highlands, to the west of a line stretching from Dumbarton in the southwest to the Moray Firth in the northeast, was nearly impossible. No carriage could climb the mountains; indeed the going was too rough even for horses, and most travel was on foot. Beyond the inconvenience and sheer arduousness of going even short distances, visitors were put off by the nature of Highland life itself. There were no cities or towns, no commerce, virtually no agriculture. The itinerant Highlanders devoted themselves entirely, it seemed to outsiders, to following herds of emaciated black cattle through the mountains, nearly starving in winter and reviving briefly in the chill far northern summer.

The hardihood of the Highlanders was inexhaustible. The clan chiefs and their principal retainers recreated themselves by taking to the high hills in winter, oblivious of the snow, to hunt for game. For days at a time they scorned shelter, sleeping on the frozen ground wrapped in their plaids, eating the game they killed and drinking the few bottles of whiskey they brought along with them. The common folk spent the winters in mean sod or turf cottages, sleeping on bare boards with heath or straw beneath them. In the summer they left the "winter towns" for the hill pastures, and lived there in temporary huts, moving on when the grazing gave out. They managed to subsist on fish and game, and on what the cattle provided—not only milk and butter and cheese but the thick pudding made from the blood of the cows, boiled and solidified.

Hardy as they were, people and cattle alike became enfeebled during the snowy winters and many did not survive to face another dark spring. In years of abnormally cold weather, famine and disease forced people down out of the Highlands into Lowland towns or across the water to Ireland. These "hungry years" decimated the countryside; in some parishes fully a third of the population died, and the abandoned pastures and winter towns did not come to life again for decades.

Such desperate hardship was almost beyond the comprehension of the few English who found their way north of the Highland Line. A scant, starveling—if ferociously combative—people clinging to their bleak hillsides and wedded to their backward customs: such was the impression the visitors received. Efforts by well-meaning outsiders to improve the lot of the Highlanders met with truculent rejection. When ryegrass and clover were introduced for use as hay for winter feed, the Scots rejected them as "English weeds" and refused absolutely to change their traditional habits. And when for military use roadways were built connecting the principal forts, the Highlanders complained that the gravel was hard on the hooves of their unshod horses, which traveled far more comfortably on heather.

Mutual incomprehension between the Highlanders and most outsiders—including Lowland Scots, who contemptuously referred to the Highlanders as "Irish"—was perhaps inevitable, for the Highlands were as remote culturally as they were geographically. The prevailing customs, particularly those of the islands off the west coast, mingled Christian and pre-Christian observances and were exotic indeed by English standards.

In his *Description of the Western Isles of Scotland,* Martin Martin, himself a Highlander, recorded his observations made on a tour of the islands in 1703.[2]

Martin found the Western Isles to be a charmed world where, as on the island of Rona, the people repeated the Lord's Prayer and Apostles' Creed in their chapel on Sunday mornings and went home to propitiate spirits with gifts of milk and oatcakes. Whenever Martin put to sea in the course of his journey the steersman and crew of the boat recited a liturgy of blessing. "Let us bless our ship," the steersman called out, and the crew answered, "God the Father bless her." "Let us bless our ship," the steersman called again, and this time the answer came, "Jesus Christ bless her." A third repetition invoked the blessing of the Holy Ghost, after which came more questions and answers, ending with the resounding cry, "We do not fear any thing!"

All this was orthodox enough, but Martin noted that the sailors hung a goat from the boat's mast to ensure a favorable wind, and consulted oracles before starting out on their journey. He also recorded that they were careful, when turning around, always to turn "sun-ways"—that is, from east to west, in the direction of the sun—lest they bring bad luck on themselves or their ventures.

A great deal of the islanders' attention and energy went into preventing misfortune. They were afraid of being carried off by ghosts, and of the fairies who came in the night to steal newborn babies. When there was a birth, friends came to stand in a circle around the cradle and guard the baby, keeping vigil all night and holding the Bible aloft to ward off danger. Another peril to be averted was that which arose from praising any animal without adding "Luck fare the beast," or admiring a child without saying "God bless the bairn" immediately afterward. Unless these propitiatory phrases were added, the cow might die or the child might grow up a cripple.

All the islanders used incantations and charms to protect themselves from *scaith,* or evil. They carried fire in a circle around their beasts to keep them safe from injury. They made pilgrimages to holy wells, where spirits lived, to seek healing or advice. They repeated magic words to make their cows give more milk and hung branches of mountain ash in their stalls to keep them healthy. On the first of May they built Beltane fires and danced around them, throwing pieces of oatcake over their shoulders and chanting, "This to thee, protect my cattle," "This to thee, O fox, spare my sheep," and "This to thee, O hooded crow, save my lambs."

Children in the Western Isles wore amulets made of beans to warn them of danger from the evil eye. The beans turned black if anyone with the "uncanny eye" came near—a likely occurrence, the Highlanders believed, because so many people possessed it.

Martin preserved vivid images of life on the more remote islands, images of young men riding at breakneck speed along the frigid beaches, whipping their horses forward with a long piece of seaweed; of stalwart fisherwomen who waded out through the freezing water to their boats, carrying their husbands on their backs in order to keep the men's feet dry; of drinking rituals lasting for several days, in which people drank whiskey distilled from oatmeal and so strong that to drink more than a spoonful of two "would presently stop a man's breath and endanger his life."[3]

Here as elsewhere in the Highlands it was difficult to grow any sort of crop. The islanders laboriously broke the salty, stony ground with small wooden-toothed harrows, which they drew themselves, sparing the horses. Then, using spades, they turned the soil over, covering it with seaweed to fertilize it. Beyond what little they grew, their diet was augmented by milk and cheese, fish, and "seapork"—the flesh of whales, hunted in the shallow island bays and driven in shoreward to beach themselves. When famine came the islanders were reduced to living on boiled goat's milk—and survived so well on it that the hardiest among them lived to a very advanced old age. Martin was introduced to one ancient islander who claimed to be a hundred and thirty years old, and who still had vigor enough to labor with his hands.

Throughout the Highlands scarcity and austerity were norms of life, for rich and poor alike. The clan chiefs lived in huge, turreted fortresses with wide moats and capacious courtyards. Yet such castles provided grandeur without luxury; indoors, the bare plaster walls were unadorned, the small, bare rooms were dark and freezing cold. Travelers were amazed to discover how simply the chiefs lived, rising early, eating gruel and oatmeal cakes from wooden or pewter plates, dressing in rather shabby plaids, and, as likely as not, slipping further and further into debt each year. Even the wealthiest and most powerful among them reckoned the value of their estates in the number of fighting men they could supply, not in money. Coins were scarce throughout Scotland; the only banks were in Edinburgh, and barter was common. Highland landowners in need of money drove their black cattle down to the market at Falkirk or Crieff and sold them to English graziers. They were a colorful sight in the cattle market, threadbare but dignified in their plaids and blue bonnets, their poniards and broadswords gleaming at their sides, speaking Gaelic and trying to make themselves understood.

The chiefs were princely, despite their relative poverty; the common folk, on the other hand, lived in uncommon squalor. "The nastiness of the lower people is really greater than can be reported," one traveler wrote. "Their faces are colored with smoke; their hair is long and almost covers their faces."[4] Indeed it was nearly impossible for them to keep clean, for the peat smoke that warmed them left their skin brown and tough, and they had to share their cramped, smoke-filled hovels with their cattle. Besides, the layers of dirt helped to keep them warm. "Muck makes luck," went one proverb. "The mair dirt the less hurt."

Prosperous cottagers had two rooms, but most families had only one, whose walls were of turf or unmortared stone. A hole in the roof let out the thick smoke, but there were no windows; the only light came through small gables—which had to be stuffed with rags or straw when the wind blew. The workday began, between March and October, at four in the morning, and went on until seven or eight in the evening—even later during harvest time. The prized self-sufficiency of the Highlanders was earned at the cost of feeding and watering the cattle, digging peat and carrying it on horseback from the moors, spinning flax and woolen yarn to weave into cloth, and dozens of similarly time-consuming tasks. And all this labor often had a sordid ending, for when the Highlanders brought their cattle to market they were at the mercy of the shrewd buyers, who knew how far they had traveled and how desperate they were to sell their emaciated beasts. More often than not the cattle brought only a few shillings a head, and the cycle of Highland poverty continued.

Such was the view outsiders had of the harsh life north of the Highland Line. Its ugliness repelled them, its inconveniences astounded them, its culture alienated them, and its squalor inspired in them more revulsion than pity.

But theirs was a partial and myopic view. For if the Highlands were not the mist-enshrouded paradise of the Romantic imagination, and if they were largely Irish in culture, their own distinctive traditions being thin in depth and recent in origin, still there was more to Highland life than most visitors perceived.[5]

For one thing, they tended to underrate the extent to which clan attachments compensated for poverty and physical hardship. "Though poor, I am noble," went one saying among the Macleans. "Thank God I am a Maclean." Who carried the clan chief's name carried at least some of his power and dignity; one chief claimed that the members of his clan, however lowly, were "all gentlemen." Pride of clan was a cohesive force that no outsider could fully comprehend; it gave each individual his or her identity, indeed it would not be much of an exaggeration to say that it gave life meaning.

The clans began and ended with the chief, the *Cean Cinne* or Head of the Kindred. As the senior member of the great extended kindred to which all clan members theoretically belonged, the chief was revered and loved with a fervor approaching idolatry. The Highlander's most sacred oath, wrote the historian John Home, was to swear by the hand of his chief. "The constant exclamation, upon any sudden accident, was, may God be with the chief, or may the chief be uppermost." Every clansman was ready to die for the chief. Highlanders had been known "to interpose their bodies between the pointed musket, and their chief, and to receive the shot which was aimed for him."[6]

The clan chiefs, and the heads of the septs (the principal cadet branches of the family), or chieftains, looked on themselves as virtually independent sovereigns, secure in the natural fortresses of the inaccessible mountains and protected by the fighting men of their clans. They feared one another, but no outside power—certainly not the power of the English king, many hundreds of miles away to the south, or his ministers or Parliament.

The chiefs were a law unto themselves, and when disputes arose between them, they went to war, as often as not, for legal decisions of the Court of Session in Edinburgh had little practical force in the Highlands. To their clansmen, the chiefs were magistrate, judge and general rolled into one. They arbitrated conflicts and the decisions made at their tribunals were final.

There was something of the feudal lord about a clan chief, and even more of the patriarch. "His habitation," Home wrote, "was the place of general resort, the scene of martial and manly exercises; a number of the clan constantly attended him both at home and abroad, the sons of the most respectable persons of the name lived a great part of the year at his house, and were bred up with his children." Though the chief was not necessarily a landholder, and the ties that bound him to his clan members were strictly ties of blood and not of place or tenancy, in many cases the chief's lands were given out to his closest relatives, who in turn divided them among their relatives and adherents. Thus territoriality, along with a common surname and common ancestry, made the clan cohere.

To be sure, by the middle of the eighteenth century, changes had begun to come to Highland society. Some chiefs' and chieftains' sons were sent to the Lowlands to college; there they learned refinement in dress, speech and manners, and unlearned to despise Lowland culture. Some chiefs had begun to cultivate business interests, with contacts in the Lowlands and elsewhere. Others invested in the West Indies trade, or speculated in land in the New World. There were small signs, here and there, that the absolute, unquestioned power of the chiefs was marginally eroding. But only marginally: if clansmen occasionally disregarded the interests of their chiefs, it was only in small things; they were still his to command, particularly in war.

Indeed it was the archaic, near-mystical force of the chief himself which made the clan system work. The Macdonald chiefs were called *Buachaille nan Eileanan,* Shepherd of the Isles, and the idea of the chief as the protective shepherd of his flock, or father of his children, was pervasive. In the Hebrides, according to Martin, the MacNeill chief took responsibility for seeing to it that every widow and widower among his people remarried—and he chose new spouses for them all. The MacNeill also gave shelter to elderly members of the clan too feeble to care for themselves, and fed the clansmen lavishly at his own table. The fact that the chiefs, in their capacity as supreme judge, sometimes hanged members of the flock who displeased them—and hanged them, it must be added, for trifling offenses—did not diminish the reverence in which they were held. Rather it was a harsh reminder of the chief's superiority, and of the stark ferocity that made him a valued leader in time of war.

That the clan chief should lead his men in battle was long-established custom. His sons or nephews were his principal subordinate commanders; together with his piper, his swordbearer and armorbearer, they fought beside him and died, if necessary, to save him. When the clan marched out to make war, the chief drew blood from the first animal he encountered, sprinkling it on his banner to baptize it for the combat to come. He and his clansmen pledged one another's health in cups of their own blood from time to time as well. Such gory rituals were commonplace in the bellicose Highlands where feuding clans did their best to exterminate each other, burning and killing with exuberance and carrying on the quest for vengeance generation after generation. One ferocious clan chief earned the admiration of his clansmen for having killed an English officer by tearing out his throat with his teeth.

In such a climate of barbarity it was not surprising that neither the king's peace nor the law of the land was heeded. Within each clan the chief's word ruled, but when it came to conflict between clans, as Home wrote, "the sword was the arbiter of all disputes." Reprisal, rapine and revenge were everpresent facts of life. "Hence, fierceness of heart, prompt to attack or defend, at all times and places, became the characteristic of the Highlanders."[7]

If they were to be perpetually ready for war, then they had to dress and arm themselves as warriors. And indeed they carried their broadswords and dirks, muskets and pistols everywhere they went—in defiance of the legislation which, in the aftermath of the Fifteen, banned all weapons in the Highlands. Even Highland clergymen carried broadswords when they went to church; their parishioners followed suit, and went to fairs, weddings, and other public gatherings accoutered as if going to war.

BONNIE PRINCE CHARLIE

It was this warlike cast of mind, combined with the outlandish magnificence of their plaids and bonnets, that made outsiders fear the Highlanders—these things plus the knowledge that in facing a Highlander in battle, one was not facing an individual but an irresistible phalanx of clansmen. As soldiers they lacked discipline, Home remarked, "but the spirit of clanship, in some measure, supplied the want of discipline, and brought them on together; for when a clan advanced to charge an enemy, the head of the kindred, the chief, was in his place, and every officer at his post, supported by his nearest relations, and most immediate dependents."[8]

The force of blood was stronger than the force of discipline. Father, son and brother stood together, with cousins and uncles on all sides. Against such a force of nature, the hastily recruited, badly trained and bedraggled government regiments might be expected to lay down their arms and run. Or so Charles hoped, as he marched his men out of Perth on September 11, intent on capturing Edinburgh.

11

At midmorning on Sunday, September 15, the alarm bell began ringing and the citizens of Edinburgh, many of whom were in church, rushed out in panic into the High Street to try to find out what was going on.

The sound of the bell shattered the normally austere silence of the old walled town on its craggy height, for Sundays in Edinburgh were devoted to worship and good works, and the citizens crept about under the watchful eye of the clergy. "Seizers" patrolled the narrow closes and wynds that led off the High Street, looking up and down every alleyway, peering around corners, listening for whispered conversations and furtive footsteps in hopes of catching truants who were breaking the Sabbath. Malefactors were reported to the church officials, and fined by the town magistrates. Nearly every sort of activity was banned on Sundays, not only such evident offenses against the Lord's Day as dancing, gambling and attending the theater, but pulling weeds, daydreaming and wandering idly in the open fields. Sundays were to be consecrated to serious and prolonged worship, and to nothing else.

Thus when the alarm bell rang it shattered the silence, and temporarily distracted even the seizers from their grim rounds. In a moment or two the High Street was filled with people, and word was spreading that the Pretender's son, with his Highland hordes, was only a few miles away.

A few weeks earlier, when the citizens of Edinburgh learned that Charles had landed on the west coast, the *Evening Courant* had belittled the threat he posed. "The Highlanders are only a pitiful crew, good for nothing," the paper assured them, "incapable of giving any reason for their proceedings, but talking only of tobacco, King James, the Regent, plunder, and new brogues." Now these pitiful good-for-nothings were about to capture the capital.

That Charles and his Highlanders had come this far meant that the government forces had been inadequate to stop them, making them seem more formidable than ever. Wild stories spread: that the French were about to land, or had already landed, in strength to join the Pretender's army; that the army was already five or ten, or even fifteen thousand strong; that Cope and his troops had been decimated; that the Highlanders would sweep into the town, waving their murderous battle-axes, and slaughter every man, woman, and child they encountered.

The hatred of the Lowlanders for the Highlanders was proverbial. Even in those towns that lay along the border between the two regions, where one segment of the population spoke Gaelic and the other spoke English, there was little or no mixing between the two groups, and a great deal of suspicion and sometimes open hostility. In Edinburgh the only Highlanders normally to be seen on the streets were servants—porters carrying their masters in sedan chairs, elbowing their way savagely along through the crowds and swearing mighty Gaelic oaths. Seen through the eyes of the Lowlanders, the Highlanders were dangerous barbarians—and now a whole host of these barbarians was about to descend on the city to seize it in the name of a Catholic and a foreigner.

Of course, there were those in the town—particularly the women, according to contemporary accounts—who were overjoyed that the dull and oppressive Hanoverian monarchy was being challenged by the Stuart heir. Ardent Jacobites, and those who since 1707 had opposed the union of the two crowns and hated the English, were inclined to welcome the Stuarts. So too were the Catholics, and the most committed of the Scottish patriots, and those Episcopalians who on religious grounds alone wanted to see the end of Presbyterian domination.

But there were others who, while not at all fond of the English, were not prepared to cast their lot with the Pretender's son. These pragmatic loyalists, among them the merchants and bankers of the capital and the more prosperous farmers, refused to risk their security for the sake of what was still a rash adventure. Late in 1743 Parliament had passed a bill of attainder against the Pretender's two sons, and against the posterity of anyone who might support either of them. To join Charles now could mean forfeiture of every coin, every stick of furniture and every acre of land. It could also, despite Charles's assurances to the contrary, mean a return to Catholicism. The Stuart succession was not yet secured into the next generation; should Charles come to the throne as regent for his aging father, his heir apparent would be his devoutly Catholic brother Henry.

If it was an exaggeration to say, as one contemporary did, that two-thirds of the Scots were loyal to George II, it was certainly true that a high percentage of them were very reluctant to support the Highland rising and make it into a general Scots revolt. (It should be noted that, of course, the rising did not represent the whole of the Highlands. Some twenty-two clans supported Charles, but the most important clans, militarily and economically, were loyal to the Hanoverians and fought against the rebels. But this is to anticipate events.)[1]

When the alarm sounded, it was perhaps to be expected that for the first few hours there would be chaos. The city was not completely defenseless; apart from the castle with its invalid garrison there was the Town Guard, plus two regiments of dragoons, a newly formed and incomplete infantry regiment and a force of Volunteers. The dragoons were some distance to the west of the town, outside the walls, but the Volunteers formed up in the College Yards as soon as the alarm was sounded, some four hundred strong. While panic and confusion deepened all around them, they waited to be joined by the other defenders, though the regimental officers lowered morale by complaining that "most of the privates were unwilling to march."

The day wore on, and the Highlanders, who were expected hourly, failed to appear. Sunday meditations forgotten, people continued to crowd into the High Street, some cheering on the bravery of the Volunteers, others treating them, as one of their number wrote later, "with scorn and derision." "In one house on the south side of the street," this writer went on, "there was a row of windows, full of ladies, who appeared to enjoy our march to danger with much levity and mirth."[2]

Meanwhile the dragoons, having received alarming reports that Charles and his men were almost at hand, and being short of food and forage, galloped off toward Leith—in full view of the townspeople on their height above. It looked like a rout, and fresh panic ensued. The Volunteers were warned, quite erroneously, as it turned out, that the rebel army, with sixteen thousand men, was in view. They lost what stomach they had had for fighting, and began to think about honorable capitulation.

Charles and his men had camped near Slateford, two miles away, and from there he issued a confident declaration to the city officials.

"Being now in a condition to make our way into this capital of his Majesty's ancient kingdom of Scotland," the declaration read, "we hereby summon you to receive us, as you are in duty bound to do." The declaration commanded the provost and magistrates to summon the town council and discuss how best to turn the city over to the forces of King James. "But if you suffer any of the Usurper's troops to enter the town," it went on, "or any of the cannon, arms, or ammunition now in it, whether belonging to the public or to private persons, to be carried off, we shall take it as a breach of your duty and a heinous offence against the King and us." Every effort would be made to protect the citizens and their property, the document went on, but "if any opposition be made to us we cannot answer for the consequences, being firmly resolved at any rate to enter the city, and in that case, if any of the inhabitants are found in arms against us, they must not expect to be treated as prisoners of war." The message was signed "Charles, Prince Regent."

In response to this a delegation representing the town government came to the camp and asked for terms—and for time to consider them. What they hoped was that Cope's forces, which having come by sea from Aberdeen, were nearing the Firth of Forth, would arrive in time to forestall a concerted attempt by Charles's men to storm the town. Charles gave them until two o'clock in the morning of the seventeenth to capitulate, and when they tried to extend even this deadline he lost patience.

Lochiel's Camerons were ordered to be ready to march "upon a minute's warning," and were sent to demand entrance through one of the gates in the town wall. The guards denied them entrance, but just then, fortuitously for the Highlanders, the coach which had carried the negotiating deputies returned, and the gate was opened to let it out. The Highlanders took advantage of the situation and rushed in, their swords and shields at the ready. It was just after dawn, and the streets were still all but deserted. The Camerons marched up the High Street—preserving their ranks, according to one eyewitness—and forced their way into the guardhouse. There was no resistance; the castle garrison neither saw nor heard the attackers, and did not fire their cannon. Within minutes there were Highland guards at every city gate, and Edinburgh was in the hands of the Jacobites.

A month after landing in Scotland, and landing without soldiers or substantial weaponry, Charles was in possession of the capital. His efforts, his sanguine temperament, his princeliness had been responsible, in no small part, for the success the Highlanders had achieved, even when the poor military preparedness of the government forces is taken into account. His energy galvanized the rising. He was interested in everything: Scotland itself, its people, even the way they wore their plaids.

At one point he asked one of the Highlanders whether he was cold, dressed as he was. The man assured him that he was so used to his plaid that he would be cold wearing anything else. At this Charles laughed heartily and asked the man how he arranged the plaid when he went to sleep. Wasn't he afraid that if he wrapped himself too tightly in it, he would be vulnerable to a surprise attack at night? No, came the answer; in time of danger every Highlander knew how to wrap his plaid in such a way that "with one spring he could start to his feet with drawn sword and cocked pistol." This elicited several more questions from Charles, and he went on questioning his informant until he had completely exhausted the subject.

He was restless, and perpetually eager for physical activity. On the march his men could hardly keep pace with him. On the way to Perth he lost a heel from one of his shoes, which slowed him down and gave the others a welcome opportunity to catch up with him. No doubt his physical vigor endeared him to the hardy Scots, who approved of the fact that he sometimes slept in a tent—though more often in the houses of chieftains or gentlemen—and did not require any pampering, though he did carry with him a "great gilt French box" containing his splendid lace-trimmed suits of silk and velvet.

Some said he had the "languid and melancholy" look of a sophisticate and a man of fashion, but everyone, Jacobite or Hanoverian, agreed that his person was extremely handsome. "He was a slender young man," wrote one who saw him at that time, "about five feet, ten inches high; of a ruddy complexion, high-nosed, large rolling brown eyes, long visage; his chin was pointed, and mouth small in proportion to his features; his hair was red [actually light brown] but at that time he wore a pale peruke."[3]

With Lochiel's men in control of the city, Charles made his entrance. People lined his path, impatient to get a glimpse of him, and he paused to let them look their fill. He wore Highland dress, a tartan coat with a blue sash over his shoulder, red velvet breeches, and a blue velvet bonnet with a white cockade. (White cockades were springing up everywhere; some of the Jacobite women were handing them out in the streets.) Even his enemies were forced to conclude that his appearance was "not ill suited to his lofty pretensions."

At noon the heralds announced, to a fanfare of trumpets, that James VIII was now king, and the declaration of regency was read out. Once again the crowds cheered, and people remarked to one another how princely—nay, kingly—Charles was.

Meanwhile Cope was supervising the landing at Dunbar of his tired, seasick men who had spent three days crowded into transports coming south from Aberdeen. Before that they had marched over half Scotland, from Stirling to Inverness and then from Inverness to Aberdeen. They were hardly fit for battle, and not at all eager for it, believing themselves to be outnumbered by the Stuart forces. Their own strength was at about twenty-five hundred, roughly equal to the Highland army, but Cope estimated that Charles had at least four thousand men.[4] Nor did it improve the morale of the government troops to be joined by the frightened dragoons, who had been avoiding a confrontation with the Highlanders for days, and who now returned to Dunbar.

Cope chose to make a stand near Prestonpans, on a wide, low stretch of ground from which the last of the harvest sheaves had been cleared only the day before. It was an ideal defensive position for him, for the two stone walls on his right, the deep moatlike ditch in front of him, and the marsh on his left and the sea behind him created a sort of natural fortification within which he was securely entrenched. However, his cavalrymen were thoroughly intimidated, his handful of gunners ludicrously incompetent—and none of his men had ever faced an opposing army before.

With Charles at their head, the Highlanders prepared to go forward to meet Cope. Sword in hand, his face "very determined," he exhorted his men. "Gentlemen, I have flung away the scabbard. With God's assistance I don't doubt of making you a free and happy people. Mr. Cope shall not escape us as he did in the Highlands."[5]

His inspiring words helped, temporarily at least, to smooth over an ominous dispute that had broken out among the men. The two largest contingents in the army were the Glengarry, Clanranald and Keppoch Macdonalds and Lochiel's Camerons (with the Stewarts of Appin). Both sought to fight on the right side, the more honorable position and, for the Macdonalds, a point of particular pride since they had fought on Robert Bruce's right at Bannockburn. Charles proposed that the issue be settled by drawing lots. But when this was done, the outcome displeased the Macdonalds, who drew the left-hand position. Only Lochiel's offer to cede to them the right side prevented a crisis—for the Macdonalds refused to fight on any other terms.

Another conflict arose when the blunt and arrogant Lord George Murray, who with the Duke of Perth had been given command of the army, found out that his Atholl men had been ordered to detach themselves from the main body of the army and take up a position guarding the road to Edinburgh, in order to prevent the government troops from marching to the capital. Murray, who at fifty-one was old enough to be Charles's father, "threw his gun on the ground in a great passion, and swore God, he'd never draw his sword for the cause, if the brigade was not brought back." Charles prudently ordered the men recalled, though Murray afterward regretted his objection and agreed to the original posting.

The squabbles did not dampen Charles's "very high spirits"; he was eager to engage Cope. He knew that his men were a ragged-looking horde compared with the smartly uniformed infantry and dragoon regiments, and that their equipment was far inferior to that of the troops they would be facing. But things had gone his way to an extraordinary extent so far. He had achieved much more during his month in Scotland than his father had in six weeks. He hoped to have French assistance before very long. And he relied on "his Highlanders," as he called them, to win it for him.

John Home, who saw the men in their camp outside Edinburgh, thought that they were "strong, active, and hardy men." They were not exceptionally tall or broad, but their legs, visible below their kilts, were "strong and muscular" and their unsmiling faces and manes of bushy uncombed hair "gave them a fierce, barbarous and imposing aspect."[6]

That they were unevenly and somewhat eccentrically armed only added to their ferocious appearance. Some had muskets or French *fusils,* others pistols, some carried hunting weapons, and in among the Highland broadswords were French swords, dirks, and knives. A considerable number of the men in the Duke of Perth's regiment carried an improvised weapon made from a stick seven or eight feet long to which was attached a scythe—"a most murderous weapon," it was observed. A few had only "bludgeons."[7]

The Jacobites came within sight of Cope's men at about midafternoon on September 20, and paused to reconnoiter.[8] The position appeared to be impregnable, until a local landowner came to Charles to tell him that there was a pathway through the marsh—a pathway Cope's scouts had neglected to take note of, leaving the marsh unguarded. Secretly, in single file, the Highlanders passed along the path after dark, without meeting any opposition. Before dawn they had formed their ranks and faced the unsuspecting Cope at a distance of two hundred paces.

The first line had about twelve hundred men, including those with the murderous scythes. A second line, commanded by Charles, was some six hundred strong. The second line was not quite through the marsh when daylight disclosed the Jacobites to their opponents, who fired an alarm gun to rouse the camp.

Caught off guard, Cope's men stumbled to arms and staggered toward some semblance of formation. Before they could prepare themselves either mentally or physically for an assault, the Highlanders were rushing at them, uttering bloodcurdling cries and firing their muskets. Cope's gunners managed to fire five of their six field pieces, but then they fled, while Charles's men, who had been told to strike at the noses of the horses, succeeded in throwing the dragoons into utter confusion. By this time many of the dragoons were already galloping as hard as they could for safety.

Smelling the panic in the ranks, Cope shouted to his infantry to hold their ground and keep firing, "and they would easily beat the rebels." But the wounded horses were plunging wildly into them, and the men were terrified. As one of their number wrote later, "There was no orders from the general what to do, and all went soon to confusion. . . . Never deers run faster before hounds than these poor betrayed men run before a rabble."[9]

The entrenched, fortresslike camp became a trap for the hundreds of fleeing men. Dropping their arms, they ran blindly away from the Jacobites—and ran into the stone walls, which had been intended to serve as their protection. The Highlanders pursued them with a vengeance, hacking at them mercilessly, Perth's men swinging their terrible scythes like the reapers who had swept the field of grain the day before.

Within a few minutes the savagely one-sided battle was over. Cope, wearing a Jacobite white cockade in his hat, somehow managed to pass through the Highland ranks without being recognized as a Hanoverian officer and escaped to England.

"The field of battle presented a spectacle of horror," wrote James Johnstone, Lord George Murray's aide-de-camp, "being covered with heads, legs, arms and mutilated bodies, for the killed all fell by the sword." Charles's men acquired the arms and baggage the government troops had left behind.

Charles himself, who had remained in the second rank through the brief encounter, stood beside the road to Prestonpans, wearing the coarse plaid and blue bonnet of a captain. His boots and knees were muddy; he had had to jump a four-foot ditch in the marsh and had stumbled on landing. He was watching the surgeons he had sent for from Edinburgh to attend the wounded on both sides. Some thirty or forty of his men had been killed and seventy or eighty wounded, most of them with gunshot wounds in the leg and thigh. But nearly a third of Cope's men had been injured, hundreds of them fatally, and they provided the surgeons with most of their work.

A young Highlander, hardly into his teens, was brought before Charles by his proud clansmen. The boy had killed fourteen of the enemy, Charles was told. When Charles asked him if this was true, he answered forthrightly. "I do not know if I killed them," he said in Gaelic, "but I brought fourteen soldiers to the ground with my sword."

Cope's men had been like sheep herded to the slaughter, so meek and defenseless that a mere boy could annihilate them. If twenty-five hundred men could be beaten in a few minutes, how long could England hold out against the invincible army of James VIII?

News of Cope's ignominious defeat at the hands of Charles Stuart's army alarmed Londoners already fearful of an invasion from France. All summer people had been expecting the French to descend on the Kentish coast or to land in Scotland.[1] In the first week of September, there were stories of thirty transports, ten men-of-war and ten thousand men massing at Dunkirk for a large-scale assault, and it was by no means certain that the British navy could protect the coasts against them. Then came the defeat at Prestonpans, and with it the realization that not only was the Jacobite army a serious foe to be reckoned with, but the government troops were cowardly and ineffectual.

Fortunately, the day before word of the battle reached London, a sizable force of Dutch troops had arrived to strengthen the home defenses. The sight of these men, and the knowledge that more Dutch troops were on their way, gave the citizens of the capital some small reassurance. Without it, in the opinion of the Duke of Newcastle, who with his brother Henry Pelham was at the head of government, "the confusion in the City of London would not have been to be described, and the King's crown, I will venture to say, in the utmost danger."[2]

No one knew for certain how large Charles's army was, for the reports that reached London varied widely in their estimates. Some said there were five thousand Jacobites, others ten thousand; there were still other stories that Charles's brother Henry was on his way to Ireland to raise rebellion there with a large invading force of his own.

"We are sadly convinced," wrote Horace Walpole, son of the former prime minister Robert Walpole and a voluminous letter writer, "that they [the Jacobites] are not such raw ragamuffins as they were represented." Walpole, who was an M.P. and privy to much that went on in government and court circles, was full of apprehension. He considered the battle of Prestonpans to be a straw in the wind, and took no comfort from the fact that few of Scotland's "men of quality and fortune" had as yet thrown in their lot with the Stuart army. He remembered his father's perennial warnings about the Jacobites, how their strategy was to lure the "meaner sort of people" into their ranks, then gradually gain the support of the more influential.

As for the reaction of the government, Walpole wrote scathingly of its "supineness" and accused the ministers of myopia. Instead of making a concerted effort to reach a consensus about how to crush the rebellion, they used it as an excuse to attack each other. And they failed miserably in persuading the king to take it seriously. "When the Ministers propose anything with regard to the rebellion," Walpole wrote, "he cries, 'Pho! Don't talk to me of that stuff.' "[3]

King George had come back from Hanover at the end of August, and had begun to wish that he had prolonged his stay. He was perennially worried about the security of his electorate, and was irritated at the thought that the increased instability in England was bound to lead to troop movements which could only weaken Hanover's defenses.

The king disliked his ministers, members of what was called the "Broadbottom Administration" because of the wide political spectrum it represented. Newcastle, his brother Henry Pelham, and their allies were anathema to the monarchy because they were outspokenly critical of any policy favoring Hanover at Britain's expense. Newcastle claimed that "the King's unjustifiable partiality for Hanover, to which he makes all other views and considerations subservient, has manifested itself so much . . . that no man can continue in the active part of the administration with honor."[4] Such sentiments were not appreciated at the palace—and Newcastle was milder in his views than some, who said flatly that "they would never rest till the Hanoverian dominions were separated from the crown."

But Hanover was not the only issue alienating the king from his ministers. George II had a strong preference for John Carteret, Earl of Granville, who had been forced out of power in 1744. Granville, a brilliant diplomatist, had made himself politically unpopular by appearing to imperil Britain's security through his handling of continental alliances. But though he was out of power, Granville retained his influence with the king, who valued his advice and sought his counsel while ignoring Newcastle. It was Granville to whom King George turned when he learned that Charles had landed in Scotland, preferring Granville's assurances that the rebellion was inconsequential to Newcastle's anxious, hand-wringing concern. (Walpole wickedly described Newcastle as all hands, "hands that are always groping and sprawling, and fluttering, and hurrying on the rest of his precipitate person.")[5]

When he learned of the astonishing events at Prestonpans, the king as usual consulted Granville, who continued to insist that the rising was of little significance and that he should take heart and pay no heed to it. Yet it was hard to ignore the widespread indications of public alarm throughout the capital. The City merchants banded together to raise money to subsidize mercenary troops. Half a dozen noblemen approached the king to ask his permission to raise regiments to defend their regions. "Loyal associations" sprang up whose members promised men and money to help fight the Pretender. There were speeches and sermons by the dozen, warning people that should the Stuarts regain the throne they would reinstate Catholicism as the only legal religion and destroy all the hard-won liberties of Englishmen. In the theaters, where the national anthem was always sung, a new verse was added:

BONNIE PRINCE CHARLIE

From France and pretender
Great Britain defend her,
    Foes let them fall:
From foreign slavery,
Priests and their knavery,
And Popish reverie,
    God help us all.[6]

No one in London knew how long it would be before the Highland army invaded England, but many thought it would be soon. Even sooner, it was feared, the French would come, or the Spanish, or the forces of some other Catholic power. The most cynical in the population saw London as the prize in a race between Hanover and Stuart forces. "England," wrote Lord Holland, "is for the first comer; and if you can tell whether the six thousand Dutch, and the ten battalions of English, or five thousand French or Spaniards will be here first, you know our fate."[7]

Meanwhile in Edinburgh, Charles had taken the time to write a letter to his father. " 'Tis impossible for me to give you a distinct journal of my proceedings because of my being so much hurried with business," he began, then went on to give a brief account of what had happened at Prestonpans, calling it "one of the most surprising actions that ever was." "We gained a complete victory over General Cope who commanded three thousand foot and two regiments of the best dragoons in the island," Charles boasted, "being advantageously posted with also batteries of cannon and mortars, we having neither horse nor artillery with us, and being [sic] to attack them in their position, and obliged to pass before their noses in a defile and bog."[8]

James, who had expressed "great astonishment" on learning that Charles had sailed to Scotland, now was overjoyed to learn that his venture was prospering. James had been doing all he could to persuade the French to support his son. He had written to Maurepas announcing his intention to abdicate in favor of Charles, something Charles himself did not publicize, if indeed he was aware of it. Thus if Louis XV decided to send arms and men to England, he would be lending his backing, not to the potential Prince of Wales, but to the potential king. (James would have been dismayed to learn with what sneering condescension his letter was received. Maurepas handed it on to his colleague Argenson with an appended note: "Do you think that the King should, or should not answer this poor King James? A word of consolation, I think, would be worthy of his Majesty's kind heart.")[9]

Meanwhile James had decided to permit his younger son to take a more active part in family politics. Late in August of 1745 Henry left Rome in secret, and made his way northward by the route Charles had taken, via Pisa to Genoa and Savona, thence by boat to Antibes. To prevent the army of Italian spies from becoming alerted to Henry's flight it was said that he was ill with smallpox and being kept in isolation. By the time they suspected the truth he was in Avignon—but there the exertion of his escape caught up with him and he fell genuinely ill. He was still recuperating there when his brother captured Edinburgh and triumphed at Prestonpans.

For Charles, the victory had the effect of widening the scope of his responsibilities. He had the wounded troops to think of, and the citizens of Edinburgh, and indeed all Scots, who were now his subjects under the terms of the declaration of regency. He had to have regard for their welfare, no longer as a conqueror, but as a ruler.

With princely compassion he took charge of providing medical care for Cope's injured men as well as his own. He tactfully forbade any public rejoicing in the town for his victory, and asked the clergy to resume the services they had ceased to perform when his men marched in, insisting that he was "resolved to inflict no penalty that could possibly look like persecution." (The clergy refused.) He continued to oversee the daily urgencies of purveyance for his army, raising money and keeping order—all the while looking ahead to the next phase of his conquest.

His success bred nuisances: in the countryside, thieves were dressing as Highlanders and terrorizing villagers, demanding money, clothing, anything of value. In Selkirk, some thirty-five miles southeast of Edinburgh, an impostor rode into town, pretending to be Prince Charles. He was not believed, and was run out of town in disgrace. But the fact that these things could happen proved how volatile the political situation was, and how difficult it was likely to be for Charles to keep it under his control. Meanwhile the area he had to govern had widened, for the Jacobites had captured Aberdeen, and were in at least nominal control of the other major towns save for the fortress town of Stirling. Charles now sent letters to the magistrates of all these towns, telling them to come to Edinburgh immediately to contribute to his treasury. Letters went out also to tax collectors and other holders of public moneys, ordering them to bring all their funds and their account books to Holyrood House on pain of high treason.

Charles was master of Scotland's capital, but not of its castle, and this quickly became a serious irritant. Realizing that the garrison was growing short of provisions, Charles decided to cut off all communication between the town and the soldiers. In response the commander ordered his men to fire on the town. The castle guns boomed out, and the narrow, tall old houses that were in their line of fire began to crumble and burn. Several people were killed before all the houses in the path of the cannon could be evacuated. The residents fled, "carrying out the aged and infirm at the imminent hazard of their lives." For five days the bombardment went on, with the hungry soldiers making sorties to plunder food from the destroyed homes. Finally, realizing that his attempt to besiege the castle was failing, Charles gave up and rescinded his order.

Quiet returned to Edinburgh, but the Jacobites knew that it could not last. Before long the British would be back in force, with more and better troops and prepared to face an enemy they had learned to respect.

The Highland army was slowly growing. Early in October three hundred of the men Lord Ogilvy had promised arrived, and three hundred more came from Aberdeenshire. There were an additional hundred and twenty from Skye, three hundred MacPhersons, and Lord Lewis Gordon, younger brother of the loyalist Duke of Gordon, guaranteed to send some recruits. Four small but important troops of Jacobite cavalry were raised as well. To offset these gains there were the losses suffered when the Highlanders, who were somewhat casual about taking prolonged leaves of absence, wandered away from the camp without bothering to seek or obtain permission.

Charles was attempting to bring more clans into his fold, telling the hesitant chiefs that he "had undoubted assurances of assistance from France and Spain" and hoping that they would be impressed by what they heard about his success at Prestonpans. To his intense disappointment, however, the principal Skye chieftains, along with most of the northerly clans, decided to support the government, partly because of the vigorous efforts of the lord president Duncan Forbes at Inverness. Forbes, having been authorized to raise twenty "independent companies" of Highlanders, was wooing the clan chiefs with the promise of a command, and achieving success.

If the Jacobites were to keep up their momentum, the French and Spanish assistance Charles seemed so confident of receiving would have to materialize, and soon.

On October 14 Alexandre Jean Baptiste de Boyer, Marquis d'Eguilles, arrived in Edinburgh, a special envoy from the French court. He brought with him four thousand guineas, nearly thirteen hundred guns and small arms, six Swedish field guns, ten French gunners and an artillery expert, Colonel James Grant, whom Charles at once made his commander of artillery. D'Eguilles, a protégé of the Marquis d'Argenson, the French foreign minister, was a well-born, pious and sober young man, and a devout Catholic. He was no diplomat, but he had the dignity and social standing to be a creditable representative of Louis XV. In fact, d'Eguilles had been chosen to go to Scotland precisely because he was neither so unimportant as to be an insult to Charles nor so important that he was authorized to bring him much help.

King Louis was inclined to back Charles, but wanted a firsthand report from one of his own courtiers before deciding to do so. D'Eguilles was under orders to see for himself how many men Charles had, how much support he had from the Scots and whether or not his conquest had the feel of permanence about it. The king had asked his naval minister Maurepas to prepare an expeditionary force of six thousand men to be sent either to England or Scotland, and to study the possibility of reviving the invasion plan that had met with disaster in 1744. Maurepas, who was vehemently against the new venture, wrote a detailed report in which he argued that it would be foolish to attempt an invasion now that the British coast was so heavily guarded, and the realm on a war footing. To convey six thousand troops would necessitate readying thirty ships—which would, according to the minister, require three months—and even if all thirty were ready in time they would have to be launched from

Brittany and sail around the west of Ireland, avoiding the Channel. So long a voyage would mean carrying a heavy load of provisions—and this in turn would mean that the number of soldiers on board each ship would have to be reduced. And then there was the weather, hazardous enough in summer, extremely hazardous in winter.

These negatives aside, Maurepas suggested that if the king was really determined to send French troops to Britain, they ought to be sent to Scotland, not England, and in fast privateer ships which would sail not as a flotilla but individually, dodging the British navy just as the *Elisabeth* had done. Even so, the weather would be a formidable obstacle. Maurepas strongly recommended sending off the ships and men before the end of October at the very latest, to avoid the worst of the winter storms.

The naval minister's report was not encouraging, especially as Maurepas calculated that the expeditionary force would cost upwards of two million livres. But the memorandum prepared for King Louis by his minister of state, the Duc de Noailles, was even harsher in its opposition to sending any French troops to Britain. In Noailles's view—and his opinion counted for a great deal with the king—the only possible landing site for a proposed French expedition was Ireland. To land men there would draw the English away from Scotland, thus giving Charles a freer hand there, and might draw in Spanish forces as well, which would take pressure off the French treasury.

Neither Maurepas nor Noailles alluded to the practical difficulties of obtaining pilots and cajoling unwilling soldiers to embark on violently stormy seas in winter. Antoine Walsh, now back in Paris, had thought of these things and had approached Maurepas about them, offering to take charge of organizing the conveyance of the French force to Britain and to guide it, if necessary, in "fisher boats" if the weather was foul.[10]

Indeed the same Irish Jacobite shipowners who had lent their support to Charles now came forward to offer their help, and King Louis, despite his ministers' dissent, was inclined to accept it.

D'Eguilles brought Charles a letter from King Louis, addressed "to his brother Prince Charles Edward" and assuring Charles of his "sincere interest" in all his affairs. In the letter the king asked

Charles to credit everything d'Eguilles said on his behalf, though he acknowledged that his envoy was not likely to say anything very specific about France's military plans. Louis was, he said, "disposed to give him [Charles] every evidence of his affection," and was praying for him. The brief letter was signed "Your good brother Louis," and was by far the most warm and intimate message the French king had ever sent him.[11]

Had the king known, when he wrote this letter, the outcome of the battle of Prestonpans it would no doubt have been warmer still. (Word of the victory took some time to reach France, arriving via English smugglers in Boulogne.) Once the Jacobites' phenomenal triumph was known, the king's determination to send an expedition grew greater than ever. A week before d'Eguilles landed in Scotland, Maurepas was instructed to go forward with preparations to launch an invasion force of six thousand men, the proposed landing site to be, not Scotland, but England. In addition, the Scots exile Lord John Drummond, brother of the Jacobite Duke of Perth, was to be sent into England with his regiment of Scots Royals—plus any volunteers from the Irish Brigade who might want to join in. A week later a formal alliance, the Treaty of Fontainebleau, was signed by representatives of the Stuarts and the foreign minister, the Marquis d'Argenson. In the treaty, France promised military aid to Charles in his conflict with the "Elector of Hanover," George II.[12]

The language of the treaty took account of the possibility that Charles might continue to be his father's regent for the kingdom of Scotland, but might not succeed in conquering England. To the most optimistic of the Stuart supporters this seemed nothing more than a diplomatic nicety, a fine point. Yet the longer Charles stayed at Holyrood House, building a fragile administration, consolidating his army, holding soirées in the evenings which drew hundreds of admirers and curious skeptics, the more sensible it seemed for him to be satisfied with his Scots kingdom, at least for the time being, and not to risk losing it for the sake of the much more difficult attempt to conquer England.

Certainly this was the view of the clan chiefs who had joined the rising with the intention of restoring the Scottish throne to the Stuarts. What happened in London, though it affected them indirectly, was not real to them; they had never imagined leading their

Highlanders there as a conquering army. From the purely military point of view, Charles's advisers counseled, he ought to stay in Edinburgh at least until spring, by which time the French would be able to send a large and well equipped support force to back him up. In the meantime he could make himself incalculably stronger within Scotland by dissolving the union between Scotland and England, making himself a hero to the entire nation. He could then summon the Scottish Parliament, impose taxes and gain supplies for his army. When the British attack came, he would be in a better position to defend himself, both legally and militarily. And perhaps the British would not be so foolish as to attack in winter in any case.

Such was the advice Charles heard every day—and every day he repeated his objections to it. Everything he had accomplished so far had come about because of swiftness, surprise and boldness. No one had dreamed he would have the daring to come to Scotland without thousands of soldiers, therefore he had not met a well entrenched, well prepared opposition when he landed. Cope had imagined his army secure against attack at Prestonpans—and an unexpected, bold frontal assault had been his downfall. The citizens of Edinburgh too had thought theselves safe until the Highlanders swarmed in and took the town. Having achieved so much in such a short time by daring and unconventional tactics, it seemed logical to take the final step of seizing England the same way. And the Highlanders thirsted for action, they would never submit to becoming a static, garrison force waiting to receive an attack. They would melt away long before it came.

Besides, there was d'Eguilles, smiling and confident, making no definite promise of any more men or money but giving every indication short of an explicit promise that both would be on their way before long. Charles knew that he had to impress d'Eguilles with his courage and élan; any further assistance from France depended on that. D'Eguilles insisted (on the basis of exaggerated reports in Paris) that once the Stuart army entered England, huge numbers of the English would rise up and join it. So far the English Jacobites had not made themselves helpful or even visible, but Charles could not let that hinder him.

Finally, Charles knew, the French were much more likely to support him in strength if he invaded England than if he stayed in

Scotland. Their aims were far wider than his; they hoped to see a Protestant Hanoverian enemy state replaced by a religiously tolerant Stuart ally. The Bank of England was financing France's continental enemies. An invasion force would create enough panic to destroy the bank and end the war subventions. None of this would happen if Charles stayed in Scotland.

"I leave for England in eight days," Charles told d'Eguilles, his face alight with joy. "England will be ours in two months." He pressed the Frenchman to give him at least an approximate date for the landing of the support force, but d'Eguilles was vague. Still, there was now a written treaty between the Stuart power and the French. He had to go forward once again, on faith. His temperament, his best judgment, his confidence in his destiny all demanded it. "As matters stand," Charles wrote to his father, "I must either conquer or perish in a little while." On November 1, the Highland army set out for England.

13

Three roads ran south from Edinburgh in 1745. The principal one went along the eastern coast, through Dunbar and Berwick to Newcastle. Another went southwestward through the most rugged of the mountainous borderlands to Carlisle. A third crossed the Lammermuir Hills to Lauder, went on to Kelso, and so continued southward to the River Esk.

Knowing that a large government army, commanded by Field Marshall Wade, was at Newcastle, Charles's first impulse was to march his men along the main coast road as quickly as possible, encountering Wade's men either at Newcastle or on the way there and overwhelming them. The clan chiefs opposed this, as did, more significantly, Charles's principal commander, Lord George Murray, who advised deploying the troops in such a way as to mislead Wade and prevent a confrontation. On reflection, Charles decided to follow Murray's advice and divided his men into three groups, none of which took the principal road.

By this time there were some five thousand foot soldiers and five hundred cavalry in the Stuart army, including a last-minute contingent of a thousand Atholl men who had arrived in Edinburgh on October 30. The heart of the army was firmly loyal to the chiefs and, through them, to Charles. But there were many men who had not joined the rebellion voluntarily, rather they had been intimidated by their chiefs or landlords. Some had had their lives threatened.[1] A magistrate in Dumfries wrote to a friend in Carlisle in mid-September that the Duke of Perth had shot three of his tenants who had refused to come out and fight, and Tullibardine was said to have shot another. It was these involuntary Jacobites, the hesitant, the waverers, who might not be relied on completely and whose vacillation might make the difference between defeat and victory in a hard-fought battle.

The uncertain loyalty of these men must have been on Charles's mind as he led his column of troops out of Dalkeith, bound for Lauder. He was concerned too about what would become of Edinburgh, now that it was virtually bereft of soldiers, and of Aberdeen, and of Perth, where he left a small body of men. Only a few days earlier, there had been a disturbing scene at Perth. On October 30, George II's birthday, a crowd of Hanoverian loyalists had attacked the residence of the deputy governor, Oliphant of Gask. The same thing had happened at Dundee, where the governor, David Fotheringham, was run out of town.[2]

Much depended on keeping the momentum of victory, and for this the army needed discipline. But discipline was not the Highlanders' strength; it was their very impetuousness, their tendency to break into spontaneous violence, that made them such a fearsome enemy.

The day book of Lord Ogilvy's regiment reveals how difficult it was to keep order in the ranks as the army made its way south. Officers were repeatedly told to reprimand their men for shooting off their weapons "in an idle fashion," for breaking into houses and stealing whatever took their fancy, for causing disturbances and even for molesting the nonmilitary members of the baggage train. The men refused to march in ranks, even when officers were placed along the flanks and at the head and rear of each column. There were constant complaints about the "scampering soldiers" who

Clementina Sobieska, wife of
James Stuart, attributed to Trevisani.

NATIONAL GALLERIES OF SCOTLAND

James Stuart, attributed to Trevisani.

NATIONAL GALLERIES OF SCOTLAND

Charles Stuart,
portrait by Antonio David.
NATIONAL GALLERIES OF SCOTLAND

The young Charles Stuart.
NATIONAL GALLERIES OF SCOTLAND

Another portrait of the
young Charles Stuart, after Blanchet.
NATIONAL GALLERIES OF SCOTLAND

Portrait of Charles Stuart,
attributed to Allan Ramsay.
DERBY ART GALLERY

Portrait of Flora MacDonald
by Allan Ramsay.
NATIONAL GALLERIES OF SCOTLAND

Flora MacDonald,
sketch by Allan Ramsay.
NATIONAL GALLERIES OF SCOTLAND

Portrait of Clementina Walkinshaw,
attributed to Allan Ramsay.

DERBY ART GALLERY

Portrait of Charlotte, Duchess of Albany,
Charles Stuart's daughter by Clementina Walkinshaw,
attributed to H. D. Hamilton.

NATIONAL GALLERIES OF SCOTLAND

wandered here and there at will. Peremptory orders had to be issued against applications for leave of absence—and this despite the fact that Ogilvy's men had only been under arms since the first week of October.

As each day passed on the journey south, new disorders were documented, and fresh directives issued in a vain attempt to stop them. The men did not want to go to England, and each day dozens of them simply decided they would not go, and left the army. "Scampering" became desertion.

Because the men were divided into several contingents taking different roads, the need for disciplined coordination was particularly acute. This was most true of the columns responsible for guarding the bread wagons (for the men were constantly "molesting" the bakers), the regimental baggage, and the artillery. The transport of heavy guns along the rutted, muddy roads and across streams and rivers was a herculean task. The soldiers could not do it alone, they needed the help of craftsmen who repaired the gun carriages and ammunition carts. Even so it was backbreaking work, and dangerous, for while repairs were being made, the entire column was vulnerable to attack.

Still, in spite of the disorder, the bad weather, and the generally lax coordination, the army managed to re-form "almost at the same instant, on a heath in England, about a mile from the town of Carlisle" on November 9.[3]

The next day, Sunday, was a foggy day, the fog so thick the men complained they could hardly see their horses' ears, much less the walls of the town. The November weather was freezing cold, and getting colder by the hour. By noon the fog had cleared sufficiently to reveal the town's crumbling red sandstone walls—but this meant that the gunners stationed there could also see the invading army, and they promptly began to fire down on it.

The city walls were in such disrepair that they could be breached without much difficulty, but the thick-walled Norman castle and Tudor citadel were another matter. The Stuart army had no siege artillery, and could not know that the forces defending the town and castle consisted of a body of militiamen and a company of invalids. Nor could they know that the commander, Colonel Durand, governor of the castle, was at odds with the deputy lieutenant and the mayor of the town and was, moreover, uncertain about whether or not he would be able to pay the militiamen.

Soon after noon the thick fog settled in again, and in midafternoon Charles sent a message to the mayor.

"Being come to recover the King our Father's just right," he declared, "for which we are arrived with all his authority, we are sorry to find that you should prepare to obstruct our passage. We, therefore, to avoid the effusion of blood, hereby require you to open your gates, and let us enter." Force would be used, Charles wrote, if the gates were not opened within two hours.

When no answer came, the besiegers began to dig trenches around the walls and to scour the countryside for ladders. Evidently they meant to settle in for a siege.

Meanwhile Charles, hearing that Wade was marching toward Carlisle, determined to meet him, and leaving part of his army to carry on the siege, marched with the rest to Brampton. As it turned out, Wade made little progress because heavy snowfalls blocked the roads; he eventually returned to Newcastle, and after several days Charles returned to Carlisle.

By the morning of November 14, however, the Stuart besiegers were ready to give up. Those in the trenches had been under direct fire from the walls for three days, and had been forced to stay at their posts despite snow and frost; they were at the point of desertion.

Yet the defenders too were exhausted and cold, and on the verge of mutiny. Some had deserted, climbing over the walls at night; all were in fear of the Highlanders, imagining that once they breached the walls they would fall on the defenders and kill them. They had not been paid, and food was running short. The militia officers presented Colonel Durand with a written statement, warning him that "having been lately extremely fatigued with duty in expectation of relief from his Majesty's force, and it appearing that no such relief is now likely to be had, and not being able to do duty or hold out any longer, they were determined to capitulate."[4]

The colonel, the mayor and the townspeople, the last hastily assembled at the town hall, all urged the militia to do their duty and defend the town, but they persisted in refusing, and in the end the castle garrison—eighty men, many of them "very infirm"—joined in the determination to capitulate. On the fifteenth both the city and the castle surrendered.

Neither the Hanoverian leaders nor their military commanders had expected the invading force to achieve such sudden and easily won success. First had come Edinburgh, then Prestonpans, now Carlisle. Neither regular troops nor militia had been able to prevent these stunning victories. Clearly Charles's men marched farther and faster than their opponents (sometimes thirty or even thirty-five miles in a single day, a remarkable pace), and were led by superb tacticians. They could no longer be dismissed as an undisciplined rabble. Undisciplined they might be, but theirs was a brand of indiscipline that terrorized more seasoned troops and was chillingly effective.

With their victories came a mystique of invincibility, heightened by the fact that no one in England was able to say precisely how many of them there were or where they would attack next. Official reports put the numbers of Charles's fighting men at between twelve and thirty thousand, and the Jacobites themselves encouraged exaggerated estimates of their strength by marching and countermarching their men through the towns, having the same troops enter and reenter by different gates on different days. Word spread throughout the north of England that the Stuart army was huge, advancing like a swarm of locusts through the countryside, destroying or sweeping aside all that stood in its path. In London, the lord chancellor Hardwicke (one of the few men in the government who estimated the size of the Jacobite force accurately) remarked that "if they do slip Wade, they will march like a torrent." The words were prophetic. The march south appeared to the local inhabitants to be nothing short of torrential, a vast flood unleashed upon a helpless populace.

It was not only the size of the army that was terrifying, but its reputed savagery. The playwright and pamphleteer Henry Fielding, who with the outbreak of the rebellion found himself in the unaccustomed role of government propagandist, described in his *True Patriot* what horrors the invading army would be likely to commit. Houses would be burned to the ground, defenseless citizens slain, women raped. No one would dare venture into the streets save priests. "The Banditti," as he called Charles's supporters, would not stop at massacre, but would add to it religious persecution, roasting Protestants alive and murdering them "with all the fury which rape, zeal, lust and wanton fierceness could inspire into the bloody hearts of Popish priestly bigots and barbarians."[5]

The English newspapers spread atrocity stories, telling how the rebels kidnapped and hanged anyone who opposed them, and set their savage dogs on people who tried to defend their towns. In order to capture Carlisle Castle, it was said, the Jacobites had seized women and children and chained them together, hand and foot, forcing the garrison to surrender lest they be harmed.[6]

With these rumors widespread, it was understandable that the capture and display of stragglers from the Stuart army caused great excitement in the northern towns. The captured soldiers were marched in or transported in carts, their appearance drawing large crowds. Barefooted, with long unkempt hair which overhung their foreheads, unwashed, and smelling of the road and the open fields, the men looked to the English like savages, and their rough manners added to the frightening effect. Their outlandish dress was in itself enough to make them suspect. They "had no breeches, nor stockings that came up to the knees," the *Chester Courant* reported of one group of Highlanders, "but a short kind of petticoat about a foot deep which they call a fillibeg." The spectacle was unnerving, even though the prisoners were more cheerful than menacing and were in fact harmless, having been relieved of their weapons and put behind bars.[7]

Even before Charles and his men crossed the border into England the merchants of the north had begun to be alarmed. They shut up their shops, hid their goods and sent their wives and children away. The roads were full of families fleeing southward, their possessions piled on top-heavy carts. Trade was at a standstill, and little or no business of any kind was done. Employment dried up, and the laboring poor, who lived from hand to mouth, suffered greatly. When word arrived that Carlisle had fallen to the rebels, evacuation began in earnest. The surrender of the fortress "cast a great damp on people's spirits," one newspaper reported, and made them distrust the capabilities of their own local militias and of the regular government troops. Nearly everywhere, friction between the lords lieutenant and town officials created chaos, as it was unclear who had primary responsibility for attending to such urgent matters as fortifying the town walls, bricking up the gates, requisitioning provisions and providing the defenders with sufficient arms and ammunition.

No one knew for certain the intended destination of the rebel army, but government intelligence suggested that it might be Wales. Fear of "a rising in the West" was added to the already great fear of the invaders from Scotland. Officials in Chester were instructed by the cabinet in London to break any bridges that might be used by the enemy, and obstruct the roads; soon afterward the orders were rescinded, however, when it was recalled that the Hanoverian troops would themselves be relying on the roads and bridges.

Rumors flew: the rebels were headed for Bristol, where they would set fire to the town and destroy its valuable shipping; they were already in the south, and the entire countryside was in arms; a French squadron was about to land on the Lancashire coast; the rebels had the government troops surrounded and were about to defeat them. In Newcastle, where there were some twenty thousand colliers who were always ripe for insurrection, the presence of thousands of regular troops gave some sense of stability, but preparations were made nonetheless to withstand a siege. In Liverpool the mayor raised a voluntary force, the "Liverpool Blues," but this did nothing to prevent panic. Shopkeepers loaded their goods onto ships and sent them out into the channel, then abandoned the town, thinking that they would be safer seeking shelter in the countryside.

The confusion was worst in Chester, where evacuees from the town ran into hordes of people from outlying districts trying to get inside the walls for protection. Many of the municipal officials had fled, and food was too scarce to provide for the influx of newcomers. Still, the substantial landowners of Cheshire assembled at Chester Castle and undertook to raise a volunteer force twenty-five hundred strong, many of them pledging as much as a year's income from their estates to maintain it.[8]

Londoners read of the crisis in the north in their newspapers, and had only to look out their windows to see evidence that the country was being roused to arms. The six City militias mustered each morning and marched to their appointed postings. Cartloads of artillery rumbled through the streets, destined for Preston and other northern towns. There were soldiers on guard at every gate and along every major avenue. And as more and more regiments of Horse and Foot Guards and Horse Grenadiers arrived from Flanders, they were encamped in the London suburbs, and swarmed through the surrounding neighborhoods, conspicuous in their regimental dress and soldierly swagger. With the streets full of soldiers, inevitably there were brawls; in the taverns and gin shops, drunken artisans assaulted soldiers with cries of "Damn you and your king too and God bless the Pretender!" before being carted off to face the magistrates. Throughout the day and long into the night, there were loud explosions as inexpert militiamen let off their firearms, the reports resounding along the narrow, dark streets and keeping the populace wakeful.

London had been on alert for several years, ever since the first alarms spread of an imminent French invasion. For two years and more the guards at the Tower and St. James's had been kept at triple strength, the parish watchmen working longer hours than usual to inform themselves of suspicious events in their parishes. Foreigners were kept under particular surveillance, as were all Catholics, foreign and native-born, and known Jacobite sympathizers. Spies kept watch at the City coffeehouses and reported to the authorities what they saw and heard there. And all expressions of disloyalty, from drunken mutterings against the king to the printing of seditious posters and pamphlets, were recorded and whenever possible rewarded with punishment.

Policing the capital was a monumental task, for its huge sprawl extended from the fashionable West End eastward through the City to the acres of crowded, warrenlike slums beyond the Tower and northward toward Islington and Hoxton. There were not enough spies or watchmen to ferret out what went on in the narrow alleys of Holborn or in the dockyards, or in the rat-infested, rubbish-strewn emigrant neighborhoods where jerrybuilt sheds and stalls blocked the streets and broken pavements fronted ruinous houses. In some areas of the city the authorities were in collusion with the criminal underworld; elsewhere they turned a blind eye to what went on in the known haunts of thieves and political conspirators.[9]

The vast areas where the Irish emigrants congregated were at once the most difficult to police and the most likely to nourish treasonable activity. Westminster, St. Giles and Marylebone, Holborn and Bloomsbury, Tower Hamlets and parts of the East End, Southwark and the docklands—all were populated by poor Irish laborers, their large families squeezed into tiny rooms or odd corners or doorways. Here, the authorities feared, the frustrations and grievances of poverty would combine with the natural preference of the Irish for the Catholic Stuart Pretender to incite rebellion. And with every passing month more Irish came into the capital, a seemingly endless stream of destitute men, women and children—so much tinder to be ignited by the Jacobite spark.[10]

From day to day, fresh alarms were sounded. Late in September, merchants began to reassure their customers that they would not for any reason refuse to accept payment in bank notes—immediately creating fear that there might be a run on the Bank of England. In the third week of October, one of the aldermen, Robert Ladbroke, reported receiving an anonymous letter warning that the Jacobites were about to set fire to the capital, and shortly afterward a rumor spread that the Catholics were plotting a massacre of Protestants. There was widespread apprehension, and immediately all the guards were ordered out to keep the peace. Two days later warrants were issued authorizing searches to be made of empty houses, which might be used as storehouses for illegal arms. Some caches of arms came to light, although some, like the store of two thousand cutlasses seized at the Saracen's Head tavern on Snow Hill, proved to be legitimate, in this instance part of the inventory of a Birmingham merchant.[11]

In the last week of October the king was reviewing the City troops. Suddenly a man darted out of the crowd and approached him, throwing a paper in his direction. The man was seized and arrested. He was a priest, and the paper was one of many broadsheets then circulating, attacking the government and upholding the rights of James III. It was a bizarre incident, as there were presumably few priests in the capital (a bounty of a hundred pounds having been offered for every priest seized within ten miles of London or its environs). Yet it demonstrated the ineffectiveness of official attempts to control the population and eliminate suspicious characters, and underscored the magnitude of the Jacobite threat. The king might easily have been assassinated, while his troops looked on in horror.

Perhaps in reaction to this frightening incident, there were loyalist demonstrations in the following weeks, and on October 30, George II's birthday, bonfires were lit in the streets and houses and public buildings were illuminated in celebration. Barrels of beer were broken open for the populace, who drank noisily to the king's health.[12]

Two weeks later, as the army of Charles Stuart was settling in to besiege Carlisle, a crowd gathered at the Royal Exchange to witness the burning of James's declaration. An effigy of James, hanging on a gibbet, was carried through the city, with six butchers in attendance as executioners. It was a virulently anti-Catholic crowd that followed the effigy, a crowd mindful of the sermons and pamphlets warning of a return to the days of Bloody Mary and the fires of Smithfield if James Stuart were to be restored to the throne. It was not, however, a particularly pro-Hanoverian crowd, and it drew its strength from outside the mercantile City proper, where the Whig government was despised. And in the outlying areas where James's declaration was passed from hand to hand and read with eager anticipation, people continued to drink quiet toasts to the Pretender's health and to wait impatiently for more news from the north.

14

On November 19 the parole, or password, in the Stuart army was "Charles and London." On previous nights it had been "Fortune and Carlisle," "Taffy and Wales," "Patrick and Ireland," and a dozen other variants. But there was something symbolic about the army's departure from Carlisle on the nineteenth, after the victorious siege of the town and the castle's humiliating surrender. The road from Carlisle led to London, and the ultimate victory. Many in the army were sure of it, and Charles surest of all.

He was thriving on the campaigning life. Its schedule was one he had been familiar with for years: early to bed, fully clothed, up long before dawn, at four o'clock or earlier, then off on the march, leading his men on foot, setting them an energetic example, until at the end of the long day it was time for a light supper and another short night's rest. It was the life of the seasoned hunter, the life Charles had enjoyed in Italy more than any other. There he had tramped the hills and marshes, his gun over his arm, winter and summer, for days at a time. Now he tramped the icy, snowbound roads of northern England, wearing thick brogues on his feet and outpacing the rugged, barefooted Highlanders who had difficulty keeping up with him.

He not only marched with the men, talking with them in his smattering of recently acquired Gaelic and dividing his time among the various regiments, moving backward and forward along the column as the day wore on, but he worked alongside them when there was work to be done, throwing off his jacket and cutting timber, wading into streams and rivers to reconnoiter the fords, making certain the men were adequately quartered at the end of the day, dispensing praise when deserved and mild blame where necessary.

His own comfort appeared to be his least concern. Even on the longest marches, after thirty grueling miles or more of walking in the freezing wind and stinging snow, he waited to assure himself of the men's safety before seeking his own quarters. To the soldiers he appeared indefatigable and so lacking in hauteur that he spoke affably to any of them who approached him, winning their loyalty and astonishing them by his even temper and moderation.[1]

It was not that Charles was superhuman, or particularly self-disciplined or self-sacrificing, merely that there was a lucky fit between his congenial, coarse-fibered hardihood and eager enjoyment of the bracing outdoors and the situation in which he found himself. He was ebullient and forward-thrusting, even cocky, by nature; he reveled in competition and adventure; and this was the ultimate adventure, the adventure of invasion, and the ultimate competition, the competition for the crown. No doubts darkened his sunny outlook. He and his men were London-bound, it was only a matter of time.

His naturalness was winning, but it had a disadvantage. He did not attempt to disguise his likes and dislikes, which were pronounced. Tact and politic behavior were foreign to him. His liking for the French and Irish officers who had come to Scotland with the Marquis d'Eguilles was obvious, and very much resented by the volunteer officers of the Lowland regiments. And his tense relationship with the man the Lowlanders revered as "the true man," Lord George Murray, precipitated a crisis.

The siege of Carlisle was no sooner over than Lord George resigned as Lieutenant-General. He was piqued at not being involved in negotiating the surrender of the town and castle (even though he had remarked when the town was first invested that he knew nothing about siege warfare), and resented Charles's permitting the Catholic Duke of Perth to represent him in the negotiations, even though under English law Catholics were forbidden to hold either civil or military offices. In truth, Murray had been resentful for weeks; the events at Carlisle had merely been the last straw. He was committed to the Stuart cause, but less than approving of Charles personally. Murray was, according to the Duke of Perth's aide-de-camp, "fierce, haughty, blunt and proud," and inclined to think himself superior to everyone else—which he was in military experience and competence. Charles, on the other hand, was blithe, carefree, and congenial, the opposite of the intense, hot-tempered Murray.

Charles felt Murray's disapproval, and resisted it. Lord Elcho wrote that Charles "loved to contradict" Murray, provoking him to irritation and making his anger flare. They were ill suited to one another, the twenty-four-year-old adventurer and his middle-aged general, and to make matters worse, several of Charles's closest advisers distrusted Murray and disparaged his loyalty.[2]

Matters reached a head at Carlisle, and Lord George wrote Charles a letter of resignation in which he complained that his advice carried too little weight. In short, he felt slighted. Charles, characteristically, accepted the letter and, without weighing the military consequences—or perhaps weighing them, and discounting Murray's value—determined to go on without the benefit of Murray's generalship.

His reply was blunt. "I think your advice ever since you joined me at Perth has had another guess [sic] weight with me than what any General Officer could claim as such," he wrote. "I am therefore extremely surprised you should throw up your commission for a reason which I believe was never heard of before." He assured Murray that he appreciated the latter's sincere desire to see his father's rights upheld, but added that he was certain James would "never take anything as proof of it but your deference to me. I accept of your demission as Lieutenant General," he concluded, "and your future service as a volunteer."

As might have been expected, the chief officers were aghast, and urged Charles to secure Murray's services again at all costs. Murray's co-commander, Perth, also resigned, to remove any lingering occasion for bad feeling and as a gesture of conciliation. Eventually a compromise was engineered: Lord George agreed to resume his command on condition that Perth and his men take over the inglorious assignment of guarding the baggage train and Murray of Broughton (whom Lord George particularly hated) remove himself from Charles's war council.

The crisis over Murray's command was but one of many. Individuals quarreled with one another, Highlanders clashed with Lowlanders, Protestants with Catholics, Scots with Irish. Each day brought new occasions for disputes. One of Lord George Murray's grievances was that, when Carlisle fell, his Atholl men were assigned miserable quarters in the vaults of the castle and in a ruined house that barely provided shelter. They were without food, and had neither candles to light their gloomy surroundings nor coal to warm them. Rightly or wrongly, Murray blamed O'Sullivan, and attributed the miserable situation of the men of Atholl to his malice. Earlier, when the town was first invested and deep trenches had to be dug in the frozen earth, the Highlanders had simply refused to do their share. They would fight wherever and whenever their leader commanded them to fight, but manual labor was beneath them. Even sentry duty made them grumble. So, no doubt occasioning a good deal of resentment, the self-sacrificing Perth ordered his men to dig the trenches, pitching in, despite his poor health, to help them with his own hands.

So it went, this group against that, officers competing against one another for prestige, slandering each other and, when they found their assignments intolerable, threatening to resign. Young Lord Ogilvy, who had brought his beautiful wife with him on the march, announced that rather than undertake the "dirty work" his regiment was given he would demote himself to being a simple volunteer in the ranks. His ego was soothed, and the assignment changed.

The bickering Stuart army moved south from Carlisle on November 21, divided into four groups: an advance guard of cavalry, the vanguard, the main body of the army led by Charles himself, and lastly the baggage and artillery. The various units traveled at different speeds and often by different roads; at most they were separated by the distance of a day's march. The road south from Carlisle led through exceedingly rough, hilly country, the hills at this season covered with snow. After a halt at Penrith, the men marched on, over more wild and barren country, reaching Kendal on the twenty-third. Charles, walking as always ahead of his troops, wearing his Highland costume and thick brogues, became badly fatigued. He trudged on, but so wearily that he appeared to be sleepwalking, and just as he reached the town he almost fainted. The people of Kendal were greatly impressed with his hardihood and lack of aristocratic pretensions—though not impressed enough to join his army—and he rested among them for a day before going on.

Meanwhile part of the army was already en route to Lancaster, taking a road that wound through hills "high as the clouds," offering a view down steep cliffs to the sea. Another easy day's march along a rare stretch of good road brought them to Preston, reputedly a stronghold of Catholicism and Jacobitism, where in fact a few dozen recruits were obtained. The townspeople cheered the army as it marched in, and there was talk in the taverns of considerable numbers of men on their way from North Wales to join Charles.[3] The mood of the soldiers was optimistic, partly because, after weeks of miserably cold weather, the temperature rose and there was a brief, almost springlike thaw.

Charles met with his officers to talk over their situation and to determine strategy. His own spirits were, as usual, high, and the men, who after their victory at Carlisle had opposed risking the dangers of a further move to the south, now favored going on to London. The ordinary soldiers too were sanguine. In a letter written on November 27, one of them said that "the army is in as great spirits as possible for troops to be in, and I have no doubt of a victory on our side against an army twice our number."[4]

The boast was plausible enough, for there was no enemy army anywhere near Preston, and the likelihood of a battle any time soon was small. But if morale was not a problem, numbers were. The

Stuart army had perhaps four thousand men, desertions having reduced it by about a thousand. More were expected to join as the invaders pressed deeper into England, and as their string of victories became more convincing. But Lancashire, a prime recruiting ground, had been disappointing so far. The Jacobite Clubs in the towns had not formed themselves into auxiliary fighting units. The villagers of Cumberland, huddled against the cold in their mud-walled huts, had shown themselves more fearful than welcoming, and had not turned out to lend their support. Some of the townspeople were hostile, or at least treacherous. At Garstang, a treasure box was stolen from one of the wagons as the baggage train passed through. The town was threatened with retribution; finally the box was unearthed from where it had been hidden—in a field behind the town hall.[5]

It was true that few men had as yet come forward to fight under the Stuart banner—but this might change. It would not take much to tip the balance, a few enthusiastic recruits might bring others, tens might grow into hundreds, and before long into thousands. The fever of rebellion could easily spread, especially among the poor, the Catholics, the tradesmen who disliked the government and its taxes, the restless and discontented, the impressionable who were sure to be swept away by the sight of the fair, athletic young man who strode the muddy roads with such authority. So volatile were the passions and loyalties of the people that anything—a rumor that the French had landed, or that King George had fled to Hanover, or that the government troops had been soundly beaten once again as at Prestonpans—could sway them. It was too soon to say that the moment would not come when they would be decisively swayed.

Charles was willing to wait for that moment, but his quarrelsome officers were beginning to wonder whether the English would ever rise in rebellion. It was not enough for the French envoy, d'Eguilles, who marched with the army, to insist that King Louis's troops were about to land somewhere on the English coast, and that their landing would precipitate an uprising in the south. They sought reinforcements closer at hand.

Charles claimed to have received letters from English Jacobites promising help soon, but this may have been an invention on his part.[6] In particular, he claimed to have written assurances from Sir

Watkin Williams Wynn, M.P. for Denbighshire and an affluent
Welsh landholder, that a regiment of three hundred mounted men
had been raised by Wynn and his Jacobite friends. This cavalry unit,
plus Wynn's own numerous tenants, armed as footsoldiers, would
represent a sizable addition to the army, and would join it at some
point on the road between Macclesfield and Derby. Another stalwart, Charles said, the Duke of Beaufort, was in the process of
raising men in South Wales and would lead them to capture Bristol.
Murray of Broughton added his hopeful message. He was in communication with a colonel in the Hanoverian army, he said, whose
regiment was in Kent. The man had assured him as solemnly as
possible that when the time came, his entire regiment would declare
for the Jacobites.

Certainly the countryside was astir, if not as yet fully awakened.
A traveling metalworker, who was constantly on the road through
Lancashire, Stafford, Shropshire and Chester, kept an ear open for
Jacobite talk. Everywhere he went he heard people raising their
tankards in the taverns "to our friends that are on the other side
of the water," "to our friends abroad," and "right to them that
suffer wrong." Having drunk the treasonable healths, the drinkers
passed along rumors of "a rising in favor of the Pretender," and of
an imminent French landing. People even went about dressed in
plaids to signal their sympathies.[7]

The country folk were well aware, in the fall of 1745, that they
were witnessing something rare and strange: an army that was not
an army, but an untidy agglomeration of people, including a great
many young boys, old men, women and children, making their way
along the roads and fanning outward in an arc miles wide when the
terrain permitted. With them were large herds of black cattle, such
horses as they were able to requisition from the towns and villages
they passed through, and wagonloads of artillery and arms.[8] Dozens
of pipers walked in the midst of the throng, which was flanked by
mounted men, some of them incongruous in their smart, if somewhat bedraggled, cavalry uniforms.

In the early morning they marched by torchlight, in the early
evening, as they sought out what quarters were available to them,
the torches were lit yet again. They were notably stoical, putting up
with the bare, cold rooms that were offered them, sometimes a

hundred of them crowded into a single house. At the end of a long
and footsore day, they were grateful for any shelter at all, since they
had no tents—their tents having been carried off by the inhabitants
of Dumfries early in the campaign—and dreaded having to spend
the night in the open.[9]

They were a miscellany of types and occupations—fillibeg-wear-
ing clansmen, farm laborers, plowmen, farmers, weavers, shoe-
makers and barbers. Merchants mingled with servants, lairds and
landowners with shepherds and shopboys. There were a great many
women among them, soldier's wives, camp followers, mistresses
acquired along the route of march. Officers had orders to permit only
wives to follow the army, but "regimental women" abounded, tolerated so long as they made themselves useful and did not take up
room in the wagons. A number of these women were left behind
when they became pregnant and could no longer keep up.[10] There
is a poignant reference in one contemporary narrative of the Stuart
army to crossing a swollen river, "without any loss but two women,
that belonged only to the public, that were drowned."[11]

Observers were struck by the large numbers of very young boys
in the Jacobite army. A man who saw the throng enter Manchester
swore that it contained as many as three thousand "boys of ten,
twelve or fourteen years old," all carrying heavy muskets, swords
and shields, and with braces of pistols strapped to their thin waists.
Some of these may have been servants, carrying their masters' arms,
but many of them were soldiers themselves. By the age of fourteen
they were expected to fight as men, however undersize or immature
they might be. Some had been forced by their clan chiefs or older
relatives to come along, others had come not only voluntarily but
eagerly, glad to leave behind stern parents or, in the case of appren-
tices, harsh masters.[12]

Seen as a moving swarm blackening the landscape, the Jacobites
were intimidating. Taken as individuals, however, they seemed less
so. "The common soldiers are a most despicable crew," wrote one
who saw them entering a town, "being in general less in stature, and
of a wan and meagre countenance, stepping along under their arms
with difficulty, and what they are about seems more of force than
inclination." Still, they knew what they were about, and left no one
in their vicinity in doubt as to their purpose. "They intend to push

on to London," the same writer added, "but do not know the route. Wherever they go they magnify their numbers, and tell the most confounded lies about themselves. In their letters to their friends in Scotland, they say that their army now consists of twenty-four thousand, and that neither ditch, dyke nor devil can turn them."[13]

Those forced to play host to the Jacobites winced at their uncouthness and marveled at the size of their appetites. A man who gave quarters to six officers and forty privates was put off by their foreign speech, which seemed to him like that of "a herd of Hottentots, wild monkies in a desert, or vagrant gipsies." Most of them, he commented, "looked like so many fiends turned out of hell, and under their plaids nothing but various sorts of butchering weapons were to be seen." They were content to sleep on straw in the hall and the laundry, although the straw soon began to reek, and the host had to replace it with fresh. At first he fed them bread and cheese, and gave them ale to drink, but by the second day of their stay they were demanding better fare, and before they left they had eaten a side of beef, eight joints of mutton, quantities of chickens and ducks, along with more cheese and bread, and had drunk enormous quantities of ale and beer.[14]

The last days of November found the Stuart army in Manchester, where their reception could hardly have been more joyful. Bells pealed, bonfires were lit, crowds gathered to cheer and call out, "God bless Your Royal Highness, Prince Charles!" It was a noisy, boisterous welcome, a foretaste, some must have thought, of the welcome the army would receive once it reached London. For Manchester, like London, was known to have strong Jacobite sympathies, and there was wild exultation when King James was proclaimed at the Market Cross. Nor was the exultation empty of substance. Three hundred volunteers enrolled under the Stuart banner. And to add to the general euphoria, Charles received a letter from his brother Henry in Paris, saying that King Louis was "absolutely resolved upon the expedition into England," and that it would be ready to embark by December 9.[15]

From Manchester they passed safely to Macclesfield, to Leek, to Ashbourne, and finally to Derby, each day expecting to encounter government troops and remaining unusually vigilant. They had intelligence that a Hanoverian army with five cavalry and fifteen infantry regiments was near; the officers allowed themselves no sleep at all on the night of December 3 in order to be ready if the alarm were raised. But they were more than ready to take on any army, no matter how large or how powerful. All the talk among the men was of London, and how close they were to getting there, and how exciting it would be to sweep in and take the capital, with the enemy falling down like matchsticks before them.

"We are now within a hundred miles of London," one soldier wrote home from Derby, "without seeing the face of one enemy, so that in a short time I hope to write to you from London, where if we get safe, the whole of our story and even what has happened already must appear to posterity more like a romance than anything of truth."[16] It had been a romance indeed, a series of events so improbable as to seem a fantasy. No one had believed the rebel army capable of surviving more than a few days once it entered England. Yet now it stood poised for a descent on the capital, the men keen for battle and their leader eager to grasp his father's throne.

15

That the Stuart army reached Derby without engaging any government troops was amazing, for only two days earlier a huge Hanoverian force, ten thousand strong, had been drawn into battle lines to take the field against them.

The government army was drawn up near the town of Stone, a few miles north of Stafford, early in the morning of December 3. Their commander, the heroic young Duke of Cumberland, had chosen the large open expanse adjacent to the town as ideal for combat between his more numerous force and the rebel army. Cumberland was certain that the Jacobites were on their way to Stone, for on the previous day Lord George Murray had taken about a quarter of the Stuart forces and marched from their encampment at Macclesfield to Congleton—only some fifteen miles from Stone—and Murray's men, in demanding billets and food in Congleton, had told their hosts that Charles was on his way there with the rest of the army. Cumberland's spies, who had been in Congleton, brought him the news, and on receiving it he confidently went ahead with his plans to meet the rebel force just outside Stone.

Cumberland had his men ready at four in the morning. They stood in their positions, teeth chattering, boots stamping on the frozen ground to keep the circulation going in their cold feet. They knew from their intelligence reports that Charles and his artillery were usually on the road long before dawn, and they meant to give him a harsh reception. But by eight o'clock there was still no sign of the rebels, and as the wintry sun rose higher in the sky the men were swaying on their feet from weariness, for they had had only a few hours' sleep in the past ten days, and had gone for a full twenty-four hours with food. They kept their ranks, for their devotion to their commander was strong, but as the hours passed and there was still no sign of the Stuart army, their fatigue began to overwhelm them. By eleven o'clock it looked as though there would be no engagement, and by afternoon Cumberland—who had had almost no sleep himself the night before—left the field. The following morning, after learning that Charles and his men were in Derby and that Lord George Murray's march to Congleton had been nothing more than a stratagem, he marched his long-suffering soldiers back to Stafford.

William Augustus, Duke of Cumberland was King George's second son and greatest favorite. Tall and forceful, with a fleshy, porcine face, long nose and sensual mouth, Duke William had been brought up to be a soldier. Unlike his elder brother Frederick, Prince of Wales, the duke did not expect to have to govern a kingdom; not being heir to the throne, he felt no particular rivalry with its present occupant. So while Frederick quarreled with King George, William busied himself in becoming the soldier his father wanted him to be.

At age twenty-two he fought beside his father at the battle of Dettingen, and was wounded in the leg. Later, given his own command, he led English, Hanoverian and mercenary troops on the continent, acquitting himself competently at Fontenoy, though the battle was lost to the French. Contemporaries thought he was everything a soldier should be: personally brave, forthright, confident, aggressive, with a straight spine and a brisk manner. He never shirked danger, but faced it head on, winning his men's respect and achieving a deserved reputation for heroism. Cumberland had "all the good qualities that ever a young prince was endowed with," the Duke of Richmond wrote. "He has justly got the love and esteem of everybody."[1]

There was new hope in the Hanoverian ranks when Cumberland was given supreme command of the armies in England on November 23. He was young, active, capable—everything General Wade, who had so far been unable to halt the advance of the rebels, was not.

Wade had become bogged down in Newcastle, a victim of weather, age, and continual frustration. He meant to do his best, but everywhere he turned things went against him. Provisioning was abysmal. When he moved his troops westward in a futile attempt to reach the Jacobites, there was not enough meat or bread to feed the men, nor enough straw or forage, nor even the minimum number of horses and carts necessary to move a large fighting force across country. An epidemic of dysentery had spread among the men, leaving them ill and weak, quite unfit to slog their way through knee-deep snow. The weather was ferocious. Men froze to death when forced, for lack of tents, to sleep in the open. Even the quarters in Newcastle were flooded. The Swiss and German soldiers, indifferent to the outcome of the rebellion, were on the verge of mutiny; the Dutch refused to leave Newcastle until their grievances over pay and horses were resolved.

All these crises plagued Wade, and made him turn despairingly to his inept Quartermaster-General and ask what was to be done. Wade was seventy-two, and felt ninety; already he was thinking ahead to the next year's campaigning season, and hoping to be relieved of command by then. He had been born in the reign of Charles II, he remembered the Glorious Revolution, and had fought his first battle soon after it. A bachelor, he had never known any life but soldiering, and now even that was becoming unendurable. According to his embittered and critical second-in-command, Lord Tyrawly, Wade was "infirm both in mind and body, forgetful, irresolute, perplexed, and snappish." He refused to listen to good advice, and refused to take steps to remedy the woeful shortcomings in provisioning and billeting that hamstrung his army. In brief, he was unfit for command—and Tyrawly privately thought that he was afraid of the rebels besides.[2] Cumberland's assessment was more blunt. He referred to the general as "Grandmother Wade," and asked that he be replaced.[3]

While stopping short of removing Wade, the government was taking the incursion of the Stuart army more and more seriously. With England at war with both France and Spain, and rapidly losing ground to the French in the Austrian Netherlands, there were no troops to spare. Yet some troops had been withdrawn from the continent to defend England, and more might have to be withdrawn soon. This placated the government's critics in the Commons, who were demanding to know why the supporters of Charles Stuart had not been crushed weeks, or even months, earlier, and who invariably objected to the expending of British men and money abroad. The king, however, was mightily displeased, protective as he was of his beloved Hanover and eager as he was to play the role of a European rather than a mere British sovereign.

Pelham was endeavoring, unsuccessfully, to broaden the base of the "Broadbottom Administration," but the interests of the various political factions kept them apart. Newcastle continued to wring his hands and issue dire warnings about the "army of ten thousand desperate men, inured to fight and fatigue" who were advancing on London. The king, impatient with the politicians and baffled by his generals' lack of military success, put his second son in command of the troops and announced that he himself would march to Finchley, where the defenders of the capital were encamped, and raise his standard at the head of the army. Was he not the hero of Dettingen, who as a young man had fought at Oudenarde and Malplaquet? After eighteen years as king he was not about to surrender his authority to a pack of insurgents led by a presumptuous boy. He intended, he swore, "to remain and die King of England."[4]

Frederick, Prince of Wales displayed a far less belligerent attitude. His wife had recently given birth to a son, and the prince celebrated his christening by giving a large and sumptuous banquet. He ordered his pastry chef to carve a likeness of the citadel of Carlisle in sugar, and served it at the banquet, where he and his guests entertained themselves by pelting it with sugar plums.[5]

Cumberland reached the Midlands at the end of November, and began the work of consolidating the various scattered units placed under his command into a single fighting force. By December 3 he

was ready to offer battle at Stone—but, as we have seen, the Jacobites eluded him and went on to Derby. Hastily the duke sent a
message to Wade, urging him to send his cavalry at least to engage
the rebels, though with the Stuarts only a few days' distance from
London Wade's cavalry would not have been likely to stop them.
And even now there was uncertainty in the government camp about
whether Charles would in fact lead his men to London or whether
he might invade Yorkshire, or turn toward Wales, or even return
to Scotland to await reinforcements from France. Whatever he did,
there was always the possibility that a second army of rebels might
be formed in Scotland, and that with Cumberland occupied in the
south, Wade would have to be relied on to march his men north to
meet them.

Meanwhile Londoners had been preparing for the worst. The
commercial City was all but deserted, the shops shuttered, the
markets shut down, the theaters closed. The merchants had sent
their valuables away, and now the last of them were leaving for safer
quarters in the countryside. "Nobody but has some fear for themselves, for their money, or for their friends in the army," Walpole
wrote. He, along with many others, "feared the rebels beyond his
reason."[6] On Friday, December 5—afterward called "Black Friday" because of the panic that swept through the city on that day—a
rumor spread that the French had landed in the south and were on
their way to seize the capital. Cumberland and all his forces were
recalled at once, but it would be four or five days at the earliest
before he arrived, and long before then the French were expected
to be in possession of all of southern England.

People shut themselves in their houses and said their prayers.
The streets were deserted, an odd silence prevailed. Even the
crowded alleyways of Westminster and the East End, usually shrill
and raucous with noise, were unnaturally quiet. For a week or more
there had been whispers of a papist plot to kill all Englishmen by
poisoning the wells. Murrain had spread among the cattle in the
vicinity of London, and it was unsafe to eat beef or even to drink
milk. The epidemic was blamed on Jacobite conspirators—or, alternately, on government provocateurs hoping to turn the populace
against the Jacobites.

There were few ordinary citizens in the streets, but many guardsmen, prominently posted in the squares and open fields, massing at the City gates, busying themselves setting up alarm posts. An Irish officer in a French regiment who was brought to London in secret by smugglers at just this time found the city hushed and expectant. The great houses of the nobles were being watched, he was told; those who were in sympathy with the rebels expected either Charles and his army or the French to arrive any day. Meanwhile, they waited, keeping their hopes and expectations to themselves, drinking the healths of "the King, the Prince, the Duke," without naming any names.[7] The sectors where the Irish congregated were being watched too, especially the docks, for Newcastle and Pelham were afraid that the Jacobite dockworkers might sabotage the naval defenses by burning the dock stores.

"Black Friday" came and went, a dark Saturday succeeded, and a dim and gloomy Sunday. Tensions rose, but there was no confirmation of the rumor of a French landing, and the camp at Finchley remained secure. Messages flew back and forth between the government and the military. Troops moved around and through the capital in an endless procession. No one had reliable information, and in the absence of reliable information, no one could feel secure.

"What in the name of wonder is become of Marshall Wade?" asked the Duke of Richmond in a letter to Newcastle. "The rebels will certainly be two days march ahead of us. . . . I make no doubt but this embarkation will go on at Dunkirk. Are we all mad? that you don't send for ten thousand more forces be they Hessians, Hanoverians, or devils, if they will but fight for us!"[8]

The Jacobites had arrived in Derby on December 4 in waves: first a party of blue-uniformed cavalrymen, then in midafternoon the Life Guards and a number of the Highland chiefs, then later on the main body of the army, marching six or eight abreast with their standards, white flags bearing a red cross. There were nearly as many soldiers as there were townspeople, and as usual they had to be crowded into their assigned quarters, dozens to each house. The mayor and several of the aldermen had left hours earlier, but Lord George Murray summoned those aldermen still in the town to assemble in their robes before the town hall, where the crier proclaimed James Stuart King of England, Scotland, France and Ireland. This done, the final contingent of troops marched in, with Charles leading them, on foot.

Though many of the townspeople were loyal to the Hanoverians, bonfires were lit to welcome Charles, church bells were rung, and at least some houses were illuminated.

Even the loyalists were impressed by Charles's appearance. "He is a fine person," one eyewitness wrote, "six foot high, a very good complexion, and presence majestic." Another found him "tall, straight, slender and handsome" in his green Scotch bonnet laced with gold, white wig, Highland plaid and broadsword. A crowd followed him as he walked across the marketplace into Full Street and on to Exeter House, the handsome, red-brick Elizabethan mansion where he was to spend the next two days.

Here good news reached him. Help from the continent had arrived. Some eight hundred Irish and Scottish troops fighting in the French army had landed at Montrose, led by Lord John Drummond, and added to these were two thousand more Scots who had come out to fight for the Jacobites since Charles left Edinburgh. Thus Drummond had an army two-thirds the size of the one at Derby, and there was every indication that still more Scotsmen would join in the coming weeks. Drummond brought with him orders from King Louis to make war against George II—referred to in the orders as the "Elector of Hanover"—and to assist Charles "in the taking possession of Scotland, England, and Ireland, if necessary, at the expense of all the men and money he is master of." Drummond claimed the title of "Commander-in-Chief of his most Christian Majesty's forces in Scotland," and he and his troops were the vanguard of a larger army yet to come from France. There was news of this larger army as well. Charles's envoy to Paris, Kelly, sent word that the rest of the invasion force would embark from France in fifteen days or at most three weeks. Meanwhile, Kelly urged, the Jacobites should "stand their ground, since a retreat must be fatal."

The following morning, December 5, the Derby streets were aswarm with soldiers, buying everything from powder flasks to buttons and handkerchiefs. According to Lord George Murray's aide-de-camp Johnstone, they expected to engage Cumberland the next day, and were eager for the fight, their "heroic ardor" high. "They were to be seen," he wrote, "during the whole day, in crowds before the shops of the cutlers, quarreling about who should be the first to sharpen and give a proper edge to his sword."[9]

The ordinary soldiers knew nothing as yet of the events in Scotland, but when Charles told the members of his council what he had learned, their view of the army's situation and prospects changed. Charles persisted in his desire to go on to London; the chiefs, Lord George Murray and the other officers were convinced that it would be preferable to retreat.

They made a forceful case. With a sizable second army in Scotland, and French reinforcements on the way, there was no need to risk the forty-five-hundred-odd men in Derby by pitting them against Cumberland's superior numbers and, after that, against the defenders of the capital massed at Finchley. Immediate victory would be gratifying but short-sighted, and in the long run wasteful and unnecessary. Besides, they argued, the taking of London had always been predicated on the cooperation of large numbers of English Jacobites, and so far these English Jacobites had proven to be a phantom.

Lord George, Ogilvy and Elcho were the staunchest proponents of this view, Elcho telling Charles bluntly that if he advanced toward London he would be in Newgate gaol within a fortnight.

To Charles, retreat was simply inconceivable, and at first he ignored the subject entirely and began considering the next day's order of march. But Lord George, whose discontent with the entire enterprise still smoldered and whose tendency to clash personally with Charles was never far below the surface, spoke up to demand a resolution of the question of whether to go on or turn back.

Charles was outraged. They were almost at the gates of London. Their objective was within their grasp. The men were excited and battle-ready, while Cumberland's army was exhausted and the rabble at Finchley was hardly an army at all. There was absolutely no reason to turn back, and every reason to go forward, he argued. They were feared, they were the better fighters, the French were on their way to help them, surely the English Jacobites would declare themselves once London was secured for King James.

At that moment Charles saw, far more accurately than his cautious officers, that the momentum of victory lay with his men. It was vital, he could not ultimately succeed without it. And he would squander it irretrievably if he retreated.

He argued on, an ebullient twenty-four-year-old convinced of the rightness of his view confronted with the equal conviction of many older and more seasoned men, most of them old enough to be his father. Murray's harsh arguing was distressingly paternal. And they were almost all against him. They even forced him to admit that, despite what he had been telling them all along, he had no actual commitments from any of the English Jacobite leaders.

The meeting ended in discord, the only agreement being to meet again in the early evening.

It was a shock, this negativity, coming as it did at the climax of three months of ever increasing, ever more astounding success. To Charles it made no logical sense whatever. He felt thwarted. To have the fruits of all this effort thrown aside as the result of an hour's heated discussion seemed monstrously wrong, totally unfair. He had to salvage the campaign if he could. He spent the afternoon in a vain search for pledges of support from the local Derbyshire gentry. But not surprisingly, they disappointed him. It was not that they were unsympathetic, merely that they lacked the daring to act then and there, with loyalist troops only a few miles away and many loyalist neighbors to confront.

The evening meeting went no better than the morning meeting had. Lord George, without waiting for any further discussion, began to give his advice on the best route of retreat. Charles tried to argue that Cumberland's men would inflict more casualties on them if they retreated than if they advanced, as he would "pursue them hotly, and be constantly at their heels." But there was no turning the clan chiefs, who had made up their minds. Even those few who had wavered earlier now announced themselves in favor of retreat.

"You ruin, abandon, and betray me if you do not march on," Charles shouted angrily, alternately bullying, shaming and pleading with the adamant men. They had named their preference. They were silent.

Filled with rage, Charles managed to maintain an icy dignity as he ordered the retreat.

"In future," he announced, "I shall summon no more councils, since I am accountable to nobody for my actions but to God and my father and therefore I shall no longer either ask or accept advice." Feeling alone and betrayed, unconsoled by the allegiance of some outside the council, such as Sheridan, who agreed with him, Charles managed to summon a façade of congeniality. Immediately after the council meeting a reception had been scheduled at Exeter House for the citizens of Derby. They rushed in by the hundreds to meet Charles, falling over one another in their haste, and upsetting the furniture. Charles withstood the assault, but the Stuart standard, placed in a prominent position nearby, was smashed.

The men, not being privy to the surprising decision their leaders had taken, marched out from Derby before dawn the next morning still believing that they were en route to London, and that they were headed for an engagement with Cumberland's army.[10] Not until the sun rose did they realize, at first with disbelief, that they were being led away from the duke and the capital. Their cheerfulness turned, Johnstone wrote, to "expressions of rage and lamentation. If we had been beaten," he added, "the grief could not have been greater."

Ten days after Charles and his enraged men left Derby for the north, a large flotilla of French ships put to sea from Dunkirk, their movements part of a vast design to concentrate men and ships at Calais and Boulogne for the invasion of England.

"Here we are at last on the eve of a great achievement," the naval minister Maurepas wrote in a letter to the Archbishop of Bourges. Elaborate naval preparations, under the direction of Antoine Walsh, were nearly complete. If all went as planned, twelve thousand French soldiers would be on English soil by the end of December.

King Louis was as enthusiastic and impatient for the invasion to begin as anyone else at his court. He supervised the coordination of the enterprise, pleased that the man he called the "Great Tyrant," George II, was to be dealt a killing blow at last, and arranged for a large sum of money to be carried across the Channel with the soldiers and delivered to Charles in person. And the king's squab-

CAROLLY ERICKSON

bling ministers, who had been at odds with one another for many months over the issue of whether or not to support the Jacobites, had finally reached agreement on this venture.[1]

The soldiers were to embark from Calais and Boulogne, under the command of Louis François Armand du Plessis, Duc de Richelieu, the great-grandnephew of the famed Cardinal Richelieu and King Louis's close friend. The aims of the invading force were set forth in a manifesto written by Voltaire, stating in English and French that, at the request of certain English supporters of the true English king, James Stuart, an army of restoration was being provided. This army intended no harm to the English, only their good—and the enthronement of their rightful ruler. Three thousand copies of the manifesto were printed and put aboard the transport ships, along with provisions, maps, arms, artillery and baggage. To preserve secrecy about the ultimate destination of the flotilla, the ships were not to be brought to their embarkation points until the last possible moment, so many stayed at Dunkirk and Ambleteuse and other coastal ports, being fitted out by local laborers pressed into service by the military.

The titular leader of the expedition was to be Henry Stuart, who had been in France for three months waiting to take his place at the head of the army of restoration. Somewhat shy, earnest, conscientious and, at twenty, still very young and sheltered, Henry had rented a house at Bagneux, where he settled in to wait for the expedition to get under way. He was introduced at court by his cousin the Duke of FitzJames, but his first meeting with Louis XV at the end of October was awkward and humiliating.

Louis forgot about having agreed to grant Henry an audience, and when the appointed day came, Henry was kept waiting for hours. Finally the error was recognized by one of the king's servants, who ushered Henry into the royal presence. Even then all was not well, for instead of greeting Henry in brotherly fashion as a prince of royal Stuart blood, Louis demanded from him the deference he expected from lesser mortals—which wounded and confused the young man. (In fact, Henry's official incognito prevented any other welcome.) Tactless remarks were made on both sides, and the interview ended badly. The queen, however, Marie Leczcinska, who was a Pole and related to Henry and his brother through their mother, was warmer toward Henry than her husband had been. And by the time the ships and men were massing at the Channel ports in December, the king too had thawed. "Cousin," he said to Henry when the latter took his leave to go to Boulogne, "I hope you will dine quietly in London in January."[2]

While the French ships gathered in Boulogne and Calais, the English experienced a new wave of panic. Admiral Vernon was informed of the movement of the flotilla from Dunkirk—in fact he had known for several days that it would embark soon. But he was not at all certain that he could intercept it should it make for the English coast. He believed, based on combined intelligence reports, that the French had twenty-three thousand fighting men in the vicinity of the Channel ports. He expected six to seven thousand of these to constitute the invasion force, sailing in fifty hundred-ton ships. But would they land on the south coast, or in Suffolk, or elsewhere? Rumor had it that they had already landed at Pevensey Bay. If a southerly wind arose, Vernon informed his superiors, his ships would be driven northward, necessarily leaving the coasts of Kent and Sussex unprotected. Moreover, while his ships put to sea in pursuit of an enemy whose location and destination were unknown, the Kentish smugglers would inform the French that the coasts were clear.

Preparedness for an invasion was stepped up. Fire beacons were set up along the coast from Cromer to Harwich. The Thames bridges were fortified, and all aids to navigation on the river removed. Alarm signals warning of invasion were agreed on: seven cannons, one to be fired every half minute from the Tower, with an answering shot every half minute from St. James's Park. Marines in the Canterbury garrison received orders to march to Sheerness, other troops were sent to Maidstone, Rochester and Chatham, to remain on alert for further orders from the Admiralty.

In London, once again there was a run on gold at the Bank of England. The frantic populace, already overwrought from weeks of sleeplessness and fear, sought a scapegoat. When some French prisoners were being marched from the coast to London where they were to be confined at the Tower, word spread through the crowd that gathered to watch them that one young man among them was none other than Henry Stuart. "The mob," Walpole wrote, "persuaded of his being the youngest Pretender, could scarcely be restrained from tearing him to pieces all the way on the road, and at his arrival."[3]

Once again, for a few torturous days, a sort of madness gripped the public. Everyone came under suspicion. If a man withdrew his funds from the bank, he was suspected of wanting to send the money northward to support the retreating Stuart army. If he left his funds intact, people said it was because he had made a private agreement with the invaders. There was talk of raising still more regiments; the weavers offered a thousand men to fight for King George, and even the lawyers and judges "formed themselves into a little army," under the command of the lord chief justice, and presented themselves to guard the royal family at St. James's while the king went off to lead his troops.

Every Frenchman was suspect, and the sight of a Scotsman in the street was enough to start a riot. Frightened people reported hearing the sound of Highland drums, or French artillery, or the tramping of French boots along the country roads. So severe was the disarray in London that the heretofore cautious English Jacobites, the Earl of Barrymore and Sir John Hynde Cotton, sent word to Charles that they would join him there with what forces they could raise, if he changed his tactics and turned once again toward the capital.[4]

On December 19, King George sent a message to Parliament. "His Majesty having received undoubted intelligence, that preparations are making at Dunkirk, and other parts of France, which are now in great forwardness, for invading this kingdom with a considerable number of forces," the message said, "in support of the rebellion carrying on here, in favor of the Pretender to his Crown . . . His Majesty having the last summer taken into his service six thousand Hessian troops . . . has judged it necessary to direct the said Hessians to be brought into these kingdoms." For once the usual parliamentary outcry against denuding the continent of troops was not heard. In view of the crisis, the importation of the Hessians was welcomed.

In Paris, where the calendar was eleven days ahead of the English reckoning, it was the Christmas season. While the soldiers were marching into position from Flanders and the shipwrights and carpenters were fitting out the transports, Versailles was brightly lit every night for the Christmas festivities. The king and queen presided at a series of holiday balls, the guests' excitement heightened by their knowledge that within days England would be at their king's mercy. In Paris, it was said that the fleet would sail on Christmas Eve; the taverns and cafes buzzed with news of the impending departure. When Christmas came, and the day after, and still there was no word that the ships had left Boulogne and Calais, people attributed the delay to the weather.

And in fact the winds, which had been harsh and unfavorable for two weeks, turned favorable two days after Christmas. On the following day Richelieu arrived at Dunkirk, intending to embark immediately. The king had promised him the rank of marshal of France if the invasion succeeded. He had nerved himself to succeed.

Almost as soon as he arrived, however, disconcerting reports began to reach him. Some of the troops were found to be unsuitable for marine operations. There was an unforeseen difficulty in equipping the transport ships with mangers for the horses, and carpenters were working night and day to get the mangers finished. Walsh, who was battling manfully to assemble some three hundred transports, discovered that the naval minister was unable to inform him precisely how many soldiers there would be in all—which made Walsh's former estimate of needed transport invalid. Walsh was also having a problem with provisions, he informed Richelieu. The officials at Versailles insisted that six months supply of food and other necessities be carried to England—far too much in Walsh's view—and it was proving to be impossible to buy this amount of foodstores in the dead of winter. It was impossible not only to buy them, but to move them: the army at Dunkirk was receiving its goods by canal from Bourbourg some ten miles inland, but the sluices froze in the cold weather, and nothing could move along the canal for days at a time. Worse still, the artillery, which had been due to arrive at Calais early in December, had yet to be loaded on the boats that would carry it to Dunkirk. Meanwhile Walsh was short of ships—and some of those he had were found to be unseaworthy.

With problems like these mounting, word arrived from England that Charles and his army had not gone on toward London from Derby but were in retreat. This was startling news, completely unexpected and demoralizing. Richelieu needed more information, and learned, via the Kentish smugglers, that the English were building up their troop strength in the capital and on the southeastern coast. So not only would the French invaders have to take London on their own, without the aid of the Jacobite troops attacking from the northwest, but they would have to take the city in spite of an increasingly large, increasingly entrenched opposing army. Briefly Richelieu considered changing his plans and landing the men somewhere in Wales. Here too, he was told, "circumstances were sadly changed." With Charles's army in retreat, the Welsh Jacobites would be less inclined to welcome a French landing and rise against the Hanoverian king.

The duke's courage, never the staunchest, began to fail him. And at the same time, his irritation with Henry Stuart rose.

Henry was no less devout in France than he had been in his father's Roman palace. He made his devotions, he confessed his sins, he went to mass. Sometimes his attendance at mass conflicted with his attendance at Richelieu's council of war. And being who he was, he gave the religious service first priority. Richelieu warned him icily that he might conquer the kingdom of heaven by attending mass, but never England—a remark whose edge of scorn even the naïve Henry could not fail to perceive. Whether Henry reprimanded the duke for his notorious and flagrant licentiousness is not recorded.

Vexed by his titular co-commander, exasperated at the incomplete preparations and the seemingly unavoidable delays, Richelieu nonetheless determined to carry on with the expedition. If the original deadline for departure could not be met, then a later one would be decided on. He would work toward this goal.

Then a series of disasters at sea further demoralized him. Two English privateers, the *Eagle* and the *Carlisle,* sprayed one of the French convoys with gunfire. One ship, loaded with much-needed artillery, was sunk, and another was seized while still at anchor, her captain not having had enough warning of the attack to cut her cables. The next day the same two privateers met a much larger artillery convoy from Dunkirk. Seventeen of the ships were either sunk or taken as prizes. And on the following day, yet another convoy was attacked, this time by royal navy ships, and considerable damage was done.

The delays were proving costly indeed. When gales blew up and made the Channel impassable, Richelieu declared that only a miracle could save the expedition. There were now eight thousand tons of shipping at Boulogne and another four thousand at Calais, but instead of marveling at the impressive size of the armada, the members of the war council fell to quarreling over the suitability of Boulogne as an embarkation point, given the nature of the tides and the size of the harbor mouth. The same favorable winds and calm seas that were hoped for to make the departure from the French coast possible were expected to result in high seas off Dungeness—which might wreck the entire flotilla.

Another departure date was set, then another. Each time the presence of English warships, or weather difficulties, or simple tergiversation prevented the launching. By the time Richelieu had been at the coast two weeks and more, it was clear that the enterprise had lost its political momentum, and even Henry was urging Richelieu not to invade England but Scotland—a project which, if feasible at all, would have to wait until spring when an escort of warships could be made available to support it.

The road north from Derby seemed endless. The dispirited men kept up a brisk pace, knowing that Cumberland and his army were not far away, but they were grim-faced and hard-eyed, their resentment evident. Their way led back through Leek and Macclesfield to Manchester, where the advance guard was stoned by the hostile populace and the Jacobite cavalry had to be called in to break up a dangerous mob. Even to obtain billets in the town was very difficult, and to prevent violence Charles ordered a curfew which forbade any two persons to walk together after the hour of nine o'clock on pain of death. There were ugly incidents. Jacobites were fired on, stragglers were seized and beaten, and in some cases killed. Militiamen opened fire and bloody skirmishes resulted. Roads that had been bad enough on the journey southward now appeared to be impassable, yet somehow the army passed along them, given added impetus by the information that a troop of cavalry under the Hanoverian Major-General Oglethorpe was in hot pursuit.

Charles, thoroughly put out at having been thwarted in his burning desire to march his men to London, was peevish and petty. He opposed Murray at every turn, refusing to issue marching orders in a timely fashion, arguing against Murray's proposed schedule, and being notably less visible and vigorous in his leadership. He no longer rose before dawn to set off on foot at the head of his soldiers. Now he slept late, rose long after the vanguard had left, and went on horseback to the next destination. He took his meals with Sheridan or O'Sullivan, dining on fresh fowls or mutton washed down, on at least one occasion, with "mountain Malaga."

After about a week his disposition improved, and he returned to his customary exertions, setting an example to the men by marching on hour after hour in heavy rain, fording swollen streams on foot, refusing to ride even when the roads were at their worst and the exhausted soldiers, soaked to the skin and miserably cold, had to struggle with baggage carts stuck in deep mud.

His unbreakable will strengthened theirs, until at last, on December 20, he led them across the River Esk. The river was four feet deep, and rising by the hour, with a swift and dangerous current. Taking all the available cavalry, he rode in, braking the current as much as possible so that the men could try to get across. They went in, O'Sullivan recalled later, "six in a breast [i.e., six abreast], in as good order, as if they were marching in a field, holding one another by the collars, every body, and every thing past, without any loss."[5] The sight of some two thousand men, their arms linked, marching in orderly fashion across a raging torrent impressed onlookers; d'Eguilles was particularly astonished. There were some near-drownings. Charles saved one man by grabbing his hair and crying "Help! Help!" in Gaelic until help came.

Once across the river, they were back in Scotland again. They lit fires to warm themselves, and as night fell the pipers played and the men, more relieved than tired, danced themselves dry.

They had made it safely through the hostile territory of England—to face an increasingly hostile Scotland.

BONNIE PRINCE CHARLIE

One of the first sights the Jacobites saw as they gained the far shore of the Esk was burning bonfires, bonfires lit by Scots loyal to the Hanoverian crown to celebrate the retreat of the rebels from England. In Glasgow, where loyalists were a solid majority, the Stuart army was received coolly. Charles's celebrated charm had no effect, and only sixty new recruits were enlisted, in contrast to the entire regiment which had been recruited for the government and which was now in Edinburgh. The Jacobites stayed in Glasgow for about a week, giving the Glaswegians time to supply the six thousand coats, shirts, bonnets, hose and pairs of shoes Charles required of them. The soldiers were badly in need of new clothes, as their own were ragged and filthy after months of dust and mud, foul weather and battle.

Early in the new year the Jacobites moved on. Charles gave the order to march to Stirling, the fortified town high on its commanding bluff overlooking the broad plain northwest of Edinburgh. At the same time he sent a message to Drummond and his men at Perth ordering them to join the rest of the army at Stirling. Drummond's French troops had artillery with them, French cannon and a dozen gunners. Again, as at Carlisle, Charles envisioned besieging Stirling Castle and, once in possession of it, using the castle as a base from which to conquer the rest of Scotland. It was a sensible strategy, at least in the abstract. One of the chief weaknesses of the campaign so far had been the Jacobites' inability to hold any of the towns they had captured. Even Carlisle had been lost when Cumberland recaptured it on December 30. If Stirling could be reduced, then strongly garrisoned, and strengthened with the army's newly acquired artillery, not only could it control a good part of the Lowlands but it could provide a safe zone of retreat for the Stuart soldiers as they progressively widened the scope of their campaigns.

Very little of Scotland was actually under Jacobite control. For the moment, the recently arrived French troops and the sizable Highland contingents that had joined them (including some Mackintoshes, some Mackenzies, Frasers and Farquharsons) dominated Perth, but as we have seen, Glasgow was hostile, Edinburgh was occupied by substantial numbers of government troops, Argyll was currently being stirred to Hanoverian loyalty, Inverness was staunchly Hanoverian, and the Highland forts—Fort William, Fort George, and Fort Augustus—were in government hands. A squadron of the royal navy lay off the ports on the east coast to intercept any French ships that might arrive with men and arms.

It would be an uphill battle to subdue all of Scotland, or even a major part of it. Yet now Charles had at hand upwards of eight thousand troops (though men were deserting by the hundreds), men who knew the terrain and could cross it at high speed, men who had accomplished marvelous feats in England and who had not known defeat. The Hanoverian army was at a great disadvantage in winter campaigning. And there was always the possibility that the French might land in the south and take London.

The orders were given, the armies marched. But before many days passed, Charles and his chief general were again at an impasse.

As always, the issue was authority, and specifically Charles's authority. This had been the sorest of sore points ever since the day Charles deferred, with a bad grace, to the prevailing opinion among the chiefs and agreed to order the retreat from Derby. For the past month he had called no councils of war, and had taken advice principally from his preferred advisers, Murray of Broughton— who, when the Derby deliberations were over, professed himself in favor of going on to London—and Sheridan. Neither man was in favor with the chiefs, which only increased the tension between them and their leader. Finally the chiefs met, and drew up a memorial in which they recommended to Charles that future decisions be made by a group of five or seven men, chosen from a larger body of fifteen or sixteen, the decisions to be made in his presence and presumably with his concurrence—though this was not stated. On the battlefield, they added, authority should reside in those in command, which, they said, "is the method of all armies."

"Had not a Council," the memorial read, "determined the retreat from Derby, what a catastrophe might have followed in two or three days? Had a Council of War been held when the army came to Lancaster, a day had [sic] not been lost. Had a Council of War been consulted as to the leaving a garrison at Carlisle, it would never have been agreed to, the place not being tenable, and so many brave men would not have been sacrificed, besides the reputation of his Royal

Highness's arms." The document ended with a reminder that the Jacobite army was a force of volunteers, not of mercenaries who could be ordered about at will.

This went beyond what had happened at Derby; it was in effect a mutiny. Charles was to be demoted to being a mere figurehead, where before he had been Commander-in-Chief.

He responded to the memorial point by point, in writing, his response full of disillusionment and anger.

"When I came into Scotland," he began, "I knew well enough what I was to expect from my enemies, but I little foresaw what I met with from my friends. I came vested with all the authority the King could give me, one chief part of which is the command of his armies, and now I am required to give this up to fifteen or sixteen persons, who may afterwards depute five or seven of their own number to exercise it for fear if they were six or eight, that I might myself pretend to be the casting vote."

If this procedure were to be adopted, he wrote, there would be nothing left to him but the dubious honor of presiding over the committee. He denied the chiefs' assertion that armies were customarily governed in this way, and denied too that his army of volunteers should expect any other form of leadership than would an army of mercenaries.

"I am often hit in the teeth, that this is an army of volunteers, and consequently very different from one composed of mercenaries. What one would naturally expect from an army whose chief officers consist of gentlemen of rank and fortune, and who came into it merely upon motives of duty and honor, is more zeal, more resolution, and more good manners, than in those that fight merely for pay. But it can be no army at all," he insisted forcefully, "where there is no general, or what is the same thing, no obedience or deference paid to him."

Warming to his theme, Charles asked the chiefs whether any of them could possibly be risking more than he himself was, with a price of thirty thousand pounds on his head and a kingdom hanging in the balance if he won, almost certain death if he lost. He denied having refused advice, and claimed that, "on more occasions than one," he had deferred to others' plans. After more detailed contradictions of the charges in the memorial, he concluded with a challenge.

"I have insensibly made my answer much longer than I intended," Charles wrote, "and might yet add much more, but I choose to cut it short, and shall only tell you that my authority may be taken from me by violence, but I shall never resign it like an idiot."[6]

It was a tribute to Charles's leadership that none of the chiefs took himself and his men off following the receipt of this firm counterblast. Instead, the army set about besieging Stirling, and by January 8 had occupied the town, though not the castle.

The soldiers were quartered in villages to the south of the high escarpment of Stirling. Charles stayed at Bannockburn House, the residence of Sir Hugh Paterson, a sixty-year-old Jacobite sympathizer whose brother-in-law, John Walkinshaw, had a long history of service to the Stuart cause. A Lanarkshire gentleman, Walkinshaw had fought for James in the Fifteen, and had been taken prisoner at Sheriffmuir. Escaping his captors, he had made his way to the continent where he was called upon to make himself useful to the court in exile in a variety of capacities until his death in 1731. Walkinshaw's devotion was all the more admirable in that he had a large and growing family. The youngest of his ten daughters was christened Clementina, named for James's bride, who was her godmother.

Clementina Walkinshaw, who was probably about the same age as Charles or a little younger, was staying with her uncle at Bannockburn House in January of 1746. She encountered Charles there, a strong rapport was established between them, and possibly they became lovers. In view of Charles's general indifference to women up until this time, it would seem that Clementina had something very special about her that appealed to him—something, that is, beyond her splendidly Jacobite pedigree.

Clementina was of average height, fair, with a freckled complexion. Her hair may have been red or auburn. Possibly she was handsome, though not a beauty, and she may well have had charm, intelligence and spirit. When Charles encountered her, he was at a low point in his life, frustrated in his bid for the conquest of London, hamstrung by his chiefs and by Lord George Murray, uncertain of his future and that of his army and his cause. He had few sincere allies, fewer confidants. Clementina may have helped to build up his confidence again, as friend or intimate or both. Whatever the nature of their rapport, it made an indelible impression on Charles, though there is no need to presuppose either a passionate erotic interlude or the romantic vow of Jacobite legend.[7]

While Charles and Clementina held communion, the siege of Stirling Castle proceeded, inconclusively, the Jacobites finding it difficult to deploy their artillery to advantage against the castle guns. As often in the past, the recalcitrance of the Highlanders was a hindrance; they refused to do the menial work of carrying sandbags needed to shore up the position of the guns.

Meanwhile the new commander in Edinburgh, Lieutenant-General Henry Hawley, decided on January 13 to advance against Charles and his men and marched toward Stirling. Hawley had a low opinion of the fighting abilities of the "rascal" Jacobites, and imagined that they would run when faced with the Hanoverian cavalry. He envisioned attacking them when and where he chose, and never imagined that they would offer battle to him, late on the afternoon of the seventeenth, with a hard rain falling and a strong wind blowing from the northwest.

In the dimming wintry light Murray led his men up the ridge of a hill called Falkirk Muir, only a mile or two from where Hawley and his men were encamped. Belatedly Hawley sent three of his cavalry regiments across the yielding, rain-soaked ground toward the hill. When they reached its summit they rode toward the Jacobites, drawn up into two lines by Murray. The men stood their ground, their muskets held at the ready, as the cavalry came on. When the horsemen were a bare ten yards away Murray gave the order to fire, and the first volley felled dozens of horses and men— perhaps as many as eighty, including the cavalry commander. At once the remaining riders closed ranks and spurred their horses to trample the Stuart infantry.

"The most singular and extraordinary combat immediately followed," James Johnstone recalled later. "The Highlanders, stretched on the ground, thrust their dirks into the bellies of the horses. Some seized the riders by their clothes, dragged them down and stabbed them with their dirks, several again used their pistols, but few of them had sufficient space to handle their swords."[8]

Faced with such savage and dogged resistance, the Hanoverians turned to retreat, throwing their own infantry into confusion as they did so. The Jacobites pursued on foot, scattering men and horses before them, for the most part spared the danger of opposing musketfire because of the rain which dampened the powder and made loading and reloading impossible.

The cry of "Stop pursuit!" flew suddenly from rank to rank, and the Stuart soldiers, who were just warming to their task, were brought up short in confusion. Night was falling, and the men, having broken ranks, were a jumble of clans and tongues, without their own officers to guide them. Some, seeing what they took to be watchfires lit in the Hanoverian camp, thought that the battle had been lost. Others sought shelter from the strong wind and lashing rain.

The men straggled back to their billets in the villages, not learning until later that night that Hawley and his army had abandoned their camp and returned toward Edinburgh. The battle of Falkirk Muir had been a Jacobite victory, sudden and brief like that of Prestonpans. Charles, who had been with the troops when they engaged Hawley, commanding the pickets, rode to Falkirk where he took over the quarters that Hawley had recently occupied and tried to assess how many men he had lost.

Hawley, humiliated in defeat and infuriated at the cowardice of his men, given their superiority in numbers and equipment, consoled himself in Edinburgh with an orgy of hangings and floggings, ordering dozens of his soldiers shot for desertion. Once again, the Jacobites had shown themselves to be the superior fighters. Once again they had humbled a Hanoverian general, the very elements conspiring with them to defeat him.

The next day, January 18, the storm raged on, the wind even stronger and the rains torrential. The weather made it nearly impossible for the Jacobites to recover the cannon that Hawley's men had left abandoned on the battlefield, but toward dusk they tried, riding slowly over the hill in small groups, picking their way by lanternlight. The horses shied when forced to step over heaps of dead bodies whose whiteness made them glimmer in the dark. They were the Hanoverian dead, some four hundred of them, their pale corpses bloated by the rain, their sightless eyes bulging horribly. Johnstone saw them lying there and recorded his revulsion. Once safely back in camp, he wrote, he felt "relieved as from an oppressive burden," and it was a long time before the "horrid spectacle" faded from his mind.

17

The winter of 1746 brought a lull in the momentum of Jacobite activity. The victory at Falkirk did not lead to further assaults on government troops, as might have been expected. Instead, Charles preferred to concentrate on the siege of Stirling, and when at the end of January this was abandoned, he allowed his chiefs to persuade him—against his better judgment—that retreat was the wisest course.

Campaigning in the dead of winter was in any case hopeless. As it was the men, marching northward to Inverness, were in sorry shape from exposure and exhaustion. To keep from freezing they carried flasks of whiskey which they shared, when the weather was at its worst, with their suffering horses.[1] Snow, hail and freezing rain slowed their progress. "Men were covered with icicles hanging on their eyebrows and beards," wrote one who made the trek, "and an entire coldness seized all their limbs, a severe contrary wind driving snow and little cutting hail bitterly down upon our faces, in such a manner that it was impossible to see ten yards before us." Morale dropped as the retreat progressed. The men felt cheated of the fruits of their victory; like Charles they wanted to push on to Edinburgh rather than to take refuge in the far north. According to Elcho's account, the men were "struck with amazement" when ordered to retreat, "for everybody expected a battle and it appeared very strange to run away from the very army that had been beat only a fortnight before."

The relatively few government troops in Inverness left as the Jacobites approached on February 21, and for the next seven weeks the town belonged to Charles, who for the most part remained there. He needed stability. His cold had worsened into pneumonia, and for a few frightening days in March it looked as if he might not recover. The unceasing cold weather, the strain and the endless disappointments and frustrations had lowered his resistance. When he did recover, it was not to his former level of conscientious leadership. He went hunting, he entertained the local aristocracy, he even danced at balls. But he left to subordinates the tasks of looking after provisioning and supplies, finding money to pay the soldiers and maintaining discipline among them. The result was that the men, still loyal to Charles and his cause but restive from long inactivity, left in large numbers for their homes and returned as and when it suited them. What military gains were made over the winter were brought about by small groups which detached themselves from the main army, and which were closely supervised by their officers.

When on April 13 Charles learned that Cumberland was rapidly approaching Inverness, he ordered his by now rather slipshod army of some forty-five hundred men to assemble immediately.

The available men scrambled to put themselves in what order they could, mindful of the large numbers of their comrades who were absent. On the fourteenth the army marched to the site O'Sullivan had chosen as a favorable battleground—Culloden Moor, about four miles from Inverness. It was a flat and featureless stretch of plain, just the sort of terrain the Hanoverians preferred and where their tactical strengths—large bodies of men, fighting as units, and powerful artillery—could be put to use with the greatest advantage.

Culloden was precisely the sort of site the Jacobites ought to have avoided, as Lord George realized right away when he learned of it. But Charles had not consulted Lord George. He had determined months earlier to rely on no one but himself, and those closest to him whom he trusted. Twice he had allowed himself to be persuaded by Murray and the chiefs that a course of action that he knew to be wrong was nonetheless advisable. Twice he and his army had been forced to throw away all they had gained. Both times his own instincts had told him what was best. He would not let those instincts be overriden again.

And now, with the Hanoverians nearly at hand, his instincts told him to meet them boldly and fearlessly, no matter how under-manned his army was or how precarious their provisioning. His men carried victory with them, they were unbeatable. They fought for a just cause, a godly cause, while the enemy fought for a wicked usurper. And the usurper's son led them. Surely in any trial of battle, God would see to it that the usurper's son and those who followed him lost.

That night the Jacobites slept near their chosen battle site, and woke the next morning to await Cumberland. By afternoon he had not arrived. He and his men were encamped at Nairn, some twelve miles to the east, apparently in no hurry to attack. It was Cumber-land's birthday, and his men were celebrating, toasting him with the brandy he had distributed among them, well fed and lying at their ease. Charles's men, by contrast, were on edge, relieved to be called into action once again but suffering, as usual, from cold and hunger. Their ration that day was a single biscuit. Not surprisingly, they left their ranks in search of food.

They could not last another day without provisions, and what few provisions existed were miles away in Inverness. The engagement had to come immediately. If Cumberland could not be brought to Culloden, Murray reasoned, the Jacobites could go to Nairn. He proposed to Charles that the men make a night march to Nairn and take the Hanoverians by surprise, before they had a chance to form up and defend themselves. It had worked at Prestonpans: the sud-den unexpected maneuver, the sudden furious attack, the sudden and precipitate flight of the enemy. It would work now, Charles reasoned. It harmonized with his instincts.

At eight o'clock that night the army marched, in two columns, toward Nairn. In his joyous excitement at the prospect of victory, Charles was moved to embrace Murray, thanking him for all that he had done and assuring him that neither his father nor he would ever forget it. Murray, inured by now to Charles's excited effusiveness and his equally passionate wrath, merely took off his bonnet and made a stiff bow in acknowledgment.

The men slogged on, their pace of necessity slow because of the darkness. When they had gone about eight miles they halted, as it was only an hour until dawn and they realized that by the time they reached Nairn the sun would be up and Cumberland's troops would be dressed and on the march themselves. They had lost the advantage of surprise. There was nothing for it but to go back—or so Murray believed. He ordered his men to turn around, and when Charles saw what was going on he was heard to mutter, " 'Tis no matter then. We shall meet them and behave like brave fellows."

The return march was punishing, coming as it did after a long hard night of walking with empty bellies. A "prodigious murmuring" was heard among the men, many of whom "exclaimed bitterly" even when Charles was within earshot. They were exhausted. The rumbling of their stomachs was louder than cannonfire. They had been pushed to their limit and beyond.

Dawn came, a sullen dawn with rain imminent. In the early morning light the train of weary men stumbled along the road, many stopping frequently to rest, others wandering off to find food, still others wrapping themselves in their plaids and lying down to sleep in the shelter of the gorse bushes. Charles, as weary as his soldiers from having made the night march on foot, managed to procure a little bread and whiskey and, after reaching Culloden, went to sleep for a while.

Within an hour or two, however, with rain pouring down and the wind rising, a Jacobite cavalryman rode up with the news that the Hanoverian cavalry were a bare four miles away. The infantry could not be far behind. Charles was up in an instant. Refusing the meal he was offered ("Would you have me sit down to dinner when my enemy is so near me?" he is alleged to have said. "Eat! I can neither eat nor rest while my poor people are starving"), he set out with Murray, Perth and Drummond to rouse the men and form them into battle lines.

All was confusion. Drums beat to arms, pipes played, trumpets sounded—a weird cacophony that underscored the general chaos. Only about a thousand of the men were ready to meet the enemy. Of the rest, some were in Inverness, where messengers were sent to summon them urgently, others were asleep, still others, kicked awake, were barely able to open their eyes and stagger to their posts. Some units were simply lost or overlooked, their posting having been turned over to old Sheridan who was so forgetful he could not account for them.[2]

Apart from their low numbers and shortage of equipment—many were without their targes, or shields—the soldiers were downcast and spiritless. Their will to fight, always in the past their preeminent characteristic, was weak. One officer recalled later the "visible damp and dejection" he observed among his men. Another remarked that "they were not the clans that had fought with such verve and vigor at Prestonpans and Falkirk." Of course they were not, how could they have been after what they had been through in the past several days?

They formed up, after a fashion, and took their positions. Looking at them, Murray concluded with a sinking heart that there were not more than three thousand men in the field, "and those not in the best order." The storm was abating, the rain giving way to drizzle and then to overcast with fitful sunshine, though the wind continued to blow. The drenching had wetted the men's muskets and powder horns, which meant that the weapons might or might not fire. Still, the order was sent along the ranks for the soldiers not to throw down their muskets—which they had a bad habit of doing when excited and ready to charge—but to keep them firmly in hand no matter what.

D'Eguilles, watching the officers in their frenzied efforts to find and order their men, and with what sorry result, became alarmed. He was responsible for the French troops Louis XV had supplied, troops whose lives were now to be put at risk because the rest of the remnant Jacobite army was in such disarray. Watching Charles, whose face was set in determination and whose eyes showed his contempt for Cumberland and his army, the Frenchman saw clearly that it would be useless to try to dissuade him from meeting the enemy. Still, faithful to his responsibility, he tried.

BONNIE PRINCE CHARLIE

In the midst of the chaos, d'Eguilles asked Charles for a brief audience, and when Charles agreed, he put his case. It was no use fighting, he argued, when half the army was absent, and the rest badly equipped. It would be far better to fall back upon Inverness, or to retreat even further, and put Inverness between themselves and the Hanoverians. After all, in the worst case they could still retreat into the Highlands, where no army could possibly reach them, and wait there for supplies of arms and money from France.

D'Eguilles threw himself at Charles's feet in supplication, but to no effect. "The Prince," he wrote to King Louis, "who believed himself invincible because he had not yet been beaten, defied by enemies whom he thoroughly despised, seeing at their head the son of the rival of his father; proud and haughty as he was, badly advised, perhaps betrayed, forgetting at this moment every other object, could not bring himself to decline battle even for a single day." Charles was "immovable in his resolve," and would fight at any cost.[3] In despair, d'Eguilles went to Inverness and burned all his papers, certain that the army would be defeated and uncertain what would happen to him when it was.

Presently the long Hanoverian line came into view, some nine thousand strong, the men marching ahead in battle order, their bayonets fixed, their step slow and steady as they paced to the solemn beat of hundreds of kettledrums. The pipes of the loyalist Campbells played, adding to the solemnity. As they advanced, twenty-odd masses of scarlet jackets topped by black tricornes, their regimental banners could be seen waving in the wind, each with its distinctive crest. They came still closer, and the sharpest Jacobite eyes could pick out their commander, the tall, many-chinned, hugely fat Cumberland, riding on a large gray horse.

The Jacobites began to call out to them, huzzaing and shouting derisively. But Cumberland's men kept silent, their discipline intact, staring straight ahead and marching mechanically, menacingly, forward. They came on, wrote an eyewitness, "like a deep sullen river," while the Jacobites, with their much smaller numbers and their fluid, not to say disordered, positions seemed more like "a streamlet running among stones, whose noise sufficiently showed its shallowness."[4]

Charles, meanwhile, rode up and down along his own lines,

cutting a fine figure on a gray gelding. He carried his leather targe decorated with the Medusa head wrought in silver, and brandished two silver-mounted pistols.

"Here they are coming, my laddies!" he shouted to the men. "We'll soon be with them. They don't forget Gladsmuir, nor Falkirk, and you have the same arms and swords—let me see yours! I'll answer this will cut off some heads and arms today."

O'Sullivan heard Charles's harangue, and recorded it later. He had often heard it before, and knew how much it heartened the men and "set them in spirits." Charles had a talent for being "most cheerful and hearty" when in the midst of the greatest danger, O'Sullivan remarked. He radiated joy and fearlessness, and knew how to communicate it to his men. Even so, on this day his effusions rang somewhat false. "Go on my lads," he shouted, "the day will be ours and we'll want for nothing after." Yet in his heart Charles "had no great hopes," O'Sullivan thought, and his conviction of invincibility began to dissolve at the sight of the nine thousand scarlet-jacketed troops that came on so resolutely.[5]

It dissolved still further as the Hanoverian guns began firing. The cannonade was fearsome. The guns fired randomly, in bursts as loud as thunderclaps, and kept on firing, the huge explosions making the earth shake and setting the men's teeth on edge. With every cannonade huge puffs of thick black smoke were thrown up into the air, and driven by the wind into the faces of the Jacobite soldiers. Their own artillery fired back, but with far less effect. According to one account, the very first Hanoverian cannon shot killed Charles's groom who was no more than thirty yards away from his master. Another struck the ground beside Charles, wounding his horse and covering him with dirt. Charles was urged to retire to a safer position, but refused until the number of balls falling near him became so great that he was virtually forced to back away. Eventually he allowed himself to be led off to Culchunaig, a rise behind and to the right of his army, which unfortunately offered only a limited view of the entire field.[6]

Men began to fall by the hundreds, the thunderous noise of the cannonade all but drowning their screams.

"Close ranks! Close ranks!" the officers yelled, and the men, too shocked at first to do anything but obey, stepped over the bloody bodies at their feet and firmed their lines. Again and again the horrible blasts came, cannonballs flying toward them through the thick smoke and ripping away arms, legs and heads. According to some accounts of the battle, by this time the sky had clouded over once again and snow and hail pelted down into the faces of Charles's soldiers as they stood waiting for the order to charge, the destructive artillery fire maddening them. Their own guns soon stopped firing altogether, silenced by the enemy gunners, and they were helpless before the cruel barrage. It was a new and devastating experience for them to find themselves thus immobilized, unable either to escape the deadly fire or to assault the enemy. One of the Hanoverian officers wrote that when his gunners had fired two rounds he could plainly see that the Jacobites "fluctuated extremely and could not remain long in the position they were in without running away or coming down upon us."[7]

Caught like dumb beasts awaiting slaughter, held back by their loyalty to their officers and chiefs yet crazed by the terrible blasting of the guns, the rain and hail and smoke that blinded them, the agonized groaning of the dying all around them, the men could not keep still. The regiments in the front were so impatient that they were "like to break their rank," Murray wrote afterward. When the enemy guns began firing grapeshot, that lethal rain of leaden balls and nails and pieces of old iron that scattered in a wide arc and did furious damage, the men could no longer restrain themselves.

Some flattened themselves on the ground, an eyewitness remembered. "Some called out to advance, and a few broke their ranks and fled." The rest began to run forward into the dark maelstrom, throwing aside their muskets, waving their swords, and yelling at the top of their lungs.

"Run, ye dogs!" "Loch Moy!" "Death or Life!"

Through the smoke they began to make out the phalanx of red jackets that stood waiting for them, muskets lowered, sharp bayonets pointed at their bellies. On they ran, and now the enemy's boots and spatterdashes became clear, and their faces, covered with soot and devoid of expression. When the Highlanders were a bare twenty paces away the front row of infantrymen fired on them, halting many who swayed and fell, impeding the advance of those behind them. They rallied, and rushed on again, this time facing the bayonets.

"They came up very boldly and fast all in a cloud together," wrote one who stood against them. But within a moment or two the cloud was shot through and stabbed and shredded out of existence. The Jacobites were advancing on the right (the Macdonalds on the left, galled at not being given the position of honor on the right, standing where they were), but raggedly, out of order, so that they were vulnerable to opposing fire on all sides. The charge was swallowed up, the men cut to pieces by the wall of bayonets and ripped through by grapeshot and musketfire. The war cries ceased. Officers and men fell in heaps, their faces contorted in grimaces of rage, their bodies twitching and writhing in the death agony.

The heroic advance had been pitifully brief. "The Highlanders fought like furies," a government soldier thought. "It was dreadful to see [their] swords circling in the air as they were raised from the strokes. And no less to see the officers of the army, some cutting with their swords, others pushing with their spontoons, the sergeants running their halberts into the throats of the opponents, the men ramming their fixed bayonets up to the sockets."[8]

The heaps of dead mounted higher, three and four deep where the charge had been fiercest. And still the murderous fire continued, the bravest of the Jacobites slashing at the muskets with their claymores, swearing, wailing in fury, individuals lifting the fallen standards of their clans and regiments and plunging forward in suicidal attacks. Fathers avenged sons, brothers sought to avenge brothers, boys and old men flinging themselves vainly into the pitiless crossfire until their swords were bent and they died where they stood.

By this time even Charles, with his limited view of the field, could begin to perceive the full extent of the terrible slaughter. Many of the officers and clan chiefs were dead or grievously wounded. Murray, whose runaway horse had carried him almost completely through the Hanoverian lines, his sword broken and his coat torn with shot, managed to dismount and fight his way back through the melée to where his own men were. He called for reinforcements, but it was too late. The clansmen, having spent their fury, were running from the field, harried like fleeing deer by the Hanoverian cavalry. Charles, after making a futile attempt to rally his men, was led away to safety by Sheridan and a few others.

BONNIE PRINCE CHARLIE

Murray managed to get his men into their ranks and to march them off, to the accompaniment of pipers, with dignity. But the rest of the remnant army was left to its fate, and to the scant mercy of Cumberland's cavalry. Excited by victory, and eager for revenge, the cavalrymen rode down the retreating soldiers and slashed at them with their swords, finishing off the wounded where they lay, stabbing at everything that moved. Their bloodlust aroused by battle, they forgot all but the urge to kill, not hesitating, as they rode toward Inverness, to harry the innocent townspeople they encountered on the roads and butcher them too. The rout brought them nothing but joy. Their dear commander, their own Billy, had won the day against the hateful rebel scum. The vermin deserved to be exterminated, down to the last shabby woman and dirty child.

Their joy went on long into the night. The streets of Inverness were full of government infantrymen dressed incongruously in the lace-trimmed coats and feathered Highland bonnets they had stripped from enemy corpses. They drank freely of the rum their commander had allotted them to celebrate their triumph, and shot off their muskets, and sang songs to serenade the subdued townspeople, while on Culloden Moor weeping women knelt to look into the faces of the naked dead by lantern-light, searching for the men they had lost.

18

Dazed and unbelieving, Charles was led off the battlefield by a few of his intimates. They rode southward to Gorthleck on Loch Mhor, where they rested on the night of April 16. There had been little enough time to react, let alone time to regroup or think through what to do next.

The enormity of the Jacobite loss had yet to reveal itself. Incomprehending as he was, and taken aback by the rout of the army he had believed to be invincible, Charles nonetheless thought, at first, that it would be possible to go on with the campaign. His aide-de-camp, Alexander Macleod, wrote soon after leaving the battlefield that "we have suffered a good deal, but hope we shall soon pay Cumberland in his own coin." Macleod was addressing Cluny Macpherson, an officer who had not been at Culloden and who was presumed to be hastening toward Inverness with his men. At least a third of the Jacobite army had not been present at the battle, and with these forces, still intact, and the regrouped survivors of Culloden, a counterattack might be launched. Macleod urged Cluny Macpherson to "make haste to join us, and bring with you all the people [*sic*] can possibly be got together." Charles, he said, had "something in view which will make ample amends for this day's ruffle."

Before long the Macpherson regiment arrived at Ruthven in Badenoch, to join with the Ogilvy regiment and a number of battle survivors—in all some fifteen hundred men. But they were never to discover what it was that Charles had had in mind for them, for by the time they assembled he had changed his mind. Even an army of only fifteen hundred men required provisions and ammunition, and neither were to be had. Cumberland's men had seized what supplies were stored at Inverness, grain was scarce and so was money to buy it. Officers too were scarce, so many having died at Culloden, and the only truly able commander, Murray, had decided that there was no point in going on.

Murray wrote to Charles asking for his demission, in a letter full of reproaches and recriminations.

"As no person in these kingdoms ventured more frankly in the cause than myself," he began, "and as I had more at stake than almost all the others put together, so to be sure I cannot but be very deeply affected with our late loss and present situation." He could bear his own ruin and that of his family with equanimity, Murray went on, but was deeply grieved by "the loss of the cause and the misfortunate and unhappy situation of my countrymen." And for this unhappy situation he blamed Charles. It was Charles's fault that the campaign had been launched without adequate guarantees of French aid, and it was his fault too that the welfare of the men had suffered so greatly during the winter months at Inverness. Charles had chosen incompetent subordinates, and he alone was responsible for the consequences—which included, Murray insisted, the loss at Culloden.

Apparently Murray's letter, plus the dawning realization that it would be impossible to feed and arm any new force that might be raised, persuaded Charles that the best course of action for him would be to go back to France and try again to raise men and arms and money. He sent Macleod to Ruthven with a message for the men assembled there: "Let every man seek his own safety the best way he can." Then, seeking his own safety, Charles rode hard for the coast.

Over the next two and a half months, he and his small group of attendants did their best to avoid capture, fleeing across the storm-ridden Sound of Arisaig to Benbecula, and then wandering up and down from Loch Boisdale on South Uist to Stornoway on North Uist, taking shelter wherever they could and living from hand to mouth.[1] The living was hard. Often there was nothing to eat but dried fish and a little brandy, plus whatever seabirds they could shoot. The near-constant rain squalls and bitter winds made foraging difficult, and on one hungry occasion they lived for a time on oatmeal mixed with salt water.

The inhabitants of the Long Island were willing enough to warn the fugitives when Cumberland's men were near, or when royal navy frigates were at hand, but they dared not take them into their homes. One Hanoverian loyalist on Scalpay actually mustered a body of men intending to capture Charles and exchange him for the thirty-thousand-pound reward promised by the government, but he was foiled in the attempt. Sailing from island to island in borrowed boats, risking their lives whenever they approached the rocky, windswept shore, endlessly pursued by hundreds of regular soldiers and in constant fear of betrayal, Charles and his handful of men were always on alert. They posed as Orkneymen, with Charles calling himself Mr. Sinclair and O'Sullivan pretending to be his father. When toward the end of June the number of soldiers on the Long Island rose to more than two thousand, Charles escaped to Skye, relying on the aid of Flora Macdonald who dressed him as a woman and convinced the soldiers that he was her maid.

The episode has taken on the lineaments of legend. Charles, after stripping to his breeches and waistcoat, put on a woman's underclothes, a quilted petticoat and calico gown sprigged with lilacs, adding to these an Irish mantle, cap, and headdress. He wanted to wear a pistol under his petticoat, but Flora advised him not to. If they were stopped and searched, she said, the pistol would betray him.

"Indeed, Miss," he is said to have answered, "if we shall happen with any that will go so narrowly to work in searching me as what you mean, they will certainly discover me at any rate."

BONNIE PRINCE CHARLIE

Thus disguised as the Irish maidservant Betty Burke, Charles
Stuart made the crossing to Skye in a small boat, narrowly escaping
capture. Once there he continued the pretense, though his height
and the length of his stride caused suspicion, as did his "awkward
way of managing the petticoats" and his constant adjustments to his
headdress, "which he cursed a thousand times."

It was an interval of farce in an increasingly dangerous situation,
for the islands were inundated with soldiers and only the remoter
reaches of the mainland could be expected to offer safety. He
managed to return there in the first week of July, to begin another
odyssey of desperate wanderings, hairbreadth escapes and extreme
discomfort. Hiding in caves by day, walking at night, always keeping to the high ground on the assumption that there would be fewer
soldiers there, Charles and his little party kept on the move, afraid
for the most part to stop lest their presence be betrayed. They knew
that there were spies among the clansmen, and that even those
clansmen who were loyal to the Stuarts and hated King George were
susceptible to threats and torture.

More than once the fugitives had to break through an enemy
cordon, coming within a few hundred feet of their patrols, so close
that they could overhear the militiamen's conversations and monitor
the cries of the sentries as they called out to one another. They
forded swift streams, clambered up the steep faces of bare hills,
slept on the ground and drank whiskey or brandy—when they could
get it—to revive themselves. There were some convivial times,
especially when they reached the remote mountain cave of Coir
a'Chait and joined the outlaw "Glenmoriston men," eight Jacobite
adventurers who were sworn enemies of Cumberland. The Glenmoriston men hid them, fed them on freshly killed game and made
surprisingly comfortable beds for them in their wilderness grotto.
For once Charles was able to rest and to feel relatively safe.

But the periods of respite and relative comfort were brief. For
most of his long months in hiding, Charles was dirty, weary and
extremely uncomfortable. When walking at night, one of his companions recalled later, "not being used with such rough and plashy
footing as is commonly to be found in the hills, braes, and glens of
the Highlands of Scotland, he was every now and then (through the
darkness of the nights) slumping into this and the other clayhole or

puddle." Often he was up to his navel in mud, with no way to wash or to keep his clothes and linen clean. One of Charles's companions, seeing that he was restless and uneasy, found that the cause was lice, and picked eighty of the voracious creatures off the royal skin.

By this time Charles was all but indistinguishable from the men he was living among. Though some, seeing him through the lens of their own adoration, insisted that he could never quite disguise his princeliness, he must have presented a shabby figure in his muddy fillibeg and dirty shirt, his old black coat and unkempt red beard. He no longer bothered with his wig, having snatched it off and stuffed it in his pocket in order to pose as a servant with a filthy handkerchief tied around his head. He carried a gun in one hand, with a pistol and dirk at his side. Altogether he must have looked more like an outlaw than like an aristocratic leader of men, heir apparent to the throne his father claimed as James VIII.

Still, he remained cheerful, jokey and optimistic in even the worst circumstances. The hard life, the danger and challenge brought out the best in him. He sang, he played with the children he encountered, he was affable and familiar. His life had been very trying in recent months, he told one of the men, but he would rather live as a fugitive, with all the hardships that entailed, for ten years than be taken by his enemies. "Since Culloden," he said, "I have endured more than would kill a hundred. Sure Providence does not design this for nothing." Providence had carried him and his remarkable army through their campaign; Providence had preserved him from his enemies though they crowded around him in their thousands. He had reason to be cheerful—and to expect ultimate vindication in the future.

For his people, though, he mourned. His own fatigues and distresses were of little importance compared to theirs. For "when he reflected upon the many brave fellows who suffered in his cause," one of his attendants remembered hearing him say, "that, he behoved to own, did strike him to the heart, and did sink very deep within him."

The Highland Scots paid a terrible price in the aftermath of the rebellion. Cumberland and his lieutenants, aided by the militia and ships of the royal navy, set out to find, capture and punish every person who had helped the Jacobite cause in any way, either directly or indirectly. The rebels were guilty of treason, the worst of crimes; they deserved no mercy or leniency. They had not only to be punished for what they had already done, they had to be deprived of the will and the means to rebel in future.

The destruction and bloodletting began in the days immediately following Culloden, when the Jacobite wounded were killed where they lay or hunted down and slaughtered like beasts. A slower death from untreated wounds and fevers came to many of the soldiers taken prisoner and shut up in the jails of Inverness. And not only the jails: barns, attics, churches, even ships were crowded with manacled men lying in their own filth. In all, nearly thirty-five hundred prisoners were taken, including the Irish and Scottish soldiers fighting in the French service who gave themselves up and expected to be returned to France. They were eventually shipped south to London, where most of them lay in their prison ships in the Thames, half starved, sickening from typhus and dysentery, until they died or were chosen for trial. Lots were cast and every twentieth prisoner was tried. Of these, the majority were convicted and sentenced to be transported to the British colonies in North America or to the West Indies; fewer than a hundred accepted forced enlistment in the British army. About a hundred and twenty were executed. Those who managed to survive in prison until 1747—an exceptionally hardy remnant—were released.

Among the released rebels was Flora Macdonald, who had been captured shortly after her escapade with Charles and imprisoned in the Tower. Later she was allowed to move to a private home where she paid for her board and enjoyed considerable freedom, though still in government custody. She became something of a celebrity, and Jacobite sympathizers raised a very generous subscription fund of fifteen hundred guineas for her which was given to her on her release in July of 1747.[2]

Cumberland invested the Highlands with soldiers, with large concentrations in the Great Glen and on the outer islands. The navy kept watch at the ports, and patrolled the sea lochs for French frigates and small boats like those Charles and his party used. People's movements were restricted, passes were issued by the militia to authorize travel in the zones where rebels were believed to be in hiding. The duke himself traveled widely, bringing to villages and hamlets written proclamations demanding that all arms be surrendered to the local authorities, and the locations of all known rebels disclosed. And having been authorized by the king to do "whatever was necessary for the suppressing of this unnatural rebellion," Cumberland ordered his officers to oversee the systematic destruction of the Highlanders' property, shelter and means of survival.

At first the plundering was orderly and properly supervised. Soldiers moved into an area and burned all the houses, from the spacious dwellings of the clan chiefs to the rude huts or shielings that gave shelter when the cattle were in their summer pastures. Everything was burned—growing things, food stores, furniture, clothing, even plows and wooden farm implements. The cattle were run off to be driven south and sold, or else slaughtered to feed the government troops. Valuables saved from destruction were divided among the plunderers according to their rank and rate of pay.

The brutal work was carried out with pitiless efficiency, leaving the devastated villagers with no shelter, no food and no means of growing any, no animals, and of course no money. With so many men killed or imprisoned, it was largely the elderly, invalids, women and young children who suffered on the land. They wandered through the barren hills in search of food, fearful of the soldiers, coming together in starveling groups when they found a cave or a shieling which had somehow escaped destruction. Many died. One officer told his superiors that he had found two women and four children "dead in the hills who perished through want, their huts being burnt." A minister wrote a pathetic letter to a Scottish newspaper telling how his parish had been "burnt to ashes" and how women and children came to him begging for food, though he had nothing to give them.[3]

By July of 1746, what had been methodical destruction became uncontrolled mayhem. Soldiers raided, pillaged and murdered indiscriminately, raping women and killing for sport. Cumberland and his officers now began to issue orders against such atrocities, but to little effect. The damage was done, the Highlands would never completely recover from it.

The wanton harm done on the islands of Raasay and Rona was particularly savage. On Raasay, three hundred cottages were destroyed, and the laird's house burned to the ground. No habitation on the entire island was spared, save two crude huts that were somehow overlooked. All the animals were killed and their carcasses left to rot. On Rona, a blind girl was raped, men were brutally flogged and the wretched inhabitants stripped of the clothes on their backs. When he learned of this, Charles made a promise to the islanders that better days would come, and that he would guarantee to replace all the burned-out cottages with better and stronger houses when his rule began.[4]

At the end of 1746 a report was drawn up for the benefit of Cumberland's successor Lord Albemarle by two spies who had been traveling in the Highlands. District by district they chronicled the horror: so many villages burned, so much land destroyed, so many inhabitants uprooted. In Glengarry, the report read, "there is neither houses nor people, only some few huts inhabited by women only in a starving condition."[5]

On September 12, Charles received word that two French ships were waiting in Loch nan Uamh to carry him over to France.

They were the latest in a series of vessels that had been sent to rescue him, some of which had been captured by the British. An Irishman, Captain Warren, whom Charles had sent to France as a messenger earlier in the year, chartered two heavily gunned privateers there, L'Heureux and Prince de Conti. The two ships had been chased, but not engaged, by British warships during their crossing from France and had found their way to Loch nan Uamh thanks to an informant on South Uist. Flying British colors themselves, the privateers anchored in the loch and waited there for Charles for two weeks, while a fierce gale hampered shipping which otherwise might have discovered their presence.

Finally on September 19 Charles went on board the Prince de Conti, accompanied by more than a hundred of his supporters who like himself had been living the lives of fugitives since Culloden. They were all lucky to be alive, yet many were seen to weep as they went on board. Even Charles, who on his way to Loch nan Uamh had been in exceptionally high spirits and had amused himself by tossing his companions' bonnets in the air and shooting at them, became more sober. After supper he moved from the *Prince de Conti* to *L'Heureux,* which set sail several hours before dawn on September 20. Nine days later both ships weighed anchor off the coast of Brittany. The great adventure of Charles's life was behind him.

19

Charles disembarked near Morlaix on the coast of Brittany on October 10,* after an uneventful voyage. On his arrival his first concerns were to see his banker, his brother, and his dog—in that order.

In Paris his banker, Waters junior, advanced him enough money to get established and to help out the exiles who had come with him to France. Charles was, as always, in want of money. He was in debt to some of the more distinguished exiles, who had loaned him money for his campaign, and he needed to dress and equip himself in princely fashion for his appearances at Louis XV's court. The rough clothes, boots and beard suitable to his Highland wanderings would now have to be replaced by finely tailored suits of velvet and silver lace, shoes with diamond buckles, smoothly shaven cheeks

---

*This was October 10 New Style (September 29 Old Style), according to the calendar in prevailing use on the continent.

and a new bag-wig. Waters was cooperative in providing the needed funds, but only up to a point. The account Charles drew on was his father's, and James had informed the banker that he would retain personal control of it from Rome.

Next Charles sent a message to his brother, whom he had not seen for nearly three years, and arranged to see him. Henry, having spent six damp and foggy months on the French and Flemish coasts earlier in the year, ostensibly in command of the invasion force that was never launched, had returned to Paris after Culloden and taken up residence at Clichy. Though willing enough to help Charles if he could, Henry had been immensely glad to leave the cheerless port towns where he had been stranded "without the least amusement," as he put it, unable to get the exercise he craved and surrounded by soldiers and other rough types who ridiculed his conspicuous piety and could not share his cultivated tastes.[1]

Henry was twenty-one, sensitive, a bit of a hypochondriac, a lover of poetry and fine music. Even after he left the seacoast and moved to his uncle's country estate near Evreux he suffered, complaining that the "thickness" of the air made him ill and took away his appetite. He moved on to Bagneux and then, in the first week of October, to Clichy, to the residence of the Cardinal of Auvergne. There he feasted on the pleasures offered by the life of a great ecclesiastic: sumptuous clothing, wigs made by the best Versailles wigmaker, a distinguished physician available on call, celebrated virtuosi to entertain on the violin and harpsichord, a famous painter to paint his portrait. In such surroundings, the contemplative, spiritual life could be pursued without fear of ridicule and without the discomforts of austerity. Henry found it appealing in the extreme.

When the two brothers met, Henry rushed to embrace Charles, crying out for joy and flinging himself into his arms with such violence that one of Charles's attendant Highlanders, not recognizing Henry, mistook him for a Hanoverian assassin.[2] So profound was Henry's pleasure in seeing his brother safely returned from his perilous adventure that he overlooked the fact that the members of Charles's entourage snubbed him, refusing to pay their respects to him and eventually becoming openly hostile. They blamed him for failing to spur the French to action the previous winter, possibly they despised him for luxuriating in comfort while Charles was risking his life for the cause. His dull, mild-mannered personality was utterly unheroic, and he certainly suffered by comparison with Charles.

After greeting his brother, Charles went to greet his dog, Marquis, left behind fifteen months earlier. Waiting for him along with Marquis was all the mail that had arrived since his departure for Scotland, most of it from his father. James had written every week during the time that Charles was away, loving, labored, occasionally pedantic letters that he knew had little chance of reaching their intended recipient. He sent his warmest affection to "his dearest Carluccio," assuring him of his continuing anxiety for his safety and his eagerness for news of him. "I cannot brag much of my health, but my chief ail at present is my concern for you." "I heartily embrace you with a heart full of love for you and confidence in the divine providence over you."[3]

Nothing in the letters was a surprise. Besides expressions of anxiety and affection there were only mundane references to the social activities of the pope and to the "fine season" in Rome. James was growing very weary of the vain pursuit of the crown. The failure of Charles's efforts, and the strain of worrying over his wellbeing, had drained away what enthusiasm he had once had. At fifty-eight, he was an old man, living through his children and wishing that they were near at hand.

James might be far away, but Charles and Henry had one relative living in the vicinity of Paris: their uncle Charles-Godefroy, Duc de Bouillon.

The duke was an important man at the French court, holding the titles of Grand Chambellan, Grand Maître, and Grand Écuyer. More important, he was a great crony of the king, dining with him, gambling with him, accompanying him in his pursuit of amusement. A contemporary described him as "a very pleasant man for society," and indeed his portrait shows such a man—baby-faced, indulgent and fleshy, with soft skin and soft features looking out of a face without any notable stamp of wit or intellect. His critics called him an overgrown child, good-looking but immature. Immature or not, he was in a position to be of use to Charles when he approached Louis XV for aid, and before going to see the king Charles consulted his uncle at length.

Both Charles and Henry went to Fontainebleau to join the court on October 21. They were graciously received, with King Louis interrupting a meeting of his council to talk briefly to "Baron Renfrew" and the "Count of Albany," as Charles and Henry were known. The dauphin too greeted them cordially, and the queen left her card table to talk to Charles, her ladies crowding around the tall, handsome adventurer about whom they had heard so much. On succeeding days Charles was entertained at lavish dinners and suppers with many of the court luminaries, including Noailles, Marshal of France and the Comte d'Argenson, war minister and one of the principal anti-Jacobite voices at the royal council table. Charles's dinner with the war minister must have been a test of his discretion—and Charles was not noted for his discretion. To dine with the man whose intransigent opposition had helped to prevent the launching of the invasion force (and thus to prevent the success of Charles's entire venture) must have strained politeness to the breaking point.

The highlight of the court visit was an evening Charles spent at supper with the royal mistress, the Marquise de Pompadour. It was an intimate party with only a dozen or so of the courtiers present, including the Duc de Bouillon and the Duc de Richelieu, who had been in charge of the would-be invasion force. During the supper the king arrived unexpectedly, strolling into the room without fanfare or formality and insisting that all the marquise's guests stay seated. He made himself comfortable, conversing with Charles in particular on every subject except politics until two in the morning and urging him to recount the adventures he had had while hiding from the Hanoverian troops. Was it true, the assembled company wanted to know, that he had been trapped for days in the heather, with hostile soldiers all around him and with nothing to eat? And that once, when he was about to be captured, the patrol that was after him suddenly and providentially turned in the opposite direction, for which there was no explanation save that God had chosen to spare his life?[4]

The familiarity King Louis displayed toward him on this evening was heartening to Charles, but he waited in vain for a private audience with the king at which the serious business of the Stuart restoration could be discussed. Finally, in desperation, Charles sent a message to the king suggesting a way for them to meet in secret: he, Charles, would have a fainting spell, whereupon he could be brought to a private apartment to recover. There King Louis could meet him, with no one the wiser—not even Henry. "I love him tenderly," Charles wrote confidentially to Louis. "I would like to avoid giving him any jealousy."

When nothing but royal silence greeted this note, Charles saw that he had been tricked. He had been put off with royal joviality and social pleasantries; he had been taken into the inner circle of the court, accepted for his pedigree, yet he had not been allowed, as an official representative of his father's interests, to ask officially for money, men and arms with which to continue his fight. He was only Baron Renfrew with his brother the Count of Albany, objects of intense but ephemeral interest in the Marquise de Pompadour's dining room.

Charles was furious. Not only had he been put off with meaningless familiarities, not only was he forced to forgo princely honors and be received as Baron Renfrew, but he had been thwarted in his quest for a private audience. Clearly the king had no intention of backing another invasion attempt. And then, insult of insults, a clerk arrived from the office of the secretary of state for foreign affairs, offering both Charles and Henry a joint income of a mere twelve thousand livres a month and the use of a mansion at Bercy, to be furnished at state expense. It was, as Charles wrote in a letter to James, a "most scandalous arrangement." He had been expecting a much higher income and a royal palace to live in, either Vincennes, Luxembourg or possibly St.-Germain, where his grandfather had held court.

In Paris, by contrast, Charles was a great celebrity. When he attended the opera with his uncle, the huge crowd that had gathered to catch a glimpse of him burst into tumultuous applause the moment he stepped from his carriage. Inside, the cheering operagoers would not let him take his seat in the royal box until he had bowed to them time and again. There were rumors about him in the capital. It was said that King Louis not only planned to install him in one of the royal palaces, but had given him eight hundred thousand livres from the royal treasury, plus a monthly stipend of another fifty thousand livres. The Parisians knew who he was and what he was truly worth; it was only the pusillanimous king and his duplicitous courtiers who failed to take his full measure.

Very well then, Charles decided, he would deal with them as a prince, even though they had not treated him as one. He sent the king an arrogant memorandum setting out his demands and justifying them with outrageous statements that fell considerably short of the truth. He refused absolutely to accept either the inferior Bercy mansion or the puny stipend of twelve thousand livres. He was "absolutely convinced," he wrote to James, "that the only way of dealing with this ***** government is to give as short and smart answer as one can, at the same time paying them in their own coin by loading them with civilities and compliments, setting apart business, for that kind of vermin the more you give them the more they'll take, and also the more room you give them the more they have to grapple at, which makes it necessary to be laconic with them, which is the only way of passifying them, and putting all their shame upon their backs."[5]

Charles's princely terseness did not produce any immediate result, but his uncle stepped in to solve at least the housing problem. Bouillon arranged for Charles and Henry to occupy two houses next to his palatial one on the Quai Malaquais, installing Henry in the structure known as the "petit hôtel de Bouillon" and Charles in the former Hôtel Transylvanie. As for their incomes, Charles continued to go to Waters for what he needed, amassing a large debt of a hundred and twenty thousand livres before the end of the year.[6]

Charles was determined to live like a prince, even if he was not officially recognized as one. He surrounded himself with his guard of Highlanders, he all but kept court at his residence. He entertained the Scottish exiles, often feeding thirty-five of them at dinner and twenty at supper. His table groaned under the weight of expensive meats and rare delicacies, his wines and liqueurs were of the finest. And when among his guests, Charles drank to princely excess—a vice in which he was encouraged, or so James's dignified, elderly envoy O'Brien believed, by his tough, hard-drinking companion-in-arms "Trebby," the Anglican parson George Kelly.

Kelly (not to be confused with Friar Kelly, Charles's Franciscan confessor, also a man who loved his bottle) was a troublemaker. He made fun of James, sneered at the pious Henry and imitated the

BONNIE PRINCE CHARLIE

French ministers in a way that Charles found very entertaining. Kelly had a gift for mimicry and ridicule, and he gossiped and spread stories about all the Jacobites, even Charles himself in the latter's absence. He outraged the proper O'Brien by suggesting that Henry ought to take a mistress, and joked and told dirty tales about O'Brien and others whom James trusted and whose rectitude he considered to be above reproach. Even the relatively unbuttoned Balhaldie was exasperated with "Trebby," whom he called the worst of the "animals" Charles kept around him, a liar and a good-for-nothing.[7]

O'Brien was eager to attribute Charles's bad habits to the influence of the scurrilous Parson Kelly, but in truth Charles was choosing his own path. He was growing older, becoming less the charming young man, eager to please and more the willful adult, quick to take offense, openly pleasure-seeking and above all self-directed. He hated having to grovel before the French ministers, knowing that no matter how able and worthy he was, he was still their creature, to be controlled at their whim. He was incapable of mastering their sort of subtlety and dissimulation, of beating them at their own game; he would make them play his game, his way, or not at all. He went to court infrequently, staying away more and more and relying on Bouillon or Cardinal Tencin—whom he hated as "an absolute rogue and rascal"—to make his excuses. The intricate etiquette of the court confused him, and his own lack of status there was a reminder of his political impotence. Besides, court appearances required a costly wardrobe. When Henry attended a ball to celebrate the dauphin's marriage in January of 1747 his clothing cost him six thousand livres.

Rather than dance attendance on those who ignored him, Charles determined to make things happen on his own initiative. He meditated a daring, if impracticable plan to marry Elizabeth, Tsarina of Russia. In lieu of a dowry he would ask her to provide him with twenty thousand soldiers, to be used on another expedition to England. He would have preferred to marry a French princess, but admitted in a letter to his father that he knew that for the present it would be futile to ask King Louis to become his father-in-law. The tsarina's ties to the Hanoverian court were an obstacle, James pointed out in his reply; why didn't Charles consider a Polish princess? But a Polish princess would be a better bride for Henry, Charles thought, and he kept after his brother—who showed no sign of wanting to marry anyone—to form an alliance with the Polish Radziwills.

Living in their separate houses, surrounded by their very different entourages, Henry cultivating his literary and artistic tastes and Charles pursuing the pleasures of the hunt and the table, while contemplating independent action of a political kind, the brothers grew wider apart. Henry, like James, seemed to accept the political status quo, seeing no alternative; he went to court on King Louis's terms and took what bounty he offered, playing his role with what dignity he could. Charles was restless, and anything but resigned. He craved activity, and was coming to accept the fact that it would have to be undertaken entirely on his own.

The divergence seemed ready to widen into a rift. One day Charles and some of his companions dined at Henry's house, and the obstreperous Kelly provoked a scene by saying what a number of the exiles had been thinking for months.

Kelly asked Henry why he hadn't ordered the French transport ships to sail to England the previous winter. Some would have been lost, he realized, but others would have succeeded in landing.

O'Brien, who was present, rushed to Henry's defense and told Kelly that Henry had been a mere figurehead, with no real authority to command.

"Is that so?" said Kelly belligerently. "And why was that, pray? For King James in 1708 had command of all troops then gathered at Dunkirk."

"Do you seriously imagine," O'Brien replied, "that if the king had had the troops at Dunkirk entirely at his command, he would have turned back without trying for Scotland, at all costs?"

The argument raged on, while Charles listened in silence and Henry felt more and more uncomfortable. At last Henry rose to answer for himself. He rounded on Kelly, telling him vehemently that at no time had it been possible to launch the ships, as Kelly knew full well. Furthermore, Kelly ought to keep silent as he was too ignorant to do otherwise. "A few months ago," Henry shouted, "you would not have dared to speak in this manner!"

The implication was clear. In the few months since Charles's arrival in France, suspicions had grown, and Henry had come under more and more unrestrained criticism. Relations between the brothers could not help but be strained.

"He does not open his heart to me," Charles told James, "and yet I perceive he is grieved which must proceed from malicious people putting things in his head, and preventing him against me. Notwithstanding, I am persuaded he loves me tenderly, which is the occasion of my grief. God almighty grant us better days!"[8]

Charles was right in sensing that Henry was not being candid with him. The extent of his secrecy would become apparent soon enough, but before it did Charles launched himself on another adventure. Toward the end of January, 1747, he left Paris, taking a few companions with him, and rode south. No one in France knew where he was going; the French courtiers speculated that he had left to organize a new expedition against England. In a sense they were right. Charles's destination was Madrid, and he hoped to convince the Spanish king Ferdinand VI to come to his aid where King Louis had not.

Before leaving, Charles had written to key English Jacobites, letting them know what his plans were. He urged them to send one of their number to serve as his Paris agent, since he did not intend to rely on any of his father's agents there any longer. He had heard that King George was in poor health, and could die. His death would cause at least temporary confusion in government circles, given the factionalism that had led to a ministerial crisis the previous year.[9] Charles was hoping that, if all went well, he would have a Spanish-backed invasion force to launch against England just when the new king's authority was at its most vulnerable.

It was the sort of daring secret escapade Charles enjoyed most: a mad dash for Madrid, ciphered letters sent to London, a strategy planned in defiance of his father and indeed of all sensible observers. But it backfired. He presented himself at the Spanish court, where King Ferdinand and his ministers received him with "many civilities" but were privately astonished that he should appear on their doorstep unannounced. His outrageous requests for money, arms and one of Ferdinand's sisters as his bride convinced them that he was either hopelessly callow or insane. They soon made it clear that his departure would be welcome.

Instead of learning from this humiliating experience, Charles became angry. The Spaniards were even greater fools than the French, he told his father. King Ferdinand was even more a creature of his ministers than King Louis was, weak and gutless. Back in Paris, Charles moved into his banker's house and refused to have anything to do with James's representatives.

What further schemes he may have had in mind were upstaged by what happened next. For many months, James and Henry had been quietly preparing in effect to abdicate their claims to the English throne. James was too old and too tired to try to guide the Stuart fortunes any longer, and Henry had decided that he had no stomach for political intrigue. The older generation of Jacobite exiles was dying off, those whom Charles had brought with him from Scotland were busily trying to ingratiate themselves with the French and gain appointments in the army, while hoping to obtain pardons from London eventually. Reports reaching Paris from England and Scotland made it plain that the Jacobites of 1745 had been decimated by imprisonment and exile in the colonies. It might still be possible for a young man to rebuild a movement capable of challenging the Hanoverian rulers, but not for an old one and his sensitive younger son.

James had decided to give up, and Henry had made an even more extreme decision: he had decided to become a cardinal.

Henry left Paris suddenly in May, leaving Charles a note to say that he was going to Rome to visit their father. Many weeks later, Charles received a letter from James.

"I know not whether you will be surprised, my dearest Carluccio," James wrote, "when I tell you that your brother will be made a Cardinal the first days of next month. Naturally speaking, you should have been consulted about a resolution of that kind before it had been executed, but as the Duke and I were unalterably determined on the matter, and that we foresaw you might probably not approve of it, we thought it would be showing you more regard, and that it would be even more agreeable to you, that the thing should be done before your answer could come here, and so have it in your power to say it was done without your knowledge or approbation."[10]

Charles was utterly stunned. Not since the decision of the chiefs at Derby to turn the Stuart army back toward Scotland had he felt so betrayed, so powerless. Unable to speak, hardly able to think, he shut himself up in his rooms. No one could reach him or talk to him.

Over the next few hours, as he began to recover from the shock and from the wave of furious anger that no doubt followed it, he must have reflected on the meaning of this unexpected turn in the family fortunes. His father and brother had conspired against him. Henry's choice of vocation had done irreparable harm, and would make his own struggle to uphold his claim to a Protestant throne much more difficult. For from now on there would be only one claimant to that throne—Charles himself. Henry could not, as a cardinal, be heir presumptive, and Henry would have no heirs. The entire burden and responsibility of the Stuart restoration now rested on Charles's sturdy shoulders.

He had the courage to face the task, and the strength of will. But did he have the other requisite qualities? The Spanish ambassador at the French court thought not. Charles, he said, lacked the intellect and presence of mind to conduct serious business, and was neither articulate enough nor sensible enough to achieve even the most modest political aims. James's conclusion was more insightful. He told Cardinal Tencin in confidence that he felt his elder son was "on the edge of a precipice."

20

In the summer of 1747 Charles Stuart was at the height of his manly beauty. Tall, lean, energetic, he radiated strength and vitality. Admirers thought his features "exceedingly noble," and compared him to the handsome Charles XII, King of Sweden. His complexion was sun-browned, his cheeks were full and his lips thicker than the ideal; his high round forehead set off lively eyes and mobile features, and drew attention away from his double chin and jaw with "pretty many pimples" under it. Restless, eager for action, full of élan, his merits, as the Marquis d'Argenson wrote deprecatingly, "were of the antique sort"; he was heroic but empty-headed, valorous but ignorant, with few ideas and fewer words to express them.[1]

Women loved him, however, and forgave him his shyness in formal situations and his inability to make witty conversation. Living at St.-Ouen this summer, far enough from the court to escape the watchful eye of the royal ministers, he dropped his incognito and entertained in style. He was much in demand by aristocratic hostesses as most of the young and middle-aged men were away on campaign in Holland.

Hunting during the day (and sometimes poaching on the king's lands, making his majesty "somewhat angry") and socializing at night, Charles's spirits lifted. He had not yet gotten over his dismay at the prospect of Henry's cardinalate—which some Jacobites were saying was a worse disaster than Culloden—but he was cheered by the war news from Holland, where a huge force led by none other than the Duke of Cumberland had been decimated at Laffeldt by the French. Cumberland himself, it was said, barely escaped with his life.

In August Charles went to his uncle's country house at Navarre, and there, during the long, warm days and sweet-scented nights, he fell in love.

He was twenty-seven, his cousin Louise, Bouillon's daughter, twenty-two. They had known each other for three years, ever since Charles first came to France; in November of the previous year, when Louise was ill with smallpox (at that time a very severe and often fatal disease), Charles had written the family in the warmest terms to say that he sympathized with her in her convalescence. But there had been no romance between the cousins until now, and when it came, it was apparently earthshaking for both of them.[2]

Louise, whose titles were Duchesse de Montbazon and Princesse de Rohan, was married to Jules-Hercule-Mériadec, Prince de Rohan, Duc de Montbazon, Prince de Guéméné, and she was the mother of a two-year-old son. Because, through her mother, Louise was a great-granddaughter of the Polish king John Sobieski, she was an exceptionally wealthy heiress, and King Louis had taken an interest in making the right match for her. Her potential wealth was of far greater interest to her contemporaries than her personality and character, and little is now known about her. Her portraits reveal a pert, determined face, less than beautiful, plump and round like her father's, and with handsome eyes shaped like a doe's.[3]

From the start the affair was difficult, for though adultery was extremely commonplace in Louise's social circle, and was widely condoned as long as it was discreet, neither she nor her young husband were practiced adulterers, and her mother-in-law kept a strict eye on her. The Prince de Guéméné was in Holland with the army, and in his absence his mother ordered her servants to guard the virtue of her daughter-in-law. In order to see Louise, Charles had to resort to secret midnight coach rides between his house in the country and hers in Paris, with his servants armed and riding along with him as bodyguards. Her suspicions aroused, the vigilant mother-in-law eventually called in the Paris police, who waited, hidden in the shrubbery, outside Charles's residence in St.-Ouen and tracked the comings and goings of his coach.

At first the lovers cared nothing for danger—in fact Charles most likely enjoyed and welcomed it as adding even more excitement to the affair. But after a month or two, Louise became pregnant with Charles's child and morning sickness made her miserable. Meanwhile her husband had come home, and she needed to make him believe that the child was his—which meant spending her nights with him and not with Charles. This in turn led the jealous Charles to redouble his efforts to see her, even if it meant waiting outside the Guéméné residence until three o'clock in the morning or later. Things went from bad to worse, with Louise feeling ill, her mother-in-law tightening the guard around the house, and Charles threatening to lay siege to it and create a scandal unless he was allowed to spend the entire night with his mistress.[4] Frustrated and enraged, he exploded, firing his pistols in front of the house after making exaggerated demands and threatening to leave Louise for another woman.

Not surprisingly, tongues began to wag and rumors to spread—although Louise's husband, whether from blindness, stupidity, cowardice or indifference, seems to have done nothing. Eventually, late in January, 1748, when Louise was three months pregnant, her father and her mother-in-law confronted her with their knowledge of the truth and forced her, after shedding floods of tears, to write to Charles and end the affair. He was to continue to see her, and his other relatives, in the conventional way so as to confute the rumors of infidelity, but it was all to be a pretense; as Bouillon told his daughter, in return for all their kindness toward him Charles had shown not only ingratitude but wickedness.

Apparently the affair did not wind down tranquilly. Louise, cut to the heart by the pain of losing Charles and the humiliation of being forced to give him up, continued to write him anguished letters in which she threatened to kill herself and their unborn child unless he responded. Respond he finally did, but not until three months later, when he agreed to a brief midnight assignation in a rented carriage. And then he had the insensitivity, or cruelty, to tell her that he had acquired another mistress.[5]

The new mistress, Princesse Marie-Louise de Talmont, was as unlike Louise as possible. At forty-seven, she was still a serene, classic beauty, elegant and quintessentially womanly. She had had many lovers, quite a few of them distinguished, and she held their admiration by her celebrated wit and intelligence as well as by her beauty. Voltaire was captivated by her taste and her skill at repartee, others noted her sound judgment and absolute independence of action. Influential, highly placed at court, and, like Charles, a cousin of the queen, Mme. de Talmont had her detractors, one of whom, Mme. du Deffand, was eloquent in her dispraise. "She believes herself to be perfect," wrote du Deffand, "she says so, and wants everyone else to believe it too." Vain, temperamental, capricious, she terrified her servants and everyone else forced to live with her. "She would like to be loved, but it is her vanity alone that demands it—her heart demands nothing."[6]

If Mme. de Talmont was cold, with a diamond-hard intelligence and a capacity for making shrewd judgments about the world, she must also have been very good company, able to entertain a man and flatter his vanity. Clearly Charles found the combination appealing, and she, in turn, desired him for his good looks and his considerable fame. They were both narcissistic; they were both ambitious, and both had daring—though hers was confined to the drawing room and the bedroom. After his ultimately disagreeable entanglement with Louise, and with her father and her vexatious mother-in-law (who had had the temerity to stage a verbal brawl with him in public), Charles must have found the older woman's frank, cosmopolitan sensuality refreshing. She did not make demands on him, or try to smother him, and though she was married, she did not seem to have any troublesome relatives to contend with.

Meanwhile, as Charles's amorous life unfolded, the War of the

Austrian Succession was finally reaching its ragged end. After years of on-again, off-again fighting, some of it glorious, much of it brutal and wasteful of lives, all of it costly, the dozen or so warring states had had enough. A peace treaty had been negotiated, and its preliminaries were ratified at the end of April, 1748. The final version would not be signed for some months, but there was no doubt that it eventually would be. As expected, the English had imposed on the French as a condition of peace that King Louis recognize the Hanoverian succession and force the Pretender, Charles Edward Stuart, to leave his realms.

But where was he to go? Rome was out of the question; to return to his father's house would be an unbearable humiliation. Yet many of the European states—even the small German-speaking principalities—were certain to refuse him entrance because to do so meant offending the reigning King of England. For Charles, the end of the war meant not only that he would have to find a new country to live in, but a new strategy to pursue. For however obliquely, the War of the Austrian Succession had been his war too; his invasion of England had been one dimension of the hostilities directed against Maria Theresa and her allies. And now that the war was over, he would have to find a new context for Stuart belligerence if he could.

The best way out of his dilemma, he was convinced, would be for him to get married. Choosing a Protestant bride would convince his future subjects in Britain that he was religiously tolerant, even if his brother was a cardinal of the Roman Church. Of course, locating the right woman would take time, the search had to begin immediately.

On May 1 Charles's agent, Sir John Graeme, left for Prussia with instructions to meet with King Frederick and propose that he give Charles his sister as a bride. If this proved unacceptable, Graeme was to ask on Charles's behalf for refuge in Prussia. Weeks went by, and finally Charles received word from Graeme that the mission had been a failure. King Frederick and the Elector of Hanover were becoming fast friends, and no marriage alliance was possible. Worse still, the Prussian king had great influence over the other German rulers, who also sought the favor of the Hanoverians.

Charles sent urgent word to Graeme to continue his search, secretly and in haste. There must be some Protestant prince who would oblige him, he insisted. He was ready to marry any woman sight unseen, provided she was a Protestant.

While Graeme went from court to court, finding rejection everywhere, Charles kept up appearances in Paris. He was seen at Mme. de Talmont's, he continued his visits to the opera and the Comédie-Française, where as always he was received with loud and prolonged applause. He also walked in the gardens of the Tuileries, where crowds gathered to catch a glimpse of him and cheer him as he passed. Everywhere he went he took his band of Highlanders, who were a spectacle in themselves, and he walked among them wearing a fur hat with a large white plume, looking larger than life and every inch a prince.

It was a display of bravado, for Charles knew that it would be only a matter of time before he was asked to leave the country. Possibly he felt that by entrenching himself sufficiently in the public eye he would have the public behind him when the authorities tried to enforce the peace treaty. The crowds he drew included more and more English tourists, who were permitted to visit France now that peace had been made. English women in particular made trips to Paris in order to attend the opera and applaud Charles, and while there they bought the souvenirs Parisian shopkeepers sold to commemorate his daring achievements in 1745. One such item was a map, with explanatory narrative, tracing Charles's route through Scotland and England. The printer sent the map to Charles for his corrections, which he obligingly gave, and the map sold well in the summer months as Parisians waited to hear that their king had asked Charles to leave.

In July and again in August, polite requests came from the French court—specifically, from the current foreign minister de Puisieux—that Charles vacate his lodgings and oblige the king by leaving the country. Each time he responded by claiming that he had a right to remain, that the king had promised him refuge, and that if the Treaty of Aix-la-Chapelle was invoked against him, he had a treaty of his own, the Treaty of Fontainebleau signed in 1745, to rely on. It was no good pointing out to him that the newer treaty took precedence; he had a formal protest ready, and copies of this protest, like copies of his itinerary in England and Scotland, sold well throughout the summer. So outwardly confident was he that he could not be dislodged that in September he rented a new and grander house than the one he had been living in and paid a year's rent in advance.

In October, however, the situation changed. The final version of the peace treaty was signed, Charles's grace period had expired. The French ministers could no longer afford to let him embarrass them, and the king, though still somewhat sympathetic, was becoming annoyed. He went to the trouble of arranging to have Charles lodged at Fribourg, where, he assured him via his messengers, he would be comfortable and treated with honor. But Fribourg was not acceptable. He then sent the humane, soft-spoken Duc de Gesvres to reason with Charles, hoping that this envoy would find him more compliant. But though the duke found Charles hospitable, he also found him adamant. Charles would not budge. And he managed to give his kindly visitor the impression that, if necessary, he would defend himself with the formidable array of muskets, sabers and other weaponry that he kept on view in his house.

By November 21, Charles's refusal to depart from Paris was the "grand topic of the day," according to Argenson's memoirs. People talked of nothing else, and cheered their hero louder than ever when he made his appearances. Rumor had it that he had threatened never to leave France alive; the king's guardsmen would have to kill him if they tried to eject him—or he would kill himself. Some blamed Mme. de Talmont for his recalcitrance, and she, prudent courtier that she was, decided to detach herself from the young man who was causing such trouble. The king warned her that she herself would be exiled if she admitted Charles to her house. She ordered her servants to refuse him entrance, but he insisted on making a nuisance of himself, just as he had done when Louise de Rohan-Guéméné ended her affair with him. He made himself conspicuous in the Talmont gardens, he shouted at his mistress's servants, and when all else failed he swore that he would break down the gates if they were shut to him again.[7]

One of Charles's more level-headed companions, Francis Bulkeley, persuaded him not to make good his threat but his provocations to the French court continued. King Louis, by now thoroughly justified in looking on Charles as a hysterical child, had some weeks earlier appealed to the child's father for help in handling him. James sent his son a letter commanding him to obey the terms of the treaty and the urgent pleas of the French ministers. Charles calmly pocketed his father's letter unread. However, Louis too had received a copy of James's letter, and took it as justification to play his final card. Late in the evening of December 3, the Duc de Gesvres delivered an ultimatum: Charles now had three days to leave Paris and nine to leave France. Otherwise he would be forcibly expelled.

On the third day following, Charles was still at his residence, holed up with his arsenal of weapons, swearing, according to his tense servants, that he would blow himself up with gunpowder the instant any French guardsman approached him. Meanwhile the king had turned the problem over to the Duc de Biron, colonel of the French Guards, ordering him to arrest Charles and leaving the logistics of the arrest to him.

On December 10, Biron invested Paris with twelve hundred royal troops, with detachments of his own French Guards placed strategically near Charles's house and vicinity. After dark that evening, Charles left his house as usual to attend the opera, accompanied by his three principal companions, Sir Henry Goring, Sir James Harrington and Michael Sheridan. In anticipation of their arrival at the opera, Biron had placed guardsmen in street clothes near the entrance, who mingled with the crowd that always collected there before a performance.

The men were watchful. They had been told that Charles would be armed, and might try to shoot himself if provoked. They were also on alert to break up the notoriously volatile crowd should any disturbance arise. The coach pulled up, the four men got out—one of them, conspicuous by his height and elegant dress, the celebrated Pretender to the British throne. As the crowd began to cheer, and Charles, preceding his companions, walked toward the opera doors, five of the plainclothed guardsmen surrounded him—so suddenly that he had no time to react. He was cut off from his friends, his arms pinioned, and carried swiftly out of sight of the dazed onlookers. One of the guardsmen produced a length of silk cord to bind him, while the others hastily searched and disarmed him, informing him that he was under arrest and that the bonds were for his own protection.[8] The remaining guardsmen and soldiers moved in to intimidate the crowd while Charles was spirited away in a coach to the prison of Vincennes where he was given relatively spacious quarters.

With the angry Charles in custody, the guardsmen proceeded to seize his companions, officers and servants. Goring, Harrington and Sheridan were taken off to the Bastille, as were seven other gentlemen of Charles's household, eleven French servants and two Savoyards, also servants, and five Scots and two Irish bodyguards. Mme. de Talmont's footman was also caught in the net; he was delivering a miniature portrait of his mistress to Charles when the arrests were made.

While Daniel O'Brien, Charles's "confidential valet," looked on to prevent breakage and theft, the soldiers searched the house and locked up the contents, including furnishings, plate, silver, papers, swords and guns (twenty-five muskets and thirty-four pistols—an arsenal indeed). In the process they turned out five miscellaneous persons who had been enjoying Charles's hospitality: three indigent Britons, one a refugee from the rebellion, a manservant and sometime wigmaker, and a fifteen-year-old Scottish boy whom Charles had taken in out of kindness. The horses and dogs were left in the care of twenty guardsmen, except for one little dog, Charlot, a gift from Charles to his friend Lady Clifford, which was taken home for safekeeping by the commander of the guard.

Clearly the French had no desire to punish Charles. His possessions were handled scrupulously, his personal papers left untouched. In the prison he was housed in two rooms, one of them large, with five fireplaces that were kept burning brightly. Excellent meals were served to him there, with the best Burgundy wine. O'Brien was even allowed to bring a number of Charles's fine suits of clothing to the prison so that he could dress as his rank deserved. Cheered somewhat by these comforts, he made the best of the situation, his anger subsiding. "Tell all my friends that I am well," he wrote to Bulkeley on December 16. "My head has never left my shoulders. It is still there."[9]

Finally on December 23, Charles was escorted to the Swiss border at Beauvoisin by a French officer. He had given his word not to make any more trouble, if only he were allowed to leave quietly with his servants and officers. Just before crossing the border, he sent his formal respects to the royal family, having assured the escorting

Frenchman several times that he would not reenter France or try to take refuge in the papal enclave of Avignon. His party moved on into Swiss territory, and the Frenchman breathed a sigh of relief. He had discharged his duty. He sent word to Maurepas that Charles was gone at last, adding that he, for one, was persuaded that he would never return.

21

George II officially proclaimed the peace late in April of 1749, and ordered a week-long series of celebrations to inaugurate it. At night buildings were hung with hundreds of lanterns, their windows lit from within, their rooftops crowned with ornamental displays outlined in strings of lights. During the day, London was as congested as a bustling country fair, the streets full of coaches arriving from all parts of the kingdom, the squares lively with hurrying servants, the shops crammed with goods demanded by an enlivened populace come to spend a holiday in the capital. Scaffolds were erected around the park, where the fireworks spectacle was to be held, and guards patrolled the vicinity of St. James's to keep the milling crowds in order and prevent their excitement from turning to riot.

At Ranelagh, the vast pleasure gardens recently rebuilt at enormous cost, a "jubilee-masquerade in the Venetian manner" was held for the entertainment of what the newspapers of the time called "people of fashion." The huge amphitheater was illuminated, and inside its arches were booths where masked shopkeepers sold crockery and trinkets and sweets. Two thousand people were accommodated, with room for more; they disported themselves at gaming tables, drank tea and wine, and danced to the music of masked musicians.

In the center of the huge open space was an artificial bower constructed of tall fir trees growing in tubs, their limbs festooned with flowers, and beneath these were rows of orange trees with small lamps inside each orange. Near the bower ran a narrow canal, where a gondola floated, gaily decorated with colored flags and streamers, and filled with musicians. Scattered here and there around the grounds were still more musicians, some playing country tunes on tabor and pipe, others dressed like huntsmen and playing hunting horns, still others disguised as Harlequins and Scaramouches. The joyous cacophony continued until late in the evening, the fashionable two thousand thronging from one masquerade scene to another, careful both to see and be seen, showing off their own rich costumes to impress one another.[1]

On the following night fireworks lit up the sky, the rockets shooting upward in a blazing display, the pinwheels spinning in place on a large "machine" erected to mount them. Pall Mall had been railed off and provided with seating for the nobility and Members of the House of Commons and their guests; King George, his favorite son Cumberland and his daughter Emily watched the spectacle from a nearby building. The Prince of Wales, no less at odds with his father than he had ever been, had not been invited to join the rest of the royal family and observed the fireworks from a separate vantage point. Despite a week of feverish preparations, the fireworks turned out to be something of a disappointment; the skyrockets were breathtaking but the squibs sputtered and fizzled and created a poor impression—and then, just when the show was well under way, one of the illuminated pavilions caught fire and burned to the ground.

The spectators were reasonably well behaved, however. There was little criminal mischief, and though two people were killed, this was thought to be a modest loss. (In similar celebrations of the peace held in Paris, forty people had been killed and nearly three hundred wounded, as a result of a violent dispute that broke out between the French and Italians who were jointly managing the fireworks display; each sought to be the first to light the fires, both lit theirs at once, and the entire battery went up in a huge explosion.)

Two further events rounded out the week's festivities. One was a "serenata" at the opera house called "Peace in Europe," the other a masked ball. The ball was by far the greater success, with all the notables of court and society attending dressed as Elizabethans and literary characters and figures from antiquity. One beauty was dressed—or rather undressed—as Iphigenia ready to be sacrificed. She was "so naked," wrote a wit who attended the ball, "that the high-priest might easily inspect the entrails of the victim."[2]

King George attended the ball "disguised in an old English habit," and very well disguised too, for another guest, not recognizing who he was, came up to him and asked him to hold his teacup while he danced. At this the king was reportedly "much pleased." Cumberland was similarly dressed, though his enormous bulk made him less easy to camouflage. He looked like a grotesque clown in a pantomime, pot-bellied and round-bottomed, his pudgy face ridiculous beneath an outmoded high curly wig.

George II was in his sixty-sixth year in 1749. For twenty-two of those years he had been king, a stiff, correct, often irascible figure who harassed his ministers and strode about restlessly when he had nothing to do. His vendetta with his son, his suffering with hemorrhoids and his intermittent struggles with his ministers, especially Newcastle whom he privately referred to as "an ass," preoccupied him, but not exclusively; he found time to go to the opera, review his troops and preside over the tame and stuffy evening entertainments that were held in his drawing rooms. In profile George's double-chinned face had become rather froglike, the heavy-lidded eyes protruding and the mouth drawn widely back in a half grimace under a large, slightly hooked nose. Aristocratic ladies, forced to listen to his ponderous monologues, found the king tedious, but in general his subjects complained about him less than they ever had. "George is Magnanimous," they sang in a new verse written after the defeat of the Jacobites,

BONNIE PRINCE CHARLIE

Subjects unanimous;
Peace to us bring:
  His fame is glorious,
  Reign meritorious,
    God save the King!

With George the Magnanimous more secure than ever on his throne, and the French danger put to rest, the fate of Charles Stuart was not of paramount interest to the English in this year of the peace. English diplomats were always eager for news of him, however, and took note of the rumors in Paris that he was in Venice, or in a Bolognese monastery, or possibly in Poland. The Parisians, who had come to look on Charles as their own particular celebrity, continued to lament his forced departure and to berate their king for engineering it. At their most histrionic they told one another that Charles was dead.

The French ministers were certain he was alive, but couldn't find him, despite extensive searching. They had reason to believe that he was somewhere in France, and probably not far from Paris, as his Parisian banker Waters was supplying him with money and forwarding his mail. Puisieux, furious at Charles for impudently ignoring his promises to stay out of the country, summoned Waters to Versailles and threatened him with execution if he didn't confess Charles's whereabouts. But Waters insisted that he was as ignorant as Puisieux himself; others took Charles his messages, Waters said, and only these others knew where to take them.[3]

In fact, after a brief stay in Avignon, where he enjoyed the hospitality of his former governor Lord Dunbar and Dunbar's sister Lady Inverness, Charles and his companion Henry Goring left for parts unknown, deliberately keeping their destination secret from nearly everyone. Charles's dilemma was acute. Under the terms of the Treaty of Aix-la-Chapelle he could not be harbored in any European state, save the anomalous spiritual domain of the pope. But even the pope was subject to pressure from the secular authorities. Three-quarters of the revenues received by the See of Rome were from France, and could at any time be cut off by the French king. And the British navy in the Mediterranean was in a position to harass papal territories by sea, as in fact the Hanoverian government threatened to do when they learned that Charles was in Avignon.

The only solution was to go into hiding, and this Charles did, showing the same skill and resourcefulness in evading the English spies and the French security forces as he had shown in evading Cumberland's forces in Scotland in 1746. He was adept at disguising himself, altering his clothes, his wig, his voice—perhaps even masquerading as a woman as he had on Skye. He had a repertoire of aliases—student, servant, clergyman, traveling Englishman. What Goring's skills may have been we can only guess. What is certain is that the two fugitives, relying chiefly on their wits, as money was scarce, managed to travel with remarkable freedom through France over the following three years, despite the guards that waited for them along the roads and in the larger towns, watching for anyone who bore a resemblance to Charles.

Catching him became something of an obsession with the French police; they distributed posters with his likeness throughout the country, and conducted random searches in Paris and elsewhere in hopes of flushing him out. But though they had good reason to believe he was there, virtually underfoot, they never found him, and his cleverness in evading capture vexed them almost as much as his earlier refusal to leave Paris had vexed the king.

Shortly before Charles and Goring left Avignon, the son Louise de Rohan-Guéméné had borne the previous July died. He was less than seven months old, and had been given the name Charles-Godefroi. Louise's relatives honored him as one of their own, burying him in the family crypt at the convent of the Feuillants and never betraying a hint of doubt as to his paternity. When and how Charles learned of the infant's death is unknown, as he never wrote a word about him that has survived—and perhaps he did not like to think about him either.

Though Charles spent the following years in a sort of internal exile in France, he did not really live a vagabond life. He had Waters's bank as his *pied-à-terre* in Paris, and Mme. de Talmont's estate at Lunéville in Lorraine as his second hidden home. From 1750 on he had a third secret residence: the Convent of St. Joseph in Paris, where the Princesse de Talmont kept an apartment for herself and where two of her friends, the Comtesse de Vasse and

Elizabeth Ferrand, also lived. The countess and Mlle. Ferrand were both staunch admirers of Charles and were committed to helping him and his cause; however, they came to find his quarrels with the princess irritating and his presence, perhaps predictably, led to jealousy among the three women. Still, he managed to rotate his residences often enough to prevent both discovery by the French authorities and excessive tedium to himself and others and occasional visits to Strasbourg, Venice (where he was soon expelled) and elsewhere gave added variety.

In the summer of 1750 Horace Mann, the waspish English envoy in Florence, was more frustrated than ever in his futile effort to locate Charles. He had heard that he was in Lorraine—but where?—and also that he was in a Bolognese convent. There were rumors that he had gone to Poland, or Hungary, and it not infrequently happened that Mann received reports of his having been seen in three or four places at once. In August Mann learned from his English counterpart in Paris that Charles had been very ill, "at the point of death for many days," and that he had been forced to reveal his identity to the physician he called to treat him in order to impress on the man how important it was that he survive.[4]

Adding to Mann's vexation was the fact that he could get no useful information from Rome. Charles continued his practice of writing periodically to his father—never to his brother—and sending news of his health. The letters were brief and perfunctory, bearing no dates and containing no clues as to their geographical origins. They were carried by various travelers, and arrived at unpredictable intervals. James was in despair at not knowing more, and Mann too despaired, for his informers relied on James and Henry for their information.

In July of 1750 James received an unexpected request from his elder son. Charles asked that his father renew his Commission of Regency—an almost certain precursor of renewed political activity. James complied, no doubt wishing that he could be privy to Charles's plans, and calling him "a continual heartbreak." He also sent him two likenesses of himself carved on gemstones.

New plans were indeed afoot. Charles was very active that summer, gathering funds and depositing them with Waters, ordering his representative in Antwerp to buy a costly shipload of arms (including muskets to the remarkable number of twenty-six thousand) and arranging for a ship to transport them. There were references in the ever-cryptic Jacobite correspondence to "the great affair of L."[5] It seems probable that "L" was London, and the "great affair" an anticipated Jacobite coup.

Wearing a monk's robes, with a black patch over one eye and blackened eyebrows, Charles embarked for England on September 12, 1750. With him was Colonel Brett, then the leader of the English Jacobites, and sometime secretary to James II's illegitimate daughter the Duchess of Buckingham. Evading the scrutiny of customs officials on the English coast, Charles and Brett traveled to London where, presumably, they were harbored by Jacobite sympathizers. Some fifty of these sympathizers gathered in a lodging in Pall Mall to welcome Charles and shake his hand.

It must have been a solemn moment, with Charles (now shorn of his disguise) looking for the first time into the faces of those who would have joined him had he marched to London four years earlier instead of halting at Derby. They in turn got their first look at the remarkable young hero whose lightning advance southward had put London into panic. They were not disappointed. "He is tall and well made," noted William King, principal of St. Mary's Hall, Oxford and another prominent Jacobite, "but stoops a little. He has a handsome face and good eyes."

On another occasion King learned from Charles that he had come to London at the urging of some of the more hotheaded and impatient of the exiles, who "had formed a scheme which was impracticable." Once in the capital he discovered just how impracticable it was, as "no preparation had been made, nor was anything ready to carry it into execution." Charles told Dr. King that "he had been deceived"—and not for the first time. Still, fifty men were fifty men, and when he recalled the event many years later Charles insisted that if those fifty would have assembled a mere four thousand from among their tenants and retainers and by hiring troops, he would have led them in a rebellion.[6]

"The great affair of L" came to nothing. Charles, presumably in disguise once again, had the pleasure of walking through the streets of his capital with Colonel Brett, seeing the parks and new fashionable squares, skirting the narrow, twisted lanes of medieval Westminster, and admiring the City monuments. No one challenged the two men as they made their way to the Tower, and stood studying its fortifications. Ultimately they concluded that it could be seized after one gate was blown in with an explosive charge.

This information Charles kept in mind for another time, as it was clear he could not hope to achieve anything during the present visit. Nothing military, that is: he did achieve something of political significance. Privately and still incognito, he renounced the Roman faith into which he had been born and was admitted to the Church of England. Thus he became the first (and only) Protestant Stuart claimant to the throne, a step which removed him further from his father and brother and brought him closer, at least in theory, to the majority of the British. This accomplished, he returned to Paris after a stay of no more than a week.[7]

What the nature of the "impracticable scheme" of 1750 was is impossible to say. But very likely it involved fomenting a riot, then taking advantage of the confusion to bring Jacobite soldiers out of carefully concealed hiding places to assault the Tower and St. James's. With these secured, more troops could be brought from Scotland to consolidate the coup and prepare to withstand any possible counterattack.

Virtually all of the Jacobite schemes put forward in the early 1750s followed this outline. London was the focus: fighting men loyal to the Stuarts were to be situated there in large numbers, then unleashed at a predetermined signal to seize the Tower, the palace, and—depending on the plot variant—the royal family. Once London was in Stuart hands, more troops would be led south from Scotland to secure the new government and Charles would arrive from the continent to lead it.

In one colorful version of this plan, fifteen hundred Irish chairmen—porters who carried the sedan chairs supported on poles in which the more affluent Londoners had themselves transported—were to be called on to assemble in Lincoln's Inn Fields "the instant they heard any particular news relative to the Pretender." A detachment of the Irishmen was to "seize the person of the King as he returned from the play, . . . knock the servants from behind his coach, extinguish the lights, and create a confusion while a party carried the King to the water side, and hurried him away to France."[8]

The proponents of these schemes, in addition to Charles himself, were adventurous exiles such as Alexander Murray, younger brother of the Jacobite Lord Elibank and a man "vastly vain and full of himself" in James Edgar's phrase, and one Mr. Seagrave, an Irish officer with only one arm, who frequented Paris cafés and claimed to have been through the 1745 campaign by Charles's side. Unfortunately for Charles, one of the adventurers was Alistair Macdonald, son of John Macdonald of Glengarry, who had become a Hanoverian spy. Young Glengarry posed as an eager conspirator while in fact sending dispatches to the government in London giving detailed accounts of everything the Jacobites were planning. As a result of Glengarry's treachery, the most ambitious of the schemes—the "Elibank Plot" which was set to come to fruition in November of 1752—went awry, and was never successfully revived.

By then, however, Charles was making major changes in his personal life which in time were to have an even greater impact on the political future of his cause.

He had continued to keep up his relationship with the Princesse de Talmont for several years, despite their quarrels and despite her growing disillusionment with him. ("You don't need friends," she wrote to him near the end of their affair, "you need victims.") He depended on her, and trusted her not to let him down emotionally, and at the same time he took comfort from her influence with the French queen and from the fact that she provided him with an entrée to ex-King Stanislas of Poland, who was her neighbor at Lunéville, and who might be expected to prove useful to the Jacobite cause. By 1751 the relationship had become troublesome. Louise was affronted when Charles, who was becoming insecure and frightened, accused her of plotting to betray him to his enemies. He, for his part, either was or professed to be suffering the pangs of unrequited love. ("I'm dying!" he wrote in one anxious billet-doux. "I love you too much and you love me too little. . . . I've spent a horrible night!")[9]

By the early months of 1752, if not before, Charles and Louise had parted, and the separation was proving to be costly. Without

Mme. de Talmont's lodgings to use, and without her influence to rely on, Charles found it hard to borrow money, even from Waters, yet his personal expenses were higher than ever. He decided to abandon the residence he had maintained in Avignon since 1749, selling off his horses and coach, dismissing all his French servants, and putting his furnishings into storage. Some of the French servants had already left voluntarily, for in Charles's absence, it seems, his feisty Irish valet Daniel O'Brien had taken to ruling the household with an iron fist, shouting and swearing at the other servants and abusing them, especially when they accused him of appropriating his master's clothes. O'Brien was an all-around nuisance: he alienated Stafford and Sheridan, could not remain on civil terms with servants in other households and even managed to cause inconvenience to James in Rome. (A local girl who claimed to be pregnant by O'Brien turned up in Rome, along with her mother, intent on appealing to James to help her financially. He managed to avoid the obligation.)

In May Charles was in Ghent, renting a house in the Place de l'Empereur and hinting about how the house had "a room in it for a friend." He was expecting a guest—none other than Clementina Walkinshaw, who after some vicissitudes had managed to make her presence in the Low Countries known to him. Clementina, still unmarried at thirty-one or so, had convinced her relatives that she meant to become a canoness in one of the convents in the Austrian Netherlands which accepted aristocratic young women and provided a luxurious situation for them without requiring much, if anything, in the way of spiritual discipline. The proposed plan was a ruse, for in fact she intended to join Charles. Yet precisely when and how he had contacted her, and what his message may have said, are unknown.[10]

Following Charles's instructions, Clementina had made her way to Paris, where she stayed with one M. Arnoud and called herself "Mme. Jackson." There she received a rather peremptory letter from the man for whose sake she had renounced home and family.

"You are to give entire credit to the bearer," Charles instructed Clementina, "and follow exactly what he tells you to do from me. That you need not fear a mistake I have given him for a token your own name written by yourself. I hereby absolutely forbid you from this instant forward never to put pen to paper for anything whatsoever." He enjoined secrecy on her, warning her that no one "must know the least thing about you or what passes betwixt us, under pain of incurring forever my displeasure." He would pose as her brother, Charles said, and she must treat him, when they met, with nothing more than sisterly friendliness.[11]

Shortly after this Clementina was escorted to Ghent, where she found that Charles had rented a house for her. The pose of sisterly fondness could now be dropped. She was willing, probably eager, to become his mistress. As for Charles, the arrangement suited him. Clementina was neither particularly young nor particularly attractive, but she was dependable and loyal, and somewhat familiar. She would make a home for him of sorts. Everyone around him was certain to disapprove of the liaison, but that was unavoidable. He had no wish to marry at present, having given up on finding a suitably highborn Protestant bride. Clementina was willing to live with him without demanding marriage, and would not throw tantrums the way Louise de Rohan-Guéméné had or leave him alone and unhappy as Mme. de Talmont had. For the time being at least, she would do very well.

22

Charles Stuart and Clementina Walkinshaw lived together for eight years, from the summer of 1752 to July of 1760. For much of that time they were spectacularly and often publicly at odds.

To outsiders, Charles and Clementina looked like a couple at war, locked in snarling, bickering, wounding combat in which he inevitably had the upper hand. It was an age when men beat their wives by right and even from necessity, women being perceived as inherently inferior and inclined to degeneracy unless severely disciplined. But even to his hardened contemporaries Charles appeared brutal in his treatment of his mistress, and the spectacle of the tall, good-looking gentleman, somewhat the worse for drink, reviling and striking the fair, sturdily built woman who passed for his wife was an all too common sight in the taverns of Liège, Ghent, Basel and Paris over the years of their liaison.

Not that Clementina was a passive martyr; she too shouted,

goaded, and provoked. In her own way she was as bold a spirit as Charles was, leaving behind family and security to join him in his exile, knowing that her relatives would never take her back or forgive her if the affair went sour, knowing too that Charles would never marry her—for if and when he married, his wife would have to be a woman of princely blood. Or perhaps this is to underestimate Clementina. Perhaps she thought that he would decide to marry her in time, especially if she gave him a son whom he would want to legitimize. Or possibly she believed that he would eventually succeed in his venture, become king of England and Scotland, and shower wealth on her as kings commonly did in rewarding their mistresses.

Clearly Clementina had many facets to her nature: daring, loyalty, and courage, along with a capacity for abject compliance. And endurance. "There is not one woman in the world," she wrote Charles after he had "pushed her to the greatest extremity" and she left him, "that would have suffered so long as what I have done."[1]

Early in October of 1753, Charles and Clementina's daughter was born. She was named Charlotte after her father, and baptized in a Catholic parish church. (The baptism was not recorded at the time, for the sake of secrecy.) Strictly speaking, this was appropriate, for as an illegitimate child she would naturally be baptized in her mother's faith, and Clementina was a Catholic. But the event caused friction. Only two weeks after Charlotte's baptism, Charles was writing to Goring announcing that he had decided to dismiss all of his "papist servants" and Clementina with them. "My mistress has behaved so unworthily," he wrote, "she has put me out of all patience, and as she is a papist too, I discard her also."[2]

Charles may have been ambivalent at first about becoming a father. When asked whether he intended ever to marry, he once responded, "No. Would you have me bring children into the world to be as miserable as I am?" In the year after Charlotte was born he remarked that, the Stuart family having had sufferings enough, he would not marry "as long as in misfortune, which would only conduce to increase misery, and subject any of the family who had the spirit of their father to be tied neck and heels."[3] Apart from not wanting to create a life marked for sorrow, Charles may have had reservations about his own skills as a parent. Here his feelings about his own hovering, cautiously overprotective father must have affected him.[4]

James continued to write him tender, solicitous, sometimes admonitory letters (with the admonitions always surrounded by expressions of sincere love). Charles wrote back less and less often, his letters being what one writer has called "jewels of vacuous concision." The gap between father and son, already wide when Charles was in his twenties, had widened considerably, and it must have caused Charles pain. He was superficially dutiful, and that was all. Looking ahead, he may have dreaded finding himself one day in James's situation, with a child who was unalterably distant from him, and from whom he was alienated.

Whatever his initial feelings about his daughter may have been, he soon became a fond parent. The infant Charlotte was plump and sturdy, with white-blond hair and large eyes in a round, broad little face. To judge from the fiercely protective statements she made about her daughter later, Clementina too adored Charlotte, doting on her all the more in that she proved to be an only child.[5]

In their early years, Charles, Clementina, Charlotte and one or two servants lived fugitive lives, coming to rest in this or that Belgian town for a few months at a time, then moving on when Charles was recognized or when he feared he soon might be. Young Glengarry had made the Hanoverian ministers aware that Charles was seriously involved in political intrigues; though the 1752–1753 plan had been circumvented, other schemes were being put forward and at any given time there were conspirators and would-be conspirators in plenty.

Few in government circles wrote Charles off as a forlorn hope, despite his loss of official French support. "No expense to be spared to find the Pretender's son," Newcastle wrote in his notes at a cabinet meeting in November of 1753. "Sir John Gooderich to be sent after him. Lord Anson to have frigates on the Scotch and Irish coasts."[6] Hanoverian agents in Rome, Paris and even Russia had dozens of spies and informers on their payrolls, and during the course of the 1750s the espionage network became more elaborate and more efficient. Hence the need for Charles and his small household to keep moving, employ disguises and aliases—one researcher has estimated that Charles used some twenty different aliases in the 1750s and early 1760s—and live as obscurely as possible.

Often Charles left Clementina and Charlotte while he pursued his most dangerous clandestine intrigues alone. The dispatches Horace Mann sent to London are full of the descriptions of Mann's spies who caught fleeting glimpses of the "Young Pretender." He was seen in Avignon, dressed as an abbé, walking abroad in the evening with three or four of his friends and attended at other times by members of his permanent, albeit much reduced, Avignon household. He was seen passing through Paris, walking in the streets on his way to the Scots College, "so disguised as to make it extremely difficult to know him, having painted his face with red, and colored his eyebrows with the deepest black, and keeping a handkerchief to his face as to keep off the cold." He was glimpsed in the Netherlands, meeting with suspected and known Jacobites, waiting for a planned insurrection in England that never occurred.[7]

When the English agents lost track of Charles, they watched the roads to Rome, waiting for couriers or servants from James's court who might be expected to lead them to him. In September of 1755, five of Charles's Scots servants, three of whom had been with him in Scotland, were seen riding through Tuscany on their way south. Horace Mann took note of their passing, and when three months later the same five men, now wearing James's livery, were seen riding back toward France, Mann sent two of his English informers to join the Scotsmen and try to discover anything they could about Charles's whereabouts and activities. The Englishmen succeeded in passing themselves off as harmless travelers, and "insinuated themselves so well" into the company of Scotsmen "as to pass the whole evening with them."

Where was Charles at present, the Englishmen asked.

The Scotsmen answered only "that they were going to Avignon and should soon know," and with considerable merriment they drank the health of "the Boy that is lost and cannot be found."

"But he will soon be found!" one of them offered—before a companion reproved him and told him to hold his tongue.[8]

Tantalizing encounters such as this convinced Mann that major Jacobite plans were afoot, yet his spies could not manage to locate

Charles or find out exactly what was being planned. Young Glengarry's usefulness had come to an end; on the death of his father the previous year he had gone back to Scotland to head his clan. Thus the spy network lost a key agent, and at times there was such a dearth of information about Charles that the English were tempted to believe that he was either dead or locked away out of reach, possibly in a madhouse.

Such speculations would doubtless have pleased Charles no end. Far from being confined in a madhouse, and very much alive, he was living with Clementina and Charlotte in Basel, posing as an English doctor—another account calls him "a private English gentleman"—named Thompson. The household consisted of the "Thompson" family, Charles's elderly servant John Stuart of Ardvorlich—who later became his major domo—and two "ordinary servants." They lived, according to the British minister at Bern, who may have got his information from Lord Elcho, "very decently, as persons of easy fortune, but without the least affectation of show or magnificence." Dr. Thompson was often away on business, and when his wife accompanied him their child was left in the care of the elderly servant.[9] Eventually the family had to move when a Basel art dealer, having been struck by the resemblance between Dr. Thompson and a portrait of Charles which he had for sale, realized that the English gentleman was none other than the Stuart Pretender. The word got out and quickly spread. Charles and his entourage were soon on their way to Flanders.

In the late 1750s Charles found a more or less permanent *pied-à-terre* for himself and his family, if a somewhat incongruous one. The Duc de Bouillon, Louise de Rohan-Guéméné's father and grandfather of Charles and Louise's dead son, offered Charles and Clementina his château of Carlsbourg at Saussure. The offer was prompted by political considerations; France was once again at war with England and Louis XV was at pains to offer comfort to one of England's most famous enemies. One wonders whether Clementina knew of the affair between Charles and Louise. Charles may have told her, or she may have heard gossip. At any event, she was very unhappy at Carlsbourg, and ultimately left the château and Charles, taking their daughter with her.

For years Clementina had lived in the shadow of Jacobite accusations. Many of Charles's advisers and supporters believed that she had an unhealthy hold over him, and accused her of undermining his cause. She was a Catholic, she was a hindrance to any future royal marriage Charles might decide to make, she made him look disreputable. Worst of all, Clementina was widely suspected of being a Hanoverian agent, as she had begun to live with Charles at about the same time that the plans for rebellion in 1752–1753 came to nothing. One of her sisters had lived in the household of the Prince and Princess of Wales since 1736, first as a seamstress and later as housekeeper. After the prince died in 1751 she stayed on as housekeeper to his widow at Leicester House. Because of her long service with the royal family, "Walky," as she was known, was in a position of trust; it was reasoned that she might have recruited Clementina to serve as an agent on behalf of her mistress the princess.

At first Charles refused to listen to the accusations, but as the years passed the voices criticizing Clementina became more and more insistent. Visitors called on him, begging him to put aside the "harlot" who was betraying him, pleading with him not to let his mistress ruin forever his chances to regain the throne his grandfather had lost. He was urged to put Clementina in a convent, forget about his illegitimate daughter and find a royal bride who could give him a true heir.

The terrible scenes that occurred between Charles and his mistress only provided more fodder to Clementina's critics. The ugly arguments in cafés, witnessed by shocked or amused patrons, the shouts and shrieks coming from the residences the couple shared, Charles's drunken rages which became the subject of common gossip—all these were terribly damaging to the man who only a few years earlier had been widely praised as a celebrity and hero. Either Clementina was driving Charles to drink, or, at the very least, she was not helping him control what had become a dangerous habit.

And she was provoking him to a level of violence unbefitting a Stuart prince. As Clementina herself told Lord Elcho, Charles mistreated and abused her physically throughout the whole time she lived with him. He frequently thrashed her with a stick as many as fifty times in a single day, she said—a claim that becomes easier to believe when it is compared with other reports that Charles was accustomed to chasing his servants with a drawn sword when they displeased him. "You pushed me to the greatest extremity and even despair," Clementina wrote to Charles seven months after she left him, "as I was always in perpetual dread of your violent passions."[10]

At midnight on July 23, Clementina bundled her six-year-old daughter into a hired carriage, got in herself, and ordered the driver to take them the hundred and sixty miles to Paris. After two long days of traveling they finally arrived, having only what little money the Earl Marischal had given Clementina for her immediate expenses. She had not dared to bring along a servant, and there was no one waiting in the city to help mother and daughter get settled. It had taken considerable daring, but Clementina had finally left Charles, choosing her time carefully to coincide with one of his many trips away from Carlsbourg and leaving behind a letter for him to find on his return.

"Your Royal Highness cannot be surprised at my having *parti* [left] when you consider one [*sic*] repeated bad treatment I have met with these eight years past," the letter read, "and the daily risk of losing my life. Not being able to bear any longer such hardships, my health being altered by them has obliged me at last to take this desperate step of removing from your Royal Highness with my child which nothing but the fear of my life would ever have made me undertake anything without your knowledge."[11]

Clementina hoped to hide herself in Paris, but Charles's elderly retainer John Stuart followed her there and confronted her once she arrived. Too feeble to force her, even if he had wanted to, the old man pleaded with her to return to the château. She would sooner "make away with herself" than go back, Clementina told him. And as for Charlotte, she would be "cut to pieces sooner than give her up."[12]

Predictably, Charles was enraged when he returned to Carlsbourg and found that Clementina had left him. When he had calmed down sufficiently, he wrote to the Abbé John Gordon, principal of the Scots College in Paris, to solicit Gordon's aid in getting Clementina and his daughter back. He was absolutely determined to recover Charlotte, he told Gordon, even if he had "to burn down every convent in Paris to find her." Gordon did his best, contacting the prefects of police and providing them with descriptions of mother and daughter. Clementina had slipped away from the servant John Stuart after only a day, and he did not know where she had gone. Gordon had reason to believe that she was looking for a convent which would accept Charlotte as a boarding pupil, but could not discover which convent.

Meanwhile Charles alternated between anger and misery. Two days after he discovered that his mistress and daughter were gone he dictated a letter to Gordon again urging him to do all he could to find them, "both of them, especially the little girl." In his own hand he wrote, "I take this affair so much to heart that I was not able to write what is here above. Shall be in the greatest affliction until I greet back the child, which was my only comfort in my misfortunes."[13]

Months went by, and Clementina proved to be as good at eluding her pursuers as Charles had always been at eluding his. Charles kept writing to Gordon, suggesting where Clementina might be—with Waters the banker, at Rouen, with the Archbishop of Toulouse, who had once offered to find a convent for her to live in—but none of his suggestions led to her discovery. By October Gordon had begun to assume that Clementina had managed to leave France and that she was likely to be in Italy, perhaps in Venice or Nice. In fact she and Charlotte were in hiding at the Convent of St. Denis four miles north of Paris, under the protection of no less a personage than King Louis.

About this time Charles discovered, to his extreme chagrin, that his father had been a party to Clementina's plot to abandon him and that James had given her his permission to take his granddaughter to Paris where she could receive a genteel education. Both mother and daughter were as good as lost to him, Charles seems to have concluded. He no longer had any power over them. Those Jacobites who had been urging him for years to get rid of Clementina now crowed with delight to discover that she was gone for good. As for Charles, he had taken to his bed, attacked by fever and in pain from hemorrhoids.

He was suffering, not only because his familiar if tumultuous domestic life had come to an end and he had lost his beloved daughter but because, only a year or so earlier, the last and most ambitious French enterprise for the invasion of Britain had collapsed in disaster.

Another continental war had begun in 1756, and at first the British had fared badly. Hanover was virtually overrun, the British forces were being defeated and even the strong British navy was scattered so widely over the vast war theater—for this was virtually a global war—that it could not adequately protect the home coasts. Renewed schemes for a French invasion of either England or Scotland with Charles at the head of the invading force had begun to reach Louis XV's council as early as June of 1755, but in January and February of 1759 the foreign minister, Choiseul, carried forth an expensive and complex plan of his own.[14]

Instead of relying on the Jacobite exiles, or on Charles's unreliable supporters in England and Scotland, Choiseul hit on the idea of landing a combined Russo-Swedish army in Scotland. He asked the Swedish government to assemble twelve thousand men in Gothenburg and requested the Russian chancellor Vorontsov to prepare to send ten to twelve thousand of his men to Scotland on board the Swedish fleet. Preparations went forward throughout the winter of 1759 and Charles, ever skeptical of the good faith of the French and still full of resentment over his expulsion from France ten years earlier, was at length persuaded to approach Choiseul for an interview. A meeting was arranged for February 7, and though the foreign minister arrived on time, Charles did not. Choiseul waited, no doubt impatiently, remembering what he had heard of the Pretender's irresponsible life and unheroic conduct. Eventually Charles arrived, thoroughly drunk, carried in the arms of one of his forbearing followers.

It was clear to the foreign minister that Charles, as he put it, "had not a steady enough head for a considerable undertaking to be run according to his views." Still, he would be put in nominal command once the enterprise was ready to be launched. Until then Charles was little more than a nuisance, protesting the successive tactics proposed by the French and determined not to let them use him as nothing more than a bluff to force the British to make peace. He refused to lead troops into either Ireland or Scotland, he said; he would invade southern England and march on London or he would have nothing to do with the venture at all.

CAROLLY ERICKSON

By mid-July of 1759 Choiseul had decided to land troops at Portsmouth, with a secondary landing at Glasgow. An extensive fleet of three hundred and thirty-seven ships carrying nearly fifty thousand men would be launched at night, protected by armed cargo boats. Preparations gathered momentum. Charles, his skepticism dissolved, envisioned the achievement of his long-deferred dream.

But the British struck first. In August the French Mediterranean fleet was severely damaged off Lagos in Portugal, while the decisive battle of Quiberon Bay south of Belle-Isle destroyed the invasion fleet and made Choiseul's scheme completely unworkable. British intelligence had discovered the plans, and the intransigence of the British prime minister, William Pitt, had ensured the French defeat.

Now, barely a year later, Charles was forced to confront a stinging personal defeat to parallel the military one. Just as he had had little or no control over Choiseul's invasion scheme, and had lost his chance when it collapsed, so he had been unable to control Clementina, and had lost her and Charlotte along with her. In the fall of 1759 he was fast approaching his fortieth birthday. His youth had run out, and his fortunes had never looked more bleak. Alienated from his father and brother, spectacularly unsuccessful as a father himself, thwarted yet again in the military arena, no longer idolized but repugned as a wife-beating drunkard, Charles faced his fifth decade depressed and alone.

23

In 1765 James Boswell was in Rome, looking for a classical subject for a large historical painting he had recently commissioned. He had the idea to consult a fellow Scot, Andrew Lumisden, who since the death of James Edgar in 1764 had been serving as secretary to James Stuart at the Palazzo Muti.

Boswell was only twenty-five, a young law student with an exceptionally observant eye, enjoying his tour of the continent before returning to Britain to begin professional life. He was naturally curious about the Old Pretender, by now a shadowy figure remembered chiefly for having fathered his much celebrated son. But Boswell was wary: might his visit to the palace be construed as treason? Not if he avoided meeting the Pretender in person, and did not discuss politics, he assured himself in his journal.

As it turned out, his worries were for nothing. James, a feeble recluse who suffered from severe stomach pains and fainting fits and periodically went into convulsions, rarely saw anyone except Lumisden and his other servants. He stayed in his room, reportedly "in very great decay," resting and praying and, when necessary, receiving those few English visitors to Rome who remembered him. His pale, long face had become chalk-white and fretted with wrinkles, his full lips drooped and had no color. His sunken eyes, always gently melancholy, were sadder than ever as he grew weaker and weaker, knowing that unless some miracle occurred he would die without the consolation of seeing his elder son once more.

James had represented the Stuart claim to the British throne for nearly sixty-four years, a far longer time than any crowned monarch had held it. His life had so far spanned five reigns and part of a sixth, the reigns being those of his father James II his half-sisters Mary (with her husband, William of Orange) and Anne, his distant cousins George I, George II and, since 1760, George III. He had ceased to be an object of interest to the Romans, and most of the English too had forgotten him. The Jacobite exiles in Rome had dwindled to an elderly few who were still clamorously dependent on their aged benefactor's bounty, but James was no longer capable of dealing with them; he left it to Lumisden to distribute his charity and placate the importunate.

In fact, Lumisden told Boswell, for some time all "uneasy things" had been concealed from James, and he gave as an example a recent minor contretemps over the Duke of York. The Stuarts and their followers had always called James's second son Henry "Duke of York," and he was generally known in Rome as "Cardinal York." So when the Hanoverian Edward, Duke of York, brother of the reigning monarch George III, came to Italy and was accorded his royal title the Stuart duke was forced to complain. He took care not to let his ailing father know anything about the matter, however, as James "would have been much hurt." As it turned out, Henry complained to the Roman authorities about Duke Edward's reception, and the English envoy Mann complained about the honors shown to Cardinal York, and the incident ended.

Had James found out about the conflict over the ducal title, he might not have cared, for in his last years politics mattered little to him. His chief concern was for Charles.

For sixteen years James had not seen his son, nor had he known where to find him. Their correspondence had dwindled away to nothing on Charles's side, though James continued to send fatherly letters out into the void, admonishing his son to "rise out of his lethargy" and show "by his actions" that he was still a force on the European stage. "I shall take it for granted that in your present situation you are not only buried alive, as you really are, but in effect you are dead and insensible to everything," James wrote in 1762. He knew where Clementina and Charlotte were, for he had helped Clementina to obtain her lodgings at the elegant old Convent of the Visitation of Our Lady in Paris and sent her twelve thousand francs every year, in addition to paying the costs of Charlotte's education. But Charles continued to be elusive.

"O my Dear Child," James wrote plaintively, "could I but once have the satisfaction of seeing you before I die!" And in another letter, written a year before Boswell came to Rome, James queried his errant son: "Will you not run straight to your father? . . . Here is no question of the past but only of saving you from utter destruction in the future. Is it possible," he concluded, "you would rather be a vagabond on the face of the earth than return to a father who is all love and tenderness for you?"[1]

Lumisden confided to Boswell that he too wrote to Charles, as his predecessor James Edgar had, to urge him to come to his elderly father's bedside, but to no avail. The secretary took his guest on a tour of the Muti Palace, showing him drawings made by Charles as a boy, carefully preserved, and inviting him to return whenever he liked. Boswell and Lumisden became friends, and in the course of the former's sojourn in Rome he availed himself of the hospitality at the Muti a number of times. He also traveled to Frascati to see Henry preside at mass, exclaiming afterward that the cardinal was most "majestic and elegant" with the face of an angel.[2]

In 1765 Henry and his father were on easy and affectionate terms, but this had not always been the case. When Henry first returned to Rome from France at the age of twenty-two, he had lived with James as before, but not as the dutiful son James wanted. Henry had developed his own tastes and habits, and was no longer inclined to spend quiet evenings with his father, reading aloud to him from the lives of the saints. Instead Henry preferred to give parties for his musician friends, and arrange for the singing of oratorios and other cultural events. James disapproved of Henry's companions, especially a young priest named Lercari, with whom Henry developed a strong and almost certainly homosexual bond.

The straitlaced James was horrified, and demanded that Henry dismiss Lercari from the household. Henry defied his father, and went on defying him even when James appealed to the pope and threatened to enter a monastery unless Henry did as he asked. The young cardinal was more stubborn than the aging nobleman. Eventually James asked his son to leave his house, and Henry obliged, warning his father that he would never speak to him again. There was a prolonged estrangement, but when after several years Henry's attachment to Lercari weakened, he made up the quarrel with his father. Still, Henry would not live with James again and kept a separate establishment.

In 1765 Henry was forty years old, popular with his flock at Frascati, influential in the curia, and extremely wealthy.[3] He held ecclesiastical preferments worth tens of thousands of pounds, chiefly in France but also in the Netherlands, Spain, and Mexico. While music was his passion, he also collected books—Bibles in many languages, classical works, many books in English—and by the time he died his collection had reached fifteen thousand volumes. To outward appearances at least, Henry was a fulfilled and happy man, unlike his older brother, and the only thing lacking to make his happiness complete was a reconciliation with Charles. As early as February of 1765, Henry had written to Charles in an attempt to persuade him to end the "disunion" that for so many years had "rendered them . . . so useless to one another." Later in the year, as James's health continued to fail, Henry wrote again, and this time Charles, knowing that his father would not last much longer, was inclined to be warmly responsive.

"Your letter of October 30, my dear brother, and that joined to it have been sent to me," Charles wrote from Bouillon. "I am most sensible of all the marks of your good heart and of your attention to my interests." Charles assured Henry that he felt once again all his old "tenderness and friendship" for him, and hoped to express them in person as soon as possible. He would prepare himself to leave France immediately, as he was just as impatient to be with

Henry as the latter was to see him again. "If I had the wings of a bird we would both be satisfied very soon," Charles concluded, calling himself "Your most affectionate brother, Charles P.R."[4]

Of course, the reunion was bound to lead to complications of protocol. Charles's return to Rome would symbolize more than just a return to the Stuart family circle; there would be the question of his rank and privileges. Charles had lived incognito for many years, now he would be returning to public life in the one city where the Stuart court had always been accorded royal status. Moreover, as James's death was imminent, Charles would be returning, not as Prince of Wales, but as king.

Through Henry, Charles asked the pope to accord him the same "marks of royalty" that James enjoyed, along with other dignities and distinctions. Henry pleaded his brother's case, but lost. The pope's reply was that he would be pleased to see Charles again, and would have him treated according to his distinguished rank, but as to according him royal status, he neither could nor wanted to. It was a courteous but cold and utterly uncompromising reply. As far as the pope was concerned, James was the last Stuart "king." A decision had been made decades earlier not to continue to acknowledge any more Pretenders, and nothing had changed since then to cause that policy to be abandoned.[5]

Apparently Charles decided not to let the question of his alleged regality stand in the way of his return to Rome, for he set out from Bouillon on December 30, 1765, the day before his forty-fifth birthday. He had decided, it seems, to drop the enduring resentment he felt toward Henry. According to the always hostile reports of Mann in Florence, he had been "very melancholy" since Clementina left him, and more inclined to seek solace in drink; it may be that his need for a family link of some sort was stronger than his old grudge against his brother. Then too, his sense of fitness, at least where his royal claims were concerned, was always strong. He was his father's successor, therefore it was fitting that he should succeed to James's palace, income and status as well as his title. And there was an additional reason for his decision, a very pressing one: he had no money left.

For years James had sent funds to Waters for Charles's use, but at some point these periodic allowances had ceased, and Charles had run through what capital he had. He could no longer afford to maintain his small personal household, plus his servants at Avignon, Paris and elsewhere. He expected to profit handsomely from James's death, and he intended to be on hand to receive his share of the estate when the time came.[6]

James died on January 1, 1766, at nine in the evening. Henry was not at his bedside, but Lumisden was, and the secretary noted that his master died as he had lived, "with his usual mild serenity in his countenance." No doubt he was at peace with himself and with God, and given his remarkably benign disposition, it may well be that on his deathbed he forgave his wayward elder son.

Charles heard the news of his father's death as he made his way southward. He would miss the obsequies, which were to be held at St. Peter's, but this was just as well. He instructed the messenger who brought him the news from Rome to tell Henry to prepare a royal welcome for him, and to get the Palazzo Muti ready for a new monarch. Either he was bluffing, or Charles sincerely expected that the pope and cardinals would soften their stance toward him once he was actually on the scene. Or he may have overestimated Henry's influence, as he was to do more than once in the years to come.

The journey was arduous, the mountain roads slippery with ice. Heavy rains and sleet led to delays and postponements. Somewhere along the way the coach in which Charles was riding had a serious accident, causing him to reinjure his sore and varicosed legs. On January 23, he finally reached the periphery of the capital and Henry met him at an inn on the Flaminian Way. The cardinal was all smiles and sympathy for his injured brother, and had him helped into his own elegant gilded coach for the remaining few miles into the city. No guard of honor waited at the Porta del Popolo to welcome King Charles III, no papal envoy greeted him. The teeming, reeking life of the Roman streets had not been interrupted to make a pathway for his arrival, and the Romans who knelt and crossed themselves as the gilded coach passed them were paying homage to the cardinal and not his long lost brother.

A large crowd had gathered, however, at the gates of the Muti Palace. They watched, noisy but intent, as Charles was helped from the coach and into the palace. Those who remembered the ebullient, golden boy who had left his father's house twenty-two years earlier stared in curiosity at the stooped, crippled, middle-aged man before them with the coarse and weary face. Could this be King Charles III, of whom so much had once been expected? Inside the palace some of the Roman nobles waited in an antechamber to pay their respects. They were curious too, for so little had been heard about Charles in recent years that many of them had believed he was dead. He passed among them, assisted by his servants and obviously in pain, returning their civilities with an effort and soon taking his leave to rest in the apartments which had been prepared for him.

It took Charles a while to recuperate from his accident and from the fatigues of his journey, but as the weeks went by the swelling in his legs went down and he was able to walk unaided through his apartments and eventually to go out riding with Henry in his coach. According to Lumisden, Charles still possessed the ingenuous charm which had made him so appealing as a younger man. He did his best to hide the resentment he felt toward the pope and College of Cardinals, leaving it to Henry to make his protests for him and hoping that in time he would be given the recognition he deserved. Henry made a great show of parading through the city with Charles seated on his right—a privilege reserved for royalty—and angered Pope Clement by encouraging others in the city to defy his mandate. One of these was Cardinal Orsini, the minister of Naples, who made a formal visit to Charles and, it was said, addressed him as he would a sovereign.

Even more gratifying to Charles was the treatment he received at the hands of the students and rector of the English Convent of St. Thomas, who turned out to welcome him attired in their ceremonial habits and conducted him to a royal chair of state. They greeted him as "Charles the Third, their Sovereign," and sang a Te Deum in his honor, even though they knew the act of defiance would lead to punishment from Pope Clement. Three days after the English students displayed their Stuart loyalties, the Irish and Scottish students did the same, causing the rectors of all three colleges to be banished from the papal city.[7]

Shortly after this Charles retired to the country to hunt, both because the weather and his health had improved and because he had little stomach for controversy, especially when it looked as though he was not going to gain the goals he sought. He stayed on, month after month, living at Albano with frequent visits to Henry at Frascati. It was a lonely life, largely devoid of society. "He says he is like one on shipboard," Lumisden wrote of Charles. "He converses only with his own little crew." As an Anglican, he was an outsider to the religion of Rome; as "Baron Douglas"—the only title the pope permitted him to use—he was an outsider to the higher ranks of aristocratic society. His only hope was that Pope Clement XIII, who was in poor health, would die soon and that his successor would be less scrupulous in his observance of protocol.

At least his financial troubles were greatly eased. James left an estate in money, jewels and plate worth many hundreds of thousands of Roman crowns, an estate which included the Crown Jewels James II had brought from England in 1688. The scepter, the collar, George and the star of the Garter and the St. Andrew's cross were all being held securely in a strongbox in one of Rome's banks. Not trusting Charles to deal prudently with his inheritance, James had left to Henry the legal responsibility for looking after his brother's money; Henry gave Charles an allowance of ten thousand Roman crowns a month—roughly twice his own income.

Pope Clement did not die, and Charles continued to live in a kind of limbo, an outsider to Roman society yet without any alternative community to belong to. Visiting Britishers, who were few and far between, found him pathetically eager for their company. An English woman who spent some time with him in 1767 noted her observations. His appearance, she thought, was "rather handsome, his face ruddy and full of pimples. He looks good natured," she went on, "and was overjoyed to see me; nothing could be more affectionately gracious." He was quite melancholy, however, and "distracted" in his conversation—he admitted to her that his memory was failing him and that he found it hard to concentrate—and his features clouded over with depression from time to time.

"He has all the reason in the world to be melancholy," wrote Charles's visitor, "for there is not a soul goes near him, not knowing what to call him. He told me time lay heavy upon him. I said I supposed he read a good deal. He made no answer. He depends entirely for his subsistence upon his brother whom he never loved, much less now, he having brought him into the scrape."

His dependence on Henry had probably become a major irritant. After more than a year of living in virtual isolation, with the well meaning but increasingly custodial Henry as his only real companion, Charles had taken to drink with a vengeance. "Could we but get the better of the nasty bottle," Henry wrote in the spring of 1767, "which every now and then comes on by spurts." Charles's "difficulties and odd notions" were driving his sedate brother mad. He had dismissed his British servants—including Lumisden—in a fit of pique and installed Italians to take their place. With these Italians in tow, he spent drunken evenings in search of pleasure, attending the theater, making a spectacle of himself at public performances, and even, with one of the men on hand to support him, trying to dance on his uncertain legs.

Time indeed hung heavy on his hands, and his brother's intolerance was even more burdensome. To Henry, Charles was nothing but an embarrassment, while to Charles Henry had come to seem like a jailer. He was shackled hand and foot: the pope kept him from enjoying his true rank and status, his brother held his purse strings, and he had no one else to turn to.

His hopes rose briefly when a papal election was held in the spring of 1769. Cardinal Stoppari, who might be expected to acknowledge Charles's titles, had a good chance of being chosen to be the new pope. But when Cardinal Ganganelli was elected instead, taking the name of Clement XIV, Charles was in despair again. This Clement looked more kindly on Charles than his predecessor had, but still felt constrained to deny him the honors he sought. He regretted having to make this decision, he told Charles in a personal interview, especially as he had once served James as chaplain and had "the greatest regard for his family." If it were not for political considerations, things would be far different.[8]

The pope's kindness was a small consolation for the despondent Charles, who sank deeper into his lethargy and isolation. A visitor who saw him the following year was struck by his excessive stoop and his corpulence. "He appears bloated and red in the face," she wrote, "his countenance heavy and sleepy, which is attributed to his having given in to excess of drinking." On the whole, she thought, he had a "melancholy, mortified appearance," though his presence was still noble and his manner graceful. At fifty, he was rapidly sinking both physically and spiritually. The Jacobite prince who had once dreamed of possessing three kingdoms had been dispossessed even of the empty name of king, and was caged like an aging beast in his brother's care.

24

In the summer of 1770, Charles broke away from the withdrawn life he had been leading in Rome and went on a tour of Tuscany. He was drinking as heavily as ever and everywhere he went his tipsy eccentricity caused comment. However, he was very gratified to find that the Tuscan peasants, unlike the Romans, were not only tolerant of his antics but called him "Majesty" when they addressed him. The title was music to his ears, and the respect he received when he walked in the streets and attended the local fairs won him over completely.

With his retinue of four footmen and two gentlemen servants he lodged at an inn in Florence, and was delighted to find that the Florentine nobles too were very courteous, if not deferential; they did not call him "Majesty," but they did pay calls on him, and invited him to call on them in return. At the theater, where, as it happened, he had a box next to that of his longtime foe Horace Mann, he enjoyed the attention he received on entering and leaving and took pleasure in paying visits to highborn ladies in their boxes.[1]

Livorno, Lucca and Pisa were as hospitable as Florence, Charles found, and he prolonged his stay in Pisa, taking the waters for his diseased legs during the day and attending the public casino at night, wearing his Garter star under his coat and his badge of St. Andrew in his waistcoat. He called himself "Count of Albany," and played cards with the notables who frequented the casino, no longer feeling like an injured outcast, as he had in Rome, but basking in the attention he received and vastly enjoying his role as a fascinating new celebrity. He was particularly pleased when several beggars suffering with what was then still called the "king's evil," scrofula, approached him and asked him to touch them with his royal hands.[2]

Charles was so pleased with the stir he caused in the Tuscan towns that he preferred to ignore the clear evidence that it was bound to turn sour. When after taking the waters at Pisa he returned to Florence for a second stay, he was pointedly ignored by the Grand Duke of Tuscany, and found that fewer of the town's nobles were willing to pay him social calls. His attendants scented conflict in the wind, and urged him to leave, but he stayed on, waving aside their entreaties. Growing increasingly anxious, his Master of the Horse Count Spada and his gentleman Count Vegha appealed to Charles's acquaintances to prevail on him to go back to Rome, but they refused to interfere. In desperation, fearful that the "natural violence" of Charles's temper, made worse by three days of nearly constant drinking, might "induce him to commit some great irregularity in public," they appealed to Henry in Rome. Finally, at Henry's urging, he agreed to leave Florence.

The following summer, however, Charles was back in Tuscany, renting a villa near the Pisan baths and, once installed in it, resuming his "irregular life" of conspicuous public drunkenness and embarrassing evening forays into society. Then, in mid-August, he disappeared.

At first it was said that he had gone to Poland, at the suggestion of the Polish Princess Tablonowsky—a Sobieski relative who had made his acquaintance in Rome. Then it was discovered that in fact he had made the difficult journey to France—particularly difficult for a man of fifty-one with bad legs—in order to attend to some "family business." Rumors flew, all the more so when Charles reappeared in Pisa, alone and secretive about his doings. There was a marriage in the air, people said—but marriage to whom? And when?

In Holy Week of 1772 the mystery was solved. Charles had himself driven in an open carriage to Macerata, a town in the Umbrian marshes near Ancona, to the palace of a local nobleman where he met his bride-to-be. She was Princess Louise of Stolberg-Gedern, a lively, intelligent and attractive nineteen-year-old with fair hair and hazel eyes. Their meeting in Macerata was their first; quite possibly, if Louise had encountered Charles before the marriage negotiations were concluded and her fate sealed, she might have refused to marry him.

Louise was spirited, youthful, brimming with energy and curiosity. An acquaintance described her expression as "bright, mischievous and sensitive," with undertones of malice. She was nothing like the coarse-fibered and compliant Clementina, and had none of Clementina's loyalty or Jacobite idealism. Louise had better breeding, was much more sure of herself, and came from royal stock—in her marriage contract she was called "Most Serene Highness." In heredity she was Charles's equal, for although her father, the late Gustav Adolf of Stolberg-Gedern, was a prince of the Holy Roman Empire and not a king, at least he had held on to his throne, unlike Charles's grandfather, and his title was not disputed.

Charles, on the other hand, had become truculent, obnoxious and at times hateful. He was far from being a physical wreck, but he was corpulent and crippled, and his flushed and puffy face, slightly pop eyes, jowly cheeks and double chins made him a grotesque figure beside his fresh young bride, even in an age when middle-aged men regularly married much younger women.[3] His relations with women had never been good, tending to veer from demanding infatuation to abusive tyranny with no middle ground between the two extremes. Certainly he expected to exercise unchallenged dominion over his wife, all the more so given the difference in their ages. He was not prepared to tolerate any degree of independence whatever, and no doubt saw himself as favoring the relatively humble Louise, daughter of a petty German princeling, with the grand title and rank of Queen Consort of England, Ireland and Scotland. That she would be queen in name only (and in Rome, not even in name) was in Charles's view an irritating detail.

Given their very different natures and expectations of one another, Louise and Charles were bound to clash. He brought out her rebelliousness, stifling her passion and making her long for escape. She in turn brought out the bully and ultimately the sadist in him, exacerbating his inherent possessiveness until he became—or tried to become—her jailer.

The partners in this ill-fated marriage were toasted and serenaded by the local notables of Macerata after the wedding, and the governor of the district made them a brief congratulatory speech. They left for Rome on Easter Sunday, and Louise became mistress of the Muti Palace, where she was nicknamed "Queen of the Apostles," because of the proximity of the palace to the Church of the Santi Apostoli. As might have been predicted the pope refused to recognize Louise as Charles's queen consort, and the longstanding battle between Charles and the curia over rank and title continued. Still, observers took it as a good sign that, now that he was married, the Count of Albany drank much less and appeared to be on the road to reform. He was even physically more active, fencing with foil, mask and gloves and playing the violin in amateur concerts—possibly at the urging of his new wife, who played the guitar.

Now, if ever, would have been the time for Charles to reconcile himself to his advancing age and physical limitations, and relax into domesticity. Had he been able to face the truth about his life—that despite his early promise, his charisma, his semi-miraculous endurance and leadership abilities, he was destined never to attain the virtually unattainable British throne—he might have spent his last decades in relative contentment. He might have written his memoirs, or become a musical or artistic dilettante (he had shown a talent for drawing in his youth), or devoted himself to raising a new generation of Stuart Pretenders. He might, in short, have made peace with his fate.

Instead, after a year or so of sobriety and uneventful living, his self-destructive side broke out with a vengeance.

He drank, steadily and heavily, morning and night. "No street-porter could equal him" in his Gargantuan thirst, one of his servants remarked. He drank "like one absent in mind," compulsively, in response to an inner darkness that drew him toward its own black void. Any slight, any vexing irritation, sent him reeling off to drink still more, until he was so drunk that he vomited on himself, on the brocaded and velvet-covered furnishings of the Muti Palace, on the upholstered chairs of his theater box. He drank until he could not control his bowels, and had to have his longsuffering servants clean up after him, both at home and in public.

When not helpless with drink, he raged, lashing out at his servants with a stick, shouting incoherently, his bloodshot eyes bulging, spitting out curses and obscenities in all directions and staggering painfully on his thick legs until he fell and had to be helped to his feet, still snarling menacingly. He lashed out at Louise as well, ranting on at her, accusing her of betraying him, of conspiring against him, of cuckolding him. She was a young and pretty woman, the household was full of men; in the second year of their marriage, Charles heard secretly from a paid informer that Louise had professed her love for one of his lackeys.[4]

Louise, not yet twenty-one and finding herself yoked to a drunken wild man, was intensely frustrated and unhappy. She was much too young and much too full of life and hope for the future to take any pleasure in the company of the elderly Jacobites who drifted in and out of the palace, and yet she was cut off from the vital younger society of the city because Charles refused to enter any Roman drawing room where he was not received as King Charles III. When she went out, it was to accompany her inebriated husband to the theater, where she sat beside him in his box and observed from a distance the people she could not meet face to face.

Things got worse when Charles decided that they should leave Rome and settle permanently in Florence, where, he imagined, he would be accorded at least a measure of royal dignity. Once there, however, the grand duke pointedly denied him the honor of having a royal canopy added to his theater box, and he and his duchess snubbed the Count and Countess of Albany when they found themselves at the same parties. Still, Charles and Louise had some companionship at last. Members of the ducal court and even foreign ministers came to visit the newcomers in their rented sixteenth-century palazzo, and Louise liked to entertain visitors of her own, particularly artists and writers.

But Charles inevitably bored guests with his endless reminiscences or was rude to them after taking offense at imagined insults. One evening at the opera, he insulted a stranger, a French military officer; when the indignant man protested that Charles did not even know who he was, the latter answered, "I know you are French—and that is enough!" At the casino, his loud remarks often caused disturbances. He told everyone who would listen that he was only planning to stay in Florence until his brother was elected pope. Then he would return to Rome in triumph. Nor was he embarrassed when Henry lost the current papal election and Cardinal Braschi won, taking the title Pope Pius VI. Charles's response to this was to draw up a protest which he hoped to persuade the Catholic bishops of England and Ireland to sign, saying that unless Pope Pius acknowledged Charles Stuart as Charles III, they would not acknowledge his title or authority.[5]

Charles's wild talk was accompanied by equally unrestrained behavior. Although by the mid-1770s he was a hopeless valetudinarian, suffering from severe varicose ulcers, violent stomach pains, and a racking cough, nevertheless he drove his febrile body mercilessly. When he could not go out walking, he went out in his carriage, with his increasingly embittered wife beside him, telling his coachman to go very slowly and to drive up and down the same streets again and again. His appetite was gone, and even the sight of food made him ill, yet he continued to preside at table every day and to entertain guests in pseudo-regal fashion. Every night he had himself driven to the theater, even when his legs and thighs were so grotesquely swollen and so painful that he could not walk at all; grimacing with pain, he had himself carried into his box, where he lay on a couch and slept through the performance, except when his severe indigestion wakened him and he was "obliged to retire in a hurry into the public passage, where two of his servants attended to give him assistance."[6]

It was as if, by clinging to a regimen of ceaseless activity, he could cling to life itself, and even prolong it. He dared not give in to bedridden immobility, for to give in would be to become a permanent invalid. There was a hideous courage in this bizarre behavior, it bespoke an unconquerable will. Just as Charles had never given up his determination to continue seeking his grandfather's throne by every means in his power, so now he directed that determination to staying active, even if it meant terrible pain for him and provoked loathing or, at best, ridicule in others.

It had long since begun to provoke rebellion in Louise. She saw nothing courageous in her husband's freakish spasms of activity, as when, at a masked ball, he attempted to dance a drunken minuet with a young girl, jerking clumsily along like a marionette, held up by Count Spada while the other guests crowded around to laugh at him.[7] Nor could Louise see anything but foolishness in Charles's self-delusion about his longevity. Though he was several times at death's door, his physicians having given up on him, convinced that he could not last long, still he insisted on taking out a lease on an expensive new residence—the grand and imposing Palazzo Guadagni, with its heavily ornamented interior and vast gardens. She knew that, when her husband died, there would be no money to pay for such a costly palace, as he had not made a will leaving her any security and she had no adequate income of her own.

Louise was rebellious, and she found an outlet for her rebellion in infidelity.

She flirted with a handsome young Englishman, Thomas Coke, who was on a tour of Italy, and encouraged him to fall in love with her. ("The young Mr. Coke is returned from his travels in love with the Pretender's Queen, who has permitted him to have her picture," Horace Walpole noted wickedly in a letter to a friend.)[8] She lost her head over an energetic Swiss, Karl Victor von Bonstetten, who was touring Europe visiting famous men and came to see Charles. Bonstetten was charmed by Louise, who, he said, "turned all heads" with her gamine looks and alert, piquant expression. He was less enraptured with her husband, who did not compare favorably with other celebrities he had visited, droning on about his past glories and repeating himself in an irritating way. When Bonstetten returned to Switzerland Louise wrote to him, telling him how he had "captured her heart, soul and spirit" and how she longed to go away with him to some hidden corner of the globe where they could be free to "follow their whim."

Bonstetten was hardly gone before Louise found another object for her awakening ardor. He was Count Vittorio Alfieri, a tall, wraithlike, red-haired poet with sharp features and a brooding expression. Alfieri came from his native Piedmont to Florence to improve his command of Italian and there he found, as he wrote later, the "beautiful, amiable and very distinguished" Louise. He was immediately attracted to her, drawn by the "outstanding beauty" of her pale complexion, fair hair and dark eyes with their "subdued fire." She was only twenty-five when he met her, yet already she had developed a love of painting and poetry, an affinity with works of art. Beyond this, she had "a golden nature."

For Louise, the passionate Alfieri became the sole ray of light in an increasingly dim world. He was everything her sodden, repugnant husband was not; he lived for his art, he believed in radical ideas, he embodied self-fulfillment. That he was reckless and temperamental only heightened his appeal. Alfieri was, in fact, a full-blown pre-Romantic given to monstrous narcissism and unwarranted self-aggrandizement, but to Louise, trapped in her splendid palace with her wreck of a husband, he seemed a demigod. They became lovers, and prayed that Charles would die.

But he clung stubbornly to life—and to Louise, seldom letting her out of his sight, reviling her to her face and to others behind her back. He accused her of taking a bribe from the Hanoverian government in return for administering a potion to make him impotent. He accused her of infidelity, and rigged up an ingenious if crude alarm system at her bedroom doors, involving tables and chairs and little bells, to give warning if an intruder tried to visit her at night. Worst of all, he made her sleep next to him, though the weeping sores on his legs gave off a terrible stench and fouled the bedclothes, and though his drunken gropings humiliated her cruelly and turned her stomach.

One night in December of 1780, things came to a head. Charles was even more "heated with wine and stronger liquors" than usual, for he had been celebrating St. Andrew's Day with debauched abandon. His servants were worried, as he had recently been more "indecent and cruel" to Louise than usual. On this night he "ill treated her in the most outrageous manner, by the most abusive language and beating her, and at night by committing the greatest indecencies upon her, in bed, and attempting to choke her." Her screams woke the household and the servants rushed in to save their mistress.[9]

Horace Mann, who learned of this incident from his informers among the servants at the Guadagni Palace, privately thought that Louise then and there made up her mind to leave Charles as soon as she could find a way to do so safely. She knew that she would need a powerful protector, and Alfieri, much as she loved him, was only a dispossessed nobleman. (In a burst of republican fervor he had surrendered his patrimony.) He would not do. Louise first appealed to Henry, who was sympathetic but did not offer her any practical help. The Duke and Duchess of Tuscany were much more forthcoming. With their assistance Louise found a refuge: the Convent of the Bianchette, not far from the Guadagni. There, behind the stone walls and locked gates, Louise would be safe from her husband's violent revenge.

A few days after the nightmarish attack on the feast of St. Andrew, Louise and a companion, Signora Orlandini, managed to persuade the ever-suspicious Charles to take them out riding in his coach. With them went the Signora's Irish lover, one Captain Gehegan, as a sort of bodyguard; Louise was afraid that Charles, who always carried loaded pistols with him, might attack her once he realized she was determined to escape.

Louise asked if she and Signora Orlandini might visit the Convent of the Bianchette to see the nuns' embroidery. Charles did not object. But when the two women rushed into the sanctuary and he tried to follow them, hobbling painfully as usual, he found that he was too late. The iron gates were shut to him, and he was informed by an official of the place that Louise, Countess of Albany, had "placed herself under the protection of the Great Duke, and that being in danger of her life, had resolutely determined never to cohabit with him any more."[10]

Charles's fury was monumental. He threatened to shoot Gehegan, or to pay someone else to shoot him. He threatened revenge against the vile seducer Alfieri, though he had never before objected to the poet's near-constant presence in his house. He sent a formal protest to the grand duke. He slandered Louise more viciously than ever. And then, having done all he could (which was very little) to punish

CAROLLY ERICKSON

those who had conspired against him, he took revenge on the nearest inanimate objects, smashing chairs and tables while the servants cowered and waited for his rage to spend itself.

Several weeks later Louise was on her way to Rome, where she had been offered lodgings at the Ursuline convent, in the very suite where, fifty-five years earlier, James's wife Clementina had taken refuge from her far less dangerous husband. Alfieri quietly followed Louise, and soon ingratiated himself with the Romans. Charles stood alone. No one took his side or came to his aid, even though Louise's indiscretions, however justifiable, made her an adulteress and entitled him to feel aggrieved. His anger gradually cooled to indignation, and then turned to a perpetual caustic melancholy.

Yet another defeat, yet another humiliation. Calling for yet another bottle, he announced that he had had enough of Florence, and intended to go to Venice for the Carnival. Or possibly Genoa. He would go somewhere, but precisely where no one could say. "He seems too much confused as yet," Mann's informers at the palace confided, "to take any fixed resolution."

25

"I am so bothered in the head," Charles wrote toward the end of his life. At times his wits were fuddled, even though he no longer drank immoderately and many of the strains that had long plagued him were now eased. He suffered from an old man's forgetfulness and could no longer focus his thoughts. At the same time memories, many of them painful, surged unbidden into his mind and made him sad. His eyes were often mournful, though they lit with satisfaction when they rested on his tall, strapping daughter Charlotte, who had become his guardian and lifeline in his old age.

Charlotte was kind to him. She nursed him, she accompanied him to the theater at night, bedecked with the magnificent Sobieski jewels, she made certain he did not exceed his allotted ration of Cyprus wine. Now in her thirties, Charlotte looked strikingly like her father had in his youth, "a tall, robust woman of a very dark complexion and a coarse-grained skin," as one who saw her wrote, "with more of a masculine boldness than feminine modesty or elegance, but easy and unassuming in her manners." Besides being husky and bold, she had a "voluble tongue," and firmness of will, which helped her to keep her ailing father in line.

Charles had made overtures to his daughter three years after Louise of Stolberg left him, legitimizing her and making her his heir. She was then living in Paris as "Lady Charlotte Stuart," unmarried and, apparently, well disposed toward the father she had not seen since the age of six. He wrote to her, calling her his "dear daughter" and telling her that everything he had would be hers when he died. In 1784 he sent his most trusted servant John Stuart to Paris to convey his sentiments in person and to escort Her Royal Highness Charlotte, Duchess of Albany, to Italy. Since then she had been his companion, his hostess, his sole family. She stood by him while he worked out his money problems (he complained of being "overcharged with debt"), she helped him arrive at a reconciliation with his brother, from whom he had been alienated. She could not cure him of the varicose ulcers, stomach complaints and dropsy that wore down his aging body, but her presence put new heart and life into him, and was a tonic in itself.[1]

Before Charlotte came to join him, Charles had been lonely, isolated in the aftermath of his separation from Louise, an object of scorn and ridicule. He had turned from public entertainments to private ones, inviting the musician Domenico Corri to his palace and sitting with Corri, night after night, in a candlelit room playing duets. Corri sat at the harpsichord, while Charles alternated between the cello, French horn, a wooden wind instrument called the flageolet and the bagpipes. Old Scottish melodies were his favorites; when he played "Lochaber no More," he wept inconsolably.

But with Charlotte beside him, Charles once more went out in public, proud to display his daughter, giving balls in her honor and pleased that the Florentine notables once again left their calling cards at the Guadagni Palace. On St. Andrew's Day, 1784, Charles honored his daughter at a banquet. He presented her with the green ribbon of the Order of the Thistle, drawing her officially into the Jacobite circle. The contrast between that evening and the sordid St. Andrew's Day of four years earlier could not have been more pronounced. Then Charles had unleashed his darkest side; now he was a benign patriarch, his melancholy lightened by the vicarious pleasure he took in his daughter and what she represented.

Charlotte worked hard to protect her father from his most poignant memories. One evening Charles was visited by an Englishman called Greathead, who wanted to hear from the old man's own lips what it had been like to live through the excitement of the Forty-Five. Charles, it seems, obliged his guest, retelling his stories of the victories and defeats of the Highland army and of his own adventures in hiding. But when he came to speak of the ghastly executions that followed his defeat, and of the sufferings of the Highlanders, he lost his animation entirely and fell to the floor in a fit. Charlotte rushed in horrified.

"Oh sir," she cried out, "what is this? You must have been speaking to my father about Scotland and the Highlanders! No one dares to mention those subjects in his presence."

Charlotte generally tried to keep Charles from talking too much, as it made him too excited and later exhausted. But she could not prevent one further exchange with the same Mr. Greathead. At a public gathering he imperiously called the Englishman to his side and said loudly, though in a voice which broke, "I will speak to my own subjects in my own way, Sir." He imitated Greathead's less than cultivated English pronunciation. "And I will soon speak to you, Sir, in Westminster Hall."[2] Such outbursts were pathetic, yet at times Charles was still capable of displaying the dignity and finesse of one born to royalty. One night at the opera house a young English officer waited to get a close look at the Pretender as he emerged from his box. Charles noticed the young man, paused, and did his best to stand alone, waving his attendants aside. Then he slowly and ceremoniously removed his cocked hat and saluted the Englishman before continuing unsteadily toward his carriage.

In December of 1785 Charlotte and Henry persuaded Charles to return to Rome, though his Florentine physicians advised against it. He had trouble breathing, all his limbs were swollen and painful, and he was plagued with recurrent nausea. He had already survived longer than anyone believed possible, long enough to become a legendary figure in Scotland, where songs were sung about his exploits which would outlast his unsavory reputation in Italy. In the popular mind he had come full circle, from youthful hero to aging debauchee to deathless, eternally youthful hero once again.

Charles had outlived most of those who fought with and for him, and many of those who had once mattered to him were also dead. One who was not was Clementina Walkinshaw. A year before he died Charles wrote Clementina a letter, signing it shakily "Charles R." "Be assured," he told her, "that I am and shall be your good friend."[3] There was no way he could reconcile himself with Louise de Rohan-Guéméné, who had been dead for six years, nor was he inclined to offer forgiveness to Louise of Stolberg, who was living happily with Alfieri and would continue to share his life for many years.

As for the thrones of England and France, the one his nemesis and the other his perpetual traducer, it was hard for him to find the energy to hate their present occupants, George III and Louis XVI. King Louis had recently settled a yearly pension of sixty thousand crowns on Charles, which enabled him to live in great comfort and luxury, and King George, who had much kindliness beneath his gruff exterior, felt sorry for Charles and privately wished there was something he could do to ease the elderly Pretender's last years.

Though more feeble than ever, once he was settled into the Muti Palace in Rome Charles would not go to bed and wait to die. He had himself driven to Albano in the warm season, where he took the waters and where peasants, many of them older and sicker than he was, came to him to plead for his healing royal touch. Charlotte never left him, and Henry too was attentive. At the head of his household staff was John Stuart, the Atholl man, whose young son was Charles's namesake. Stuart hovered near him, as the months passed and the last of his master's strength ebbed.

Charles's sixty-seventh birthday came, and not long after it he had a stroke. One side of his body was paralyzed, and he could not speak. He lingered for several days, semiconscious, Charlotte and John Stuart at his bedside. Then either on the night of January 30 or the morning of January 31 he died, surrounded by those who loved him best.

There was gossip in Rome that the official announcement of the time of death was a fabrication. Because January 30 was the anniversary of the execution of Charles II, it was thought to be an ill omen that Charles III had also died on that date, so the servants put abroad the fiction that he had not died until the following morning. The Stuart stigma that had dogged Charles throughout his life beclouded his death as well.

His obsequies, however, were as grand and regal as his brother could make them. In the Muti Palace, six altars were erected in the antechamber where two hundred masses were said for Charles's soul. (He had been persuaded to return to the Catholic fold before his death.) The Irish Franciscans of St. Isidoro chanted the office of the dead. A cast was taken of his face, and his body was embalmed, dressed royally and with a carved wooden crown and scepter placed under the coffin lid. "Charles III, King of Great Britain" read the leaden inscription.

Because the pope forbade a royal funeral within the walls of Rome, Henry ordered his brother's remains removed to Frascati, where the interior of the cathedral was draped in black cloth with gilded trim. More than a hundred large tapers burned around the high catafalque, and scores of black-clad mourners, many of them English, filed in to hear the cardinal perform the funeral mass.

In his will Charles left all his earthly possessions to his daughter, but Charlotte died less than two years after her father, the victim of what may have been liver cancer. In any case, it was Henry who was heir to the Stuart claims and cause. He lived on for another two decades, preserving the outward symbols of monarchy but never pressing its political claims. He called himself "Henry IX, King of Great Britain, France, and Ireland, Defender of the Faith," and dressed his footmen in liveries of the English royal house. But though Henry gave formal acknowledgment to Charles-Emanuel IV, King of Sardinia, as his heir (the king was the great-grandson of Henrietta, Duchess of Orléans, sister of Charles II, and as such the next Stuart claimant), events in Europe soon swept monarchy and many of its representatives from the stage.

Soon after the outbreak of the French Revolution, the majority of Henry's benefices and revenues were confiscated, and not long afterward he was forced to sell the Sobieski jewels to raise money to help pay the huge fine Napoleon levied on Pope Pius VI. Early in 1798, when the French occupied Rome, Henry fled to Naples, then was taken in a British warship to Messina. With other displaced ecclesiastics he ultimately made his way to Venice, where a defiant conclave-in-exile elected Pius VII pope. An old man in his seventies, dependent on charity for his sustenance, Henry was in every sense a relic of the past. George III, now aging himself and beleaguered by war, intermittent ill health and a bevy of disappointing children, took pity on the last Stuart Pretender and gave him a life pension of four thousand pounds.

NOTES

CHAPTER 1

1. Christopher Sinclair-Stevenson, *Inglorious Rebellion: The Jacobite Risings of 1708, 1715 and 1719* (London, 1971), p. 53.

2. W. A. Speck, *Stability and Strife: England 1714–1760* (Cambridge, Mass., 1977), pp. 173–74.

3. Charles Petrie, *The Jacobite Movement: The First Phase 1688–1716* (London, 1948), p. 154.

4. *Ibid.*, 177–78.

5. Mar's circular letter is printed in Robert Patten, *The History of the Late Rebellion* (London, 1717), pp. 221–22.

6. Quoted in Sinclair-Stevenson, p. 126.

7. Patten, p. 245.

8. Mar's *Journal,* cited in Patten, p. 242.

9. Patten, pp. 229–30.

NOTES

CHAPTER 2

1. Marchesa Nobili-Vitelleschi [Amy Cochrane-Baillie], *A Court in Exile: Charles Edward Stuart and the Romance of the Countess d'Albanie* (London, 1903), I, 102.

2. *Ibid.*, 104, citing the *Cracas,* or Roman newsletter, for May 16, 1719.

3. Alistair and Henrietta Tayler, eds., *The Stuart Papers at Windsor* (London, 1939), pp. 63–64.

4. Nobili-Vitelleschi, I, 115–16, citing the Roman *Cracas* of January 4, 1721.

5. These are the names that appear on Charles's baptismal certificate; the Roman *Cracas* adds the name "Severino."

CHAPTER 3

1. Blandford's letter is in Alexander Charles Ewald, *The Life and Times of Prince Charles Stuart* (London, 1883), pp. 6–10.

2. Quoted in Clennell Wilkinson, *Bonnie Prince Charlie* (Philadelphia, 1932), p. 34.

3. Ewald, p. 17.

CHAPTER 4

1. A. J. Youngson, *The Prince and the Pretender* (London, 1985), p. 174, citing a letter of James, January 10, 1742.

2. *Stuart Papers,* p. 84.

3. *Ibid.*, 85.

4. *Ibid.*, 85–86.

5. Youngson, p. 174.

6. *Stuart Papers,* p. 89.

7. Murray's long account of events at Gaeta is in *Stuart Papers,* pp. 90–97.

8. Ewald, pp. 28–29.

9. *Stuart Papers,* p. 95.

10. Ewald, p. 29.

11. *Ibid.*, 30.

NOTES

12. *Stuart Papers,* p. 97.
13. *Ibid.,* 98.
14. *Ibid.*
15. *Ibid.,* 86.
16. Ewald, p. 32.

CHAPTER 5

1. Youngson, p. 175.
2. *Stuart Papers,* p. 104.
3. *Ibid.,* 125.
4. Ewald, pp. 44–45.
5. *Stuart Papers,* pp. 106–9.
6. In fairness to Henry it must be noted that Murray's description of him is unlike any other, and that other observers thought him to be "lively," "virtuous," "exceedingly good natured and well bred," and able to converse well with "a keen interest in English affairs." Ewald, pp. 45–46.
7. Ewald, pp. 43–44.
8. Cited in Youngson, p. 183.

CHAPTER 6

1. William Cobbett, *The Parliamentary History of England* (London, 1806–20), X, 402–3.
2. *Ibid.,* 400–1.
3. Cited in Paul S. Fritz, *The English Ministers and Jacobitism between the Rebellions of 1715 and 1745* (Toronto and Buffalo, 1975), p. 105.
4. *Ibid.,* 111.
5. Lesley Lewis, *Connoisseurs and Secret Agents in Eighteenth Century Rome* (London, 1961), p. 90.
6. Lady Mary Wortley Montagu, "Account of the Court of George I," in *Letters and Works,* ed. Lord Wharncliffe (London, 1837), I, 107–8.
7. John Hervey, *Some Materials Towards Memoirs of the Reign of King George II,* ed. R. Sedgwick (London, 1931), II, 485–88.
8. *Ibid.*

NOTES

CHAPTER 7

1. Lewis, p. 24.
2. Ewald, p. 52.
3. Andrew Lang, *Prince Charles Edward Stuart* (London, 1903), p. 63.
4. F. J. McLynn, *France and the Jacobite Rising of 1745* (Edinburgh, 1981), is the best background work on French policy and the French involvement with the Jacobites in the 1740s.
5. Cited in Lang, p. 71.
6. Cited in Lang, p. 70.
7. *Stuart Papers,* pp. 113–14.
8. *Ibid.,* 112.
9. *Ibid.,* 116.
10. Cited in Lang, p. 78.

CHAPTER 8

1. Cited in Ewald, p. 59.
2. Cited in David Daiches, *Charles Edward Stuart: The Life and Times of Bonnie Prince Charlie* (London, 1973), p. 100.
3. W. Drummond Norie, *Life and Adventures of Prince Charles Edward Stuart* (London, 1903), I, 106.
4. The memorandum is in *Stuart Papers,* pp. 122–23.
5. Drummond Norie, I, 122.
6. Lang, p. 82.
7. *Stuart Papers,* pp. 118–19.
8. John S. Gibson, *Ships of the '45: The Rescue of the Young Pretender* (London, 1967), p. 11.
9. McLynn, *France and the Jacobite Rising,* p. 32, states that the *Elisabeth* had "about a hundred marines" aboard; other authorities say that there were from five hundred to seven hundred fighting men. Charles gave a figure of seven hundred (*Stuart Papers,* p. 132). In the subsequent battle with the H.M.S. *Lyon,* the *Elisabeth* lost 57 men killed and 176 wounded—numbers which argue for a fighting complement of many hundreds of men.
10. *Stuart Papers,* p. 120.
11. Charles's letter is in Ewald, pp. 61–63.
12. *Stuart Papers,* pp. 126–27.
13. Drummond Norie, I, 128.

NOTES

CHAPTER 9

1. *Stuart Papers,* p. 137.
2. *Ibid.,* 135.
3. *Ibid.,* 139.
4. There were in all, Youngson, p. 191, reckons, seven hundred Camerons and six hundred others for a total of thirteen hundred.
5. Details of Cope's march northward are in Katherine Tomasson and F. Buist, *Battles of the '45* (London, 1967), pp. 30ff.
6. Cited in Ewald, p. 101.

CHAPTER 10

1. Cited in Henry Grey Graham, *The Social Life of Scotland in the Eighteenth Century,* 3rd ed. (London, 1909), p. 3.
2. Martin Martin, *Description of the Western Islands of Scotland,* in John Pinkerton, ed., *A General Collection of the Best and Most Interesting Voyages and Travels in All Parts of the World* III (London, 1809), 572–699.
3. Martin, p. 575.
4. Cited in Graham, p. 178.
5. The myth of the romantic Highlands is exploded in Hugh Trevor-Roper, "The Invention of Tradition: The Highland Tradition of Scotland," in *The Invention of Tradition,* ed. Eric Hobsbawm and Terence Ranger (Cambridge University Press, 1983), 15–41. Trevor-Roper's merciless and sardonic demythologizing reveals the modernity of the Scottish "national apparatus" of kilt, clan and bagpipe and shows how "the whole concept of a distinctive Highland culture and tradition is a retrospective invention." Western Scotland was, culturally, "the overflow of Ireland," he points out, and it was only in the aftermath of the Jacobite rising, when the Highlanders "combined the romance of a primitive people with the charm of an endangered species," that new Highland traditions were artificially created and presented as old and original. This is a tonic reminder that the Romantics were indeed responsible for a gross historical distortion, but Trevor-Roper goes too far in implying that the "inventors" of Highland tradition built on no foundation more substantial than their own imaginations.
6. John Home, *History of the Rebellion* (London, 1802), pp. 3–13.
7. *Ibid.,* 3–12.
8. *Ibid.*

NOTES

CHAPTER 11

1. According to one estimate, there were twenty-five to thirty-five thousand men fit to bear arms in the Highlands in 1745; Charles never had more than twelve thousand men, and not all of those were Highlanders. David Smurthwaite, *Battlefields of Britain* (New York, 1984), p. 181. In the far north, the Mackays, Munros and Sutherlands were Hanoverian, as were, of course, the Argyll Campbells. The Macdonalds, Macphersons, and most Macleods and Grants stayed out of the conflict. Others were divided in their loyalties.

2. *The Autobiography of Alexander Carlyle of Inveresk,* cited in Daiches, p. 130.

3. Cited in Lang, p. 150.

4. Later, at his trial, Cope testified that "the rebels were about fifty-five hundred in the field." Lang, pp. 152–53.

5. Charles was quoted in the *Caledonian Mercury,* cited in Lang, p. 155.

6. Youngson, p. 93.

7. Chevalier de Johnstone [James Johnstone], *A Memoir of the Forty-Five,* ed. Brian Rawson (London, 1958), p. 34.

8. This account of the battle of Prestonpans is taken in large part from Johnstone, pp. 34ff.

9. Cited in Daiches, p. 139.

CHAPTER 12

1. Newcastle wrote to Argyll on August 14 that he had never been so fearful that the French, having conquered all of Flanders, would embark from Ostend or Dunkirk intent on invading Britain. State Papers, Scotland, August 14, 1745.

2. Cited in Tomasson and Buist, p. 79.

3. *The Letters of Horace Walpole, Fourth Earl of Orford,* ed. Peter Cunningham (Edinburgh, 1906), I, 386–87, 389, 392.

4. W. Coxe, *Memoirs of the Administration of . . . Henry Pelham* (London, 1829), I, 21.

5. *Walpole Letters,* I, 381.

6. Tomasson and Buist, p. 79.

7. *Walpole Letters,* I, 389–90 note. Holland added that "had five thousand landed in any part of this island a week ago, I verily believe the entire conquest would not have cost them a battle."

8. Cited in Lang, p. 167.

9. *Ibid.*, 181–82.

10. *Stuart Papers,* p. 161.

11. *Ibid.*, 162.

12. McLynn, *France and the Jacobite Rising,* pp. 86–87.

CHAPTER 13

1. It is difficult to estimate in how many cases coercion was used to enlarge the army of Charles Stuart. Naturally enough, the Jacobites in 1745 and afterward claimed that it was rare, and the Hanoverian partisans were inclined to exaggerate its frequency. Bruce Lenman, *The Jacobite Risings in Britain, 1689–1746* (London, 1980), pp. 257–58, is convinced that the incidence of coercion is far greater than most historians have realized. The rank and file of the Stuart army contained, he writes, "a very high percentage" of men who had been forced out. The legal evidence accumulated after the end of the rebellion is "overwhelming in this respect," even after allowances are made for the fact that those testifying were eager to exonerate themselves in the eyes of the British.

Lenman bases his conclusion in part on the correspondence of Lord Lewis Gordon, Lord Lieutenant of Aberdeenshire and Banffshire in late 1745 and 1746. These letters, Lenman writes, "show quite clearly that the normal Jacobite technique for beating up recruits in the later stages of the rebellion was to threaten local landlords that their estates would be ravaged with fire and sword if they did not produce a set quota of men." The same techniques were used, according to Lenman, to force people to provide food for the army and to collect local taxes which were used to finance the rebellion.

2. Lenman, *Jacobite Risings,* p. 257.

3. Johnstone, p. 49.

4. Ewald, pp. 156–57.

5. Henry Fielding, *True Patriot,* November 19, 1745, cited in Rupert C. Jarvis, *Collected Papers on the Jacobite Risings* (Manchester, 1971–72), II, 28, 121 and *passim.*

6. *Ibid.*, II, 29; Lang, p. 186; F. J. McLynn, *The Jacobite Army in England: 1745, The Final Campaign* (Edinburgh, 1983), p. 49. The provincial newspapers used language that was sometimes genteel and sometimes coarse, referring to the rebels as, in one case, "nothing but a ragged crew of miscreants who commit every outrage without regard to life and

decency," and in another, as "those shabby, scabby, scratchy, lowly, shitten Rebels."

7. *Chester Courant,* December 18, 1745, cited in Jarvis, II, 24.

8. R. C. Jarvis, *Collected Papers on the Jacobite Risings* supplies much detailed information on the local reactions to the rising of 1745 and measures taken to counteract it.

9. A. A. Mitchell, "London and the Forty-Five," *History Today* XV (November 1965), p. 722. A report drawn up on September 11, 1745 noted that "most of the public houses near St. James, Charing Cross, Whitehall and the hither end of Kings Street and Downing Street Westminster are not under the inspection of the justices for the liberty of Westminster, but solely under the clerks of the green, who never give themselves any trouble to do their duty, but leave it entirely to those known villains the 'Marshal Men' who get money by protecting these men, *viz.* Irishmen of all kinds, and the houses they use do every night swarm with multitudes of them to what intent anyone may easily imagine."

10. Fritz, p. 136. The Bishop of London observed with alarm in the fall of 1745 that "many poor Irish are making their way to London . . . London and Westminster are fuller of Irish papists than ever." However, within the City itself, municipal returns indicate a population of fewer than five hundred recusants. Mitchell, pp. 721–22.

11. Mitchell, p. 722; *Walpole Letters,* I, 398; Nicholas Rogers, "Popular Disaffection in London During the Forty-Five," *The London Journal* I, 1 (May 1975), 5–27.

12. Rogers summarizes the events of fall 1745 in London and concludes that there was a strong undercurrent of anti-Hanoverian sentiment but that it was chiefly confined to Catholics, and in particular to the Irish. However, the City was staunchly Tory, and as the City aldermen were responsible for law and order within the capital, London's loyalty could not have been relied on had the army of Charles Stuart reached it.

CHAPTER 14

1. The foregoing summarizes O'Sullivan's judgment of Charles, and is understandably biased, though not as extravagant in its bias as the reverential comments of Lord Balmerino, who in his scaffold speech praised Charles for "the incomparable sweetness of his nature, his affability, his compassion, his justice, his temperance and his courage." "He wants no qualifications," Balmerino said, "requisite to make a great man."

NOTES

2. Although Lord George had at one time taken an oath of allegiance to George II, his loyalty to the Stuart cause was beyond dispute. As he wrote to his brother Tullibardine in September of 1745, "My life, my fortune, my expectations, the happiness of my wife and children, are all at stake (and the chances are against me), and yet a principle of (what seems to me) honor, and my duty to King and country, outweighs everything." Cited in Daiches, pp. 122–23.

3. Lang, p. 164.

4. *Ibid.*

5. McLynn, *Jacobite Army,* p. 77.

6. *Ibid.,* 80. McLynn concludes that it was "doubtful, though not impossible" that Charles had such letters.

7. Jarvis, I, 251. Charles was sending out "recruiting letters" at this time, telling prospective recruits that, given his successes in Scotland, and the longstanding promises of support offered by the English, he now presented them with an opportunity to "shake off a foreign yoke" and join his army. "I am persuaded you will not baulk my expectations," he wrote, "and you need not doubt but I shall always remember to your advantage the example you shall thus have put to your neighbors, and consequently to all England." Lang, p. 166.

8. The Jacobite army benefited from the capture of Carlisle in capturing with it 1,500 arms of various types, 160 barrels of powder, 500 grenades and about 120 good horses. *The Orderly Book of Lord Ogilvy's Regiment in the Army of Prince Charles Edward Stuart, Journal of the Society of Army Historical Research,* II (December 1923), 16–17, notes 1 and 2.

9. *Orderly Book of Lord Ogilvy's Regiment,* p. 15 note 1.

10. Lord Ogilvy's regiment book refers often to "women and children," though it also records "orders against all women but soldiers' wives," and notes that officers were told to "absolutely forbid to suffer any woman to follow" the men. *Orderly Book of Lord Ogilvy's Regiment,* pp. 17, 27. Jarvis, I, 273, counts eighteen women who "took a more or less prominent part in the rising," and fifty-six "regimental women" whose names appear in various sources. After the rebellion, some of the women, with their infants, accompanied their men into exile or overseas to the plantations, where it was their fate to die of disease or live out their lives in semislavery.

11. Daiches, p. 176.

12. Lists of prisoners tried after the rebellion reveal many young boys among those tried for treason: Thomas Warrington, a "boy of fourteen or fifteen," John Forrest of Elgin, "not fifteen yet," many unnamed boys

listed as "under fifteen" or "not yet fifteen years old." Prisoners held at Chester included a boy of fifteen, three boys of fourteen, one of thirteen and two of eleven, plus two children aged six and eight, and Clementine Macdonald, aged twelve, and Margaret Douglas, aged three. Jarvis, II, 297ff.

13. Lang, p. 177.

14. *Ibid.*, 220–21, citing "Letter from a Gentleman at Derby," in Marchant's 1746 *History of the Present Rebellion.*

15. Lang, p. 167.

16. Mitchell, p. 720.

CHAPTER 15

1. W. S. Speck, *The Butcher: The Duke of Cumberland and the Suppression of the '45* (London, 1981), pp. 4–5 and *passim.* Horace Walpole noted that "for bravery, His Royal Highness [Cumberland] is certainly no Stuart, but literally loves to be in the act of fighting." According to Walpole, the men in Cumberland's command went north to meet the rebels "in the greatest spirits" because of their attachment to their commander and their confidence in him. *Walpole Letters,* I, 107.

2. Lang, pp. 167–68.

3. McLynn, *Jacobite Army,* p. 122.

4. Speck, p. 90. King George did not, as the Chevalier de Johnstone wrote in his memoirs, prepare the royal yacht and resign himself to abandoning his kingdom if the rebels reached London.

5. *Walpole Letters,* I, 407.

6. *Ibid.,* I, 408–9.

7. Eveline Cruickshanks, *Political Untouchables: The Tories and the '45* (London, 1979), pp. 90–91.

8. Cited in Cruickshanks, pp. 92–93.

9. Johnstone, p. 58.

10. *Ibid.,* 61.

CHAPTER 16

1. In his *France and the Jacobite Rising* and elsewhere, F. J. McLynn demonstrates persuasively that the view of the French commonly met with in the secondary literature on the Jacobites is misguided. Far from being

devious or insincere in their avowed intentions to aid the Jacobites, the French ministers were merely deeply divided in opinion. In 1745–46, McLynn points out, French foreign-policy-making was fragmented and chaotic. Six ministers competed with one another in Louis XV's council of state, with no clear leader among them. Even to refer to "France" or "the French" implies a coherence of policy that simply did not exist. Instead, different *ad hoc* factions gained the upper hand in the council at different times.

2. McLynn, *France and the Jacobite Rising*, p. 136.

3. *Walpole Letters*, I, 409–10.

4. Cruickshanks, p. 101.

5. O'Sullivan's narrative, cited in Daiches, p. 176.

6. Ewald, pp. 193–94.

7. Very little is known about Clementina Walkinshaw. C. Leo Berry, "Portraits of Clementine Walkinshaw," *Notes and Queries* (November 1951), pp. 491–95, discusses the question of authentic portraiture of Clementina. Walter Scott's florid description of her in *Redgauntlet* as "tall, fair, and commanding in her aspect," with "locks of paley gold," "open, blue eyes" and a Junoesque figure "inclined to embonpoint" has no foundation in fact. Charles himself described her at the age of forty as "fair, of average height, freckled, with a thin face." That she was spirited is a reasonable inference, given her later history. Both her age and place of birth are uncertain, though the story that she and Charles knew one another as children in Rome is clearly legendary.

According to Berry, *The Young Pretender's Mistress* (Edinburgh and London, 1977), p. 21, Clementina spent her youth and early womanhood with her mother and sisters in or near Edinburgh, though in 1731, when her father died, she was "out of the kingdom," possibly being educated abroad.

Clementina's mother, Katharine Walkinshaw, was, according to her great-granddaughter who wrote of her in 1822, "a woman of superior abilities" with "a firm undaunted, I may say manly, character" whose boast it was that "she had never leaned back in a chair." She ruled her ten daughters with firmness, refusing to let any of them sit in her presence without her permission and regulating their lives energetically. Family tradition had it that when important relations came to call, Katharine permitted only the most attractive of her daughters to present themselves, locking the others in the garret until the visitors left. She lived to be at least ninety, and was still capable of dancing vigorously to country tunes into her tenth decade. (Berry, pp. 7–8.)

NOTES

Although Lord Elcho claimed in his memoirs that Clementina became Charles's mistress at Bannockburn House in January of 1746, there is no substantiation for this, and Elcho's animus against Charles makes his assertion suspect.

8. Johnstone, p. 87.

CHAPTER 17

1. "A True Account of Mr. John Daniel's Progress with Prince Charles," *Origins of the Forty-Five*, ed. Walter Biggar Blaikie, *Publications of the Scottish History Society*, Second Series, Vol. II (Edinburgh, 1916), 167–224. John Daniel wrote how he took pity on his poor horse, "of a delicate and tender breed," and, knowing that the horse could drink beer, tried him on whiskey. He poured the spirits into the crown of his hat, and dissolved some snow in it to dilute it. The horse drank it down, "his mouth," Daniel noted, "being so cold that he did not know what he drank."

2. Tomasson and Buist, p. 146. The following account of the battle of Culloden relies in part on Tomasson and Buist's narrative, pp. 145–204.

3. Quoted in Blaikie, ed., *Origins of the Forty-Five*, pp. lxix–lxx.

4. Daniel's narrative, in Blaikie, ed., *Origins of the Forty-Five*, pp. 213–14.

5. Tomasson and Buist, p. 145.

6. That this position was ill chosen had important consequences. The lie of the land was such that Charles could not see the results of Cumberland's cannonade. One of the men with him, John Macdonald, was convinced that the Hanoverian guns were doing little damage to the Jacobite line, and presumably Charles was led to the same conclusion. Consequently Charles did not realize how urgent it was to give the command to advance, and when he finally gave it, the losses were already grave and the situation irremediable. Tomasson and Buist, p. 170.

7. *Ibid.*, 170.

8. *Ibid.*, 175.

CHAPTER 18

1. The following account of Charles's wanderings in Scotland between April and September, 1746, comes in part from Robert Forbes, *The Lyon*

in Mourning, ed. Henry Paton, *Publications of the Scottish History Society,* Vols. XX–XXIII (Edinburgh, 1895), W. B. Blaikie, *Itinerary of Prince Charles Edward Stuart, Publications of the Scottish History Society,* Second Series, Vol. XXIII (Edinburgh, 1897), Eric Linklater, *The Prince in the Heather* (London, 1965), and "Account of the Young Pretender's Escape," *The Lockhart Papers* (London, 1817), II, 539–62.

2. Flora returned home to Scotland, where she settled down and had ten children. In 1774 she and her husband emigrated to America— surviving, on the journey, an attack by a French privateer that left Flora slightly wounded. Having settled in North Carolina, she and her husband were dismayed by the American revolutionaries and he fought for the British against the colonists. In 1779 they returned to Scotland.

3. John Prebble, *Culloden* (London, 1967), p. 194.

4. Linklater, p. 102.

5. George Hilton Jones, *The Main Stream of Jacobitism* (Cambridge, Mass., 1954), pp. 240–41. While it is true that the scale of the destruction was maximized by Jacobite writers and annalists, such as Bishop Forbes, even the most dispassionate late-twentieth-century scholars agree that massive damage was done accompanied by widespread suffering.

CHAPTER 19

1. Henry complained to O'Brien in a letter written from Boulogne in March 1746 that his health was bound to suffer if he stayed there any longer, housebound, bored, and increasingly convinced that his martyrdom was of no use to Charles's cause. "Our enemies know better than we ourselves that we can't do anything for England," he wrote, begging O'Brien to do all he could to get him released from "this vile hole" and at least moved inland, if not to Paris. "Who could bear to stay in a place like Boulogne, three months, with such worrisome news and events and on top of all else with such people as ours? I can't do it any more." *Stuart Papers,* pp. 166–67.

2. L. L. Bongie, *The Love of a Prince: Bonnie Prince Charlie in France, 1744–1748* (Vancouver, 1986), p. 144.

3. *Stuart Papers,* pp. 169ff.

4. Bongie, p. 143.

5. *Stuart Papers,* p. 187. The editors of the *Stuart Papers* omitted the offensive word.

6. *The Lockhart Papers* contain a Jacobite pamphlet describing in glowing terms Charles's arrival, reception and celebrity in France. Many of

Charles's biographers have relied on it as an authentic account of events, but in fact it is mostly wishful thinking. According to the pamphleteer, Henry met Charles immediately when he disembarked; Louis XV greeted him as a princely hero at Versailles, not Fontainebleau, and made him a lengthy speech of honor; the queen greeted him like a son and made him so welcome that he went back to the palace several times a week to regale her and her ladies with his adventures. There is even a hint that one of the princesses was infatuated with him. The pamphlet goes on to describe his formal reception at Versailles, arriving there accompanied by a train of coaches complete with pages, footmen and gentlemen of the bedchamber. For this, the pamphleteer noted, Charles wore a velvet coat embroidered with silver and a waistcoat of gold brocade, and his every ornament, from the cockade in his hat and the buckles on his shoes to the buttons on his waistcoat, was covered with diamonds. "He glittered all over like the star which they tell you appeared at his nativity." *Lockhart Papers,* II, 565–86.

7. Bongie, pp. 150, 152.

8. *Ibid.,* 151–52.

9. A contretemps between the government and the king had led all the ministers to resign en masse early in 1746, following which two of them had attempted in vain to form a new government. After a few days they gave up, defeated; wits referred to this brief hiatus as "the Long Administration." Had George II died in the early months of 1747, there would certainly have been a struggle for power between his ministers and the faction loyal to the Prince of Wales, who would have become King Frederick I. As it was, George survived, and in the elections of 1747 the Whigs tried to blacken their opponents by accusing them of Jacobitism. One Tory politician lamented that "the phantom of Jacobitism is made to appear in terrible shapes." Rogers, p. 5.

10. Bongie, p. 166.

CHAPTER 20

1. *Journal et mémoires du Marquis d'Argenson,* V, 303–4.

2. The love affair between Charles and Louise has been brought to light in L. L. Bongie, *The Love of a Prince: Bonnie Prince Charlie in France 1744–1748.* Bongie's research in the Stuart Archives unearthed a one-sided amorous correspondence which, he believes, points to a love affair between the Young Pretender and Louise de la Tour d'Au-

vergne, Duchesse de Montbazon and Princesse de Rohan. Bongie speculates that Charles's letters to Louise were destroyed, only hers to him remain. However, one is always skeptical of any one-sided correspondence, and as Bongie himself writes, "it is puzzling that not one word of this tragic romance seems to have seeped down through the gossipy annals of a century that generally loved to record such juicy incidents in intimate detail." (Bongie, p. 13.) It was also a century, be it noted, that loved to fabricate amorous correspondences. Still, his conjecture is plausible, if far from indisputable, and Charles's behavior with Louise fits the pattern of his later treatment of other women.

3. Apart from Clementina Walkinshaw, Charles had never shown much interest in women. Bongie suggests that he may have taken a vow of chastity, and that he abandoned it, possibly as a gesture of defiance toward his father, in 1747. On one occasion, Charles told James's agent O'Brien that, far from complaining about Henry's sexual purity, he approved of it, adding, "And I'll even confess to you that in some things, I think myself as virtuous as he." (Bongie, p. 150.) Balhaldie wrote to James in February 1748 that Charles's Irish companions "had at last succeeded in corrupting" him, and that he had lost his innocence the previous summer. This fall from grace was all the more tragic, according to Balhaldie, "because of the resolution he [Charles] had taken of being singular in that virtue." By the time Balhaldie wrote his letter, Bongie says, Charles's affair with Louise was well advanced.

4. Bongie, pp. 5–6.

5. *Ibid.*, 11.

6. *Ibid.*, 219–21.

7. *Journal et mémoires du Marquis d'Argenson*, V, 288.

8. According to Horace Walpole, not all the onlookers stood by passively. "It is said," he wrote to Horace Mann on December 15, "that a Mr. Dun, who married Alderman Parson's eldest daughter, is in the Bastille for having struck the officer when the young man [Charles] was arrested." *Walpole Letters*, II, 137. Walpole added, "What a mercy that we had not him here! With a temper so impetuous and obstinate, as to provoke a French government when in their power, what would he have done with an English government in his power?" *Walpole Letters*, II, 136–37.

9. Bongie, p. 268. Details of Charles's capture and imprisonment, together with an account of his own somewhat embroidered narrative of the experience, are in Bongie, pp. 252–62.

NOTES

CHAPTER 21

1. Horace Walpole described the masquerade at Ranelagh, and the other peace celebrations, in his *Letters*, II, 150–52.

2. *Walpole Letters*, II, 153 note.

3. Viscount Mahon, ed., *The Decline of the Last Stuarts: Extracts from the Despatches of British Envoys to the Secretary of State* (London, 1893), p. 9.

4. *Ibid.*, 9.

5. Lang, p. 363.

6. *Extracts from Despatches*, p. 77. King himself had made a list of 275 Midlands gentlemen who were sympathetic Jacobites. Petrie, II, 142–43.

7. Charles himself claimed late in his life that he had stayed two weeks in London in 1750, with "the government never having the least notice of it." *Extracts from Despatches*, p. 77. But a note in his handwriting among the *Stuart Papers at Windsor* indicates that only eight days separated his arrival in London from his return to Paris. Lang, p. 345 note.

8. Petrie, II, p. 152. This "Irish chairman" scheme was said to have been concocted by Charles and others while Charles was in England, but Petrie argues convincingly that he was only in England once after 1745; other purported trips to England were the result of confused chronology or faulty memories on the part of memoirists. Petrie, II, 157.

9. Bongie, p. 273.

10. Correspondence relating to Clementina's acceptance by a Netherlands convent spanned several years, so presumably Charles got word to her sometime in 1750, if not before. See Berry, pp. 34–45. This, like so much else about Charles and Clementina, is murky with uncertainty.

11. Berry, pp. 43–44.

CHAPTER 22

1. Berry, p. 65.

2. *Ibid.*, 50.

3. Frank Brady and Frederick A. Pottle, eds., *Boswell on the Grand Tour* (New York, 1955), p. 249; James Lees-Milne, *The Last Stuarts* (London, 1983), p. 85.

4. Bruce Lenman attributes many of Charles's personality aberrations in later life—including in particular his alcoholism—to the all-pervasive effect of his incompatibility with his father. That Charles and James were radically different, and that Charles's petulance toward James gradually

hardened into punishing indifference, are undeniable; certainly Charles attempted to sidestep his father from 1746 on, in order to be free to lead his own quixotic life. It would be a mistake, however, to attempt to attribute too much to one overriding deep-seated psychological influence. James's influence on his son was one strong influence among many, and by the time he reached his thirties, Charles was very much his own man—albeit a sadly flawed one.

5. In 1754, John Edgar, nephew of James's servant James Edgar, wrote that Clementina had had two children by Charles, and other contemporary references allude to a second child, a son. If Clementina had a son, he presumably died in infancy, although there is a very slim possibility that he survived into adulthood. Here Jacobite wishful thinking is most likely heavily overlaid on sober fact; still, it is impossible to rule out a second surviving child altogether. Berry, pp. 52–53.

6. Berry, p. 51.

7. *Extracts from Despatches,* pp. 13–15.

8. *Ibid.,* 16–17.

9. Berry, pp. 58–59.

10. *Ibid.,* 55–56, 80. Lord Elcho's account of Charles's mistreatment of Clementina contains the story that he was so jealous of her that he surrounded her bed with chairs placed on tables, and little bells on the chairs, so that if anyone came near her during the night the bells would ring an alarm. Though this memorable anecdote is often recounted by Charles's biographers, it is suspect, as the same story is told of Charles and Louise of Stolberg years later. Of course, it is possible that Charles rigged the same alarm system for Louise that he had once used with Clementina, and given his increasingly irrational behavior the story is not too far-fetched to have been true in both cases.

11. Berry, p. 65.

12. *Ibid.,* 72.

13. *Ibid.,* 70–71.

14. For the 1759 invasion and what led up to it see Claude Nordmann, "Choiseul and the Last Jacobite Attempt of 1759," in Eveline Cruickshanks, ed., *Ideology and Conspiracy: Aspects of Jacobitism, 1689–1759* (Edinburgh, 1982), pp. 201–17.

CHAPTER 23

1. Frank McLynn, *The Jacobites* (London, 1985), p. 190.

2. *Boswell on the Grand Tour,* p. 84. The dissolute young Boswell also

availed himself of the skills of James's physician, Dr. James Murray, to treat him for a venereal disease. *Ibid.,* 71.

3. Henry appears to have had a somewhat bovine placidity, which led Pope Benedict XIV to make the oft-quoted remark that "if all the Stuarts were as boring as the Cardinal," he did not wonder the English had driven them out." *Stuart Papers,* p. 164.

4. *Extracts from Despatches,* p. 27.

5. *Ibid.,* 21–22.

6. According to Mann's reports, James had stopped making payments to Waters for Charles's use at some unspecified time, probably in the 1760s. He did, however, give Charles the money he had been holding in the public funds in Paris—an amount which Mann estimated to be between four and five hundred thousand French livres. Apparently Charles ran through this within a fairly short time, for in 1766 he was reported to be so hard up that he had to cease buying the English newspapers.

In 1761 Mann reported that Charles had to some extent paved his way for a return to Rome whenever James died, adding that he did not expect him to live there permanently, "as he has so great an aversion to his brother." *Extracts from Despatches,* p. 20. As for Charles's alcoholism, Mann passed on the observation of one of his informants that Charles was "drunk as soon as he rises" and was always "senselessly so at night, when his servants carried him to bed." If this was true even half the time, it clearly indicates a serious condition.

7. *Extracts from Despatches,* pp. 31, 34. The rectors were eventually readmitted.

8. *Ibid.,* 36.

CHAPTER 24

1. *Extracts from Despatches,* pp. 37–39.

2. *Ibid.,* 39.

3. As to Charles's general physical state, it is worth noting that in 1769, three years before his marriage to Louise of Stolberg, the Jacobite Bishop Robert Gordon wrote that he was "jolly and plump, though not to excess, being still agile and fit for undergoing toil." Lees-Milne, pp. 98–99.

4. Lees-Milne, p. 107.

5. *Extracts from Despatches,* pp. 49–51.

6. *Ibid.,* 53–54.

7. *Ibid.,* 56.

NOTES

8. *Walpole Letters,* VI, 109.
9. *Extracts from Despatches,* p. 57.
10. *Ibid.,* 58.

CHAPTER 25

1. *Extracts from Despatches,* pp. 83–86. The claim that Charlotte had several illegitimate children before she went to live with her father lacks foundation.
2. Cited in Ewald, p. 414.
3. Berry, p. 80.

SUGGESTIONS
FOR FURTHER READING

Of the hundreds of books and articles about Charles Stuart, his relatives, his times and his cause, the following are among the best and most accessible recent studies:

Cruickshanks, Eveline, ed. *Ideology and Conspiracy: Aspects of Jacobitism 1689–1759*. Edinburgh: John Donald, 1982.
———. *Political Untouchables: The Tories and the Forty-Five*. London: Duckworth, 1979.
Daiches, David. *Charles Edward Stuart: The Life and Times of Bonnie Prince Charlie*. London: Thames and Hudson, 1973.
Fritz, Paul S. *The English Ministers and Jacobitism between the Rebellions of 1715 and 1745*. Toronto and Buffalo: University of Toronto Press, 1975.
Jones, George H. *The Mainstream of Jacobitism*. Boston, Mass.: Harvard University Press, 1954.
Lees-Milne, James. *The Last Stuarts: British Royalty in Exile*. New York: Charles Scribner's Sons, 1984.

SUGGESTIONS FOR FURTHER READING

Lenman, Bruce. *The Jacobite Risings in Britain 1689–1746.* London: Eyre Methuen, 1980.

McLynn, F. J. *France and the Jacobite Rising of 1745.* Edinburgh: Edinburgh University Press, 1981.

Mitchell, A. A. "London and the Forty-Five." *History Today* XV (November 1965), 719–26.

Tomasson, Katherine, and F. Buist. *Battles of the Forty-Five.* New York: Macmillan, 1962.

INDEX

INDEX

INDEX

INDEX

INDEX